REGIONALISM AND AFRICA'S DEVELOPMENT

Also by S. K. B. Asante

AFRICAN DEVELOPMENT: Adebayo Adedeji's Alternative Strategies

PAN-AFRICAN PROTEST: West Africa and the Italo-Ethiopian Crisis

POLITICAL ECONOMY OF REGIONALISM IN AFRICA: A Decade of the Economic Community of West African States (ECOWAS)

Regionalism and Africa's Development

Expectations, Reality and Challenges

S. K. B. Asante
*Senior Regional Adviser in Economic Cooperation and Integration
and Coordinator, Southern Africa Desk and Task Force
Cabinet Office, Economic Commission for Africa
Addis Ababa, Ethiopia*

Foreword by K. Y. Amoako
*United Nations Under-Secretary-General
and Executive Secretary of the Economic Commission for Africa*

First published in Great Britain 1997 by
MACMILLAN PRESS LTD
Houndmills, Basingstoke, Hampshire RG21 6XS and London
Companies and representatives throughout the world

A catalogue record for this book is available from the British Library.

ISBN 0–333–71128–9

First published in the United States of America 1997 by
ST. MARTIN'S PRESS, INC.,
Scholarly and Reference Division,
175 Fifth Avenue, New York, N.Y. 10010

ISBN 0–312–17697–X

Library of Congress Cataloging-in-Publication Data
Asante, S. K. B.
Regionalism and Africa's development : expectations, reality, and
challenges / S.K.B. Asante ; foreword by K. Y. Amoako.
    p.   cm.
Includes bibliographical references and index.
ISBN 0–312–17697–X (cloth)
1. Africa—Economic policy.   2. Africa—Economic integration.
3. Regionalism—Africa.   I. Title.
HC800.A854 1997
337.1'6—dc21   97–18971
                                                           CIP

This book is printed on paper suitable for recycling and made from fully managed and
sustained forest sources.

10   9   8   7   6   5   4   3   2   1
06 05 04 03 02 01 00 99 98 97

Printed in Great Britain by
The Ipswich Book Company Ltd
Ipswich, Suffolk

For my three lovely granddaughters: Akua and
Abena Adu-Nyarko and Afuah Agyeiwa Asante

Contents

List of Tables

List of Abbreviations and Acronyms

AAF-SAP	African Alternative Framework to Structural Adjustment Programmes for Socio-economic Recovery and Transformation
ADB	African Development Bank
AEC	African Economic Community
AMU	Arab Maghreb Union
APEC	Asia-Pacific Economic Cooperation
APPER	African Priority Programme for Economic Recovery
ASEAN	Association of South-East Asian Nations
CACH	Central African Clearing House
CACM	Central American Common Market
CBI	Cross-Border Initiative
CCH	COMESA Clearing House
CEAO	Communauté économique de l'Afrique de l'Ouest
CEMAC	Communauté économique et monétaire de l'Afrique Centrale
CEPGL	Communauté économique des Pays des Grands Lacs
COMESA	Common Market for Eastern and Southern Africa
EAI	Enterprise for the Americas Initiative
ECA	Economic Commission for Africa
ECCAS	Economic Community of Central African States
ECLAC	Economic Commission for Latin America and the Caribbean
ECOWAS	Economic Community of West African States
ECSC	European Coal and Steel Community
EEC	European Economic Community
EFTA	European Free Trade Association
EU	European Union
FAL	Final Act of Lagos
FTAA	Free Trade Area of the Americas
GATT	General Agreement on Tariffs and Trade
IMF	International Monetary Fund
LAFTA	Latin American Free Trade Association
LPA	*Lagos Plan of Action*

MRU	Mano River Union
NAFTA	North American Free Trade Agreement
OAU	Organization of African Unity
PTA	Preferential Trade Area of Eastern and Southern African States
SADCC	Southern African Development Coordination Conference
SADC	Southern African Development Community
SEM	Single European Market
SAP	Structural Adjustment Programme
TNC	Transnational Corporation
UDEAC	Union douanière et économique de l'Afrique Centrale
UEMOA	Union économique et monétaire ouest-africaine
UNCTAD	United Nations Conference on Trade and Development
UN-NADAF	United Nations New Agenda for the Development of Africa in the 1990s
UN-PAAERD	United Nations Programme of Action for African Economic Recovery and Development
WTO	World Trade Organization

Foreword

No publication could be as timely as Professor Asante's *Regionalism and Africa's Development: Expectations, Reality and Challenges.* This comprehensive and thought-provoking resource comes at a time of heightened interest in regional integration, the emergence of trading blocs in Europe, the Americas and Asia, and an increasing awareness among African countries of the imperative of integration for growth and development. Professor Asante's well-researched work provides the historical relevance, contextual background, theoretical constructs, and persuasive rationale for economic regionalism in Africa. His balanced representation of the issues and prescriptions for a 'new direction' set the stage for a greater understanding of the dynamic potential of regional cooperation and integration.

Regionalism and Africa's Development makes a significant contribution to the body of practical and theoretical knowledge that support regional integration – a process which will enable African countries to overcome the constraints of small markets, increase intra-African trade, and achieve economies of scale in production. The concepts Professor Asante examines in this book occupy the centre stage of the Economic Commission for Africa's (ECA) work programme. ECA advocates economic integration and considers it key to Africa's development.

Professor Asante proposes measures to expedite the implementation process of the Abuja Treaty; strengthen subregional organizations and activities; develop cross-border trade liberalization; develop robust transport, communications, and energy infrastructures; and build and enhance agriculture and business production capacities. Virtually all recent internal and external action programmes and guidelines for Africa consistently reflect the tenets of subregional and regional integration that he highlights: the *Lagos Plan of Action* (1980), the United Nations Programme of Action for African Economic Recovery and Development (1986–90) (UN-PAAERD), the United Nations New Agenda for the Development of Africa in the 1990s (UN-NADAF), and the *Cairo Agenda for Action* (1995), to name a few.

The measures detailed in this book support ECA's new core work programme (1996–2001) and set the stage for successful and expeditious regional cooperation and integration throughout the continent. Currently undergoing a renewal process to create a more responsive and tactical organization, ECA maintains a comparative advantage in institution-building within the integration framework. We have created several sponsored institutions in Africa and have catalysed the subregional integration process by creating requisite organizations throughout Africa, such as the Economic Community of West African States (ECOWAS) and the Preferential Trade Area of Eastern and Southern African States (PTA), now transformed into the Common Market for Eastern and Southern Africa (COMESA).

This pivotal volume makes a strong case for mobilizing support for economic integration at all levels, for ensuring adequate financial support for Africa's integration from within the continent, and for a committed constituency for Africa's economic future. It proposes measures towards rapid diversification of African countries' exports, increased export processing, expansion of intra-African trade, promoting South–South trade, and rationalization and revitalization of African integration process as some of the relevant policy responses to the emerging regional age. While one may not accept every idea or rationale that the author has proffered, we can all agree that he has clearly and concisely articulated the benefits and challenges of African regionalism and has defined a distinctly African strategy.

Professor Asante's approach will surely stimulate greater attention of scholars, researchers, and policy makers, particularly the member states of the ECA, to further intellectual exploration of the prospects and the promise of regionalism in the 1990s and beyond. I applaud Professor Asante's construction of a contemporary and challenging book that can assist our understanding of and interest in regionalism in Africa.

Dr K.Y. Amoako
United Nations Under-Secretary-General
and Executive Secretary of the
Economic Commission for Africa

Preface

Regional and subregional economic cooperation and integration is widely recognised and accepted as a necessary condition for the long-term sustainable development of African countries. The African countries themselves and the international community, in various convergent policy declarations and statements, have underlined intra-African economic integration and cooperation as indispensable for the socio-economic transformation of the continent. The consolidation of the African economic space, in particular, through the formation of subregional common markets leading eventually to a continental common market and economic community has been perceived as a primary goal. This objective has provided the main rationale for the establishment of regional and subregional economic cooperation and integration groupings in Africa.

By the 1980s, frustration with the growing gap between the high initial expectations and the actual achievements of the first phase of integration considerably reduced the interest in economic cooperation and integration as a policy issue. As the economic crisis deepened, concern over national stabilisation and structural adjustment gradually began to take precedence over subregional and regional considerations. Member states of the economic communities resorted to purely national measures of short-term crisis management thereby often compromising their obligations to their respective groupings.

Recently, however, following the new wave of regional integration in the early 1990s, the question of economic integration is once again at the top of the policy agenda in almost all the subregions of Africa. This is partly in line with recent worldwide trends which have increased the force of the economic argument in favour of regional solidarity. Integration is being looked at again as a way to achieve faster, more diversified, and sustainable economic growth that would enable Africa to effectively respond to the challenges of the emerging world of trading blocs, rapid changes in technology and the globalization of world production. Hence the reassessment, in the early 1990s, of the entire integration project, which has led to fresh initiatives resulting in the creation of new regional and subregional economic integration schemes, revitalization of the existing economic communities and transformation of others into more dynamic groupings that would enable them to adjust to the rapidly changing economic landscape in many regions of the world.

This book is concerned with the objectives, challenges and prospects of the two distinct phases of regionalism in Africa which have hitherto not received adequate attention in the various studies on economic cooperation and integration in Africa. The impetus for exploring the themes of this volume comes from several significant sources. First and foremost, the assumption of office by Dr K.Y. Amoako as United Nations Under-Secretary-General and Executive Secretary of the Economic Commission for Africa (ECA), in July 1995, has given a renewed emphasis on economic integration not only as a major mandate of the ECA but also as a priority issue in Africa's development strategy. Promotion of regional economic cooperation and integration has been identified as one of the five new programme directions offered as the foci of the ECA's work over the next six years, 1996–2001. As Senior Regional Adviser in Economic Cooperation and Integration at the Cabinet Office of the Executive Secretary and Coordinator of the ECA-Multidisciplinary Regional Advisory Group (ECA-MRAG) for three consecutive years (1992–4), I considered it necessary to produce a book setting out the lessons learnt in regionalism in Africa and posing questions of a theoretical and policy nature. Through this modest effort, I hope to make some contribution to the achievement of the ECA's renewal objective which is to serve Africa better. It is indeed proper and fitting therefore that Dr Amoako has consented to write the Foreword to this study.

The sustained impact which my annual special two-week course module on Economic Cooperation and Integration in Africa has had on the students of the Diploma and Masters programmes of the United Nations African Institute for Economic Development and Planning (IDEP); the Institute of Diplomacy and International Studies (IDIS) at the University of Nairobi, Kenya; the Zambia Institute for Diplomatic Studies (ZIDS); the International Relations Institute of Cameroon (IRIC) and the Legon Centre for International Affairs (LECIA) at the University of Ghana, has been more than sufficient to rekindle my interest in doing further work towards the publication of this volume. Similarly, the favourable reaction to my annual series of lectures and training workshops on regionalism and Africa's development to both staff and graduate students of such South African universities and research centres as the University of Pretoria, where I serve as Extraordinary Professor, and the Africa Institute of South Africa, as Fellow, greatly inspired me to write this book.

Furthermore, the various technical advisory and training missions to ECA member states, intergovernmental organizations, and the regional and subregional economic communities on substantive issues in economic integration, coupled with my participation in the revitalization of the Economic Community of West African States (ECOWAS) as a member of the

Committee of Eminent Persons for the Revision of the ECOWAS Treaty headed by Nigeria's former Head of State, Dr Yakubu Gowon (May 1991 to June 1992), and in the drawing up of the treaties establishing the Common Market for Eastern and Southern Africa (COMESA) (1992–3) and the African Economic Community (AEC) (1989–90) – all this stimulated and sharpened my interest in writing this book.

I owe a debt of gratitude first, to the Ministers, Permanent, and Principal Secretaries and Directors of Ministries of Planning and/or African Regional Integration whose requests for technical advisory and training services provided the opportunity to study closely the management and challenges of economic integration at the national level which has hitherto been neglected; Secretaries-General and Executive Secretaries of the African regional economic communities and directors of the institutes who invited me on several occasions to assess their economic integration process, identify problems and prospects of their management of regional economic integration and to provide training programmes on the technology of regional cooperation and integration. Special thanks are due to the following who, among others, initiated the various requests and invitations: Hon. Hidipo Hamutenya, Minister of Trade and Industry, and Hon. Dr Mose P. Tjitendero, Speaker of the National Assembly, both of the Republic of Namibia; Mr F.M. Kuindwa, Permanent Secretary, Office of the Vice-President and Ministry of Planning and National Development, Republic of Kenya; Hon. Dean M. Mongomba, former Deputy Minister of Planning and Development Cooperation, Office of the President, Republic of Zambia; Dr Louk de la Rive Box, Director of the European Centre for Development Policy Management based in Maastricht, The Netherlands; Dr Jeggan C. Senghor, Director of IDEP; Professor Joshua Olewe-Nyunya, Director of IDIS, University of Nairobi; Dr Bingu Wa Mutharika, Secretary-General of COMESA; Dr Abbas Bundu, former Executive Secretary of ECOWAS; Dr Kaire Mbuende, Executive Secretary of the Southern African Development Community (SADC); Professor Geert de Wet, Head, Department of Economics, University of Pretoria, Pretoria, South Africa; Dr Denis Venter, Executive Director, Africa Institute of South Africa, Pretoria, South Africa; and Dr Garth le Pere, Executive Director, Foundation for Global Dialogue, Johannesburg, South Africa.

I am extremely grateful to Professor H.M.A. Onitiri, who showed special interest in the preparation of this volume at the very beginning, critically reviewed its Contents page and provided the relevant material of his own work in this area. I should also like to express sincere thanks to my colleagues Dr M.J. Balogun, Senior Regional Adviser in Public Sector Management, and Professor W.A. Ndongko, Senior Regional Adviser in Macro-economics and Policy Reform, both of ECA-MRAG, who participated in our special multidisciplinary missions to Cameroon, Ghana, Kenya, Namibia, Seychelles, South Africa, Sudan, Tanzania, Zambia and Zimbabwe, and to the headquarters of COMESA, ECOWAS and SADC. These two colleagues provided an intellectual atmosphere, at once stimulating and relaxed, that creates the ideal conditions for research.

I am greatly indebted to Ms Sissay Tadesse and Mrs Charlotte Mfasoni who typed the manuscript with their usual speed, care and professional skill, who I always have in mind as my first audience, and whose many kindnesses are part of the background to my work. I am also grateful for secretarial and other much-valued assistance, at various stages of the project, to Ms Roman Alemayehu of ECA-MRAG, Mrs Nancy Wanjala of the Institute of Diplomacy and International Studies, University of Nairobi, Kenya and Ms Noelle Lawson of the Foundation for Global Dialogue, Johannesburg, South Africa.

Most of all I wish to thank my dear wife, Jane, my cleverest and most inspiring critic, about whom I do not have words to say enough. Her insight and her passion for ideas have been vital to this book, as to everything I write.

S.K.B. Asante
Senior Regional Adviser,
Economic Cooperation and Integration,
ECA-Multidisciplinary Regional Advisory Group,
Cabinet Office of the Executive Secretary
November 1996

1 Introduction: Africa and the World of Regionalism: Old and New

Regional integration is not new. It has been a continuing part of the post-World War II trade landscape. Recently, however, interest in regionalism has revived in both developed and developing countries. Existing arrangements have been, or are being, extended in their coverage; old arrangements are being revived; and new regional groupings are being formed. The three distinctive features of this trend are: the 'conversion' of the United States to the regional approach; the emergence of regional arrangements among industrial and developing countries; and an apparent move away from inward-oriented towards more outward-oriented arrangements among developing countries, particularly in the Western Hemisphere. In developing countries, these developments are being accompanied in many cases by unilateral trade liberalization.

The renewed interest in regionalism, particularly in view of the difficulties in concluding the Uruguay Round of multilateral trade negotiations, has created a concern that the world trade system may gravitate towards regional trade blocs aligned around the European Community, now the European Union (EU), the United States, and Japan (the triad). There is the tendency of these blocs to provide their members with guaranteed access to large markets, while poor non-member countries, like those in Africa, will suffer from the loss of access to world markets if trading blocs become a reality.

Against the background of the implications of these arrangements for Africa, a global consensus has emerged on the need for closer regional cooperation and integration in Africa if the continent is to be able to face up to the challenges of the 1990s and beyond. It is widely recognized that regionalism will have a crucial role to play in relaunching development and growth in Africa and to improve the economic outlook in the continent. This introductory chapter attempts a brief overview of both the first and second waves of regionalism and their implications for Africa. It then highlights the scope of this study.

THE FIRST WAVE OF REGIONALISM

Four decades ago, boosted by the creation of the European Economic Community (EEC), a first wave of regionalism spread across the world. Many countries that were close neighbours or had common problems of economic development tended to strive to maintain some degree of economic cooperation. Economic integration has now become such a worldwide phenomenon that the post-World War II period has been to some extent described as an 'era of regional integration', or, as scholars like Haberler would have it, 'the age of integration'. So much is this the case that nowhere in the world today do the policy makers and economists tackle any problem of economic development without first taking into consideration theories and trends of economic integration both at home and abroad. Vague notions about improved relations employ the term 'integration' as a magic formula that can be invoked at random in order to draw the world's attention to the conditions under which joint beneficial developments can arise. For economists and social scientists today economic integration is an essential aspect of the dynamics of modern society in its continuous process of transformation. Moreover it is acknowledged as an important factor of economic development in the developing countries and of more rapid growth in the industrial ones.

Linking the concept of regionalism with development has become so important that some scholars like John Sloan would prefer to substitute the term 'developmental regionalism'[1] for that of regional economic integration, because the latter, they contend, is imprecise, static, and irrelevant to the development issue. In most recent economic literature, the terms 'integration' or 'common market' have tended to become nearly synonymous with 'rapid economic growth', 'acceleration of economic development' or 'big push'. Regardless of the terminology used, there can be no doubt that the process of regional integration is now inextricably linked to that of economic development.

The European Coal and Steel Community (ECSC), established in 1951, the EEC (1957) and, to a lesser degree, the European Free Trade Association (EFTA) (1960) are undoubtedly the best known schemes in this first wave of regionalism. The United States, then a staunch supporter of the General Agreement on Tariffs and Trade (GATT) and of the multilateral approach, and therefore philosophically opposed to regionalism, saw a united Western Europe as an effective deterrent to the growing Soviet threat and threw its weight behind the European Community. The post-war progress towards integration in Europe made a considerable impression on many countries, as the idea of economic integration became attractive to political and economic leaders of the Third World. Hence the proliferation of regional arrangements around the world, especially in the developing countries of Africa and Latin America. The potential power of the EEC triggered a desire for emulation both to reap the alleged benefits and to seek protection against the EEC's capacity to export and import goods.

Free trade areas and customs unions mushroomed in Latin America and Africa during the 1960s and early 1970s. The Latin American Free Trade Association (LAFTA) (1960), Central American Common Market (CACM) (1961), the Central African Economic and Customs Union (1964), the Association of South-East Asian Nations (ASEAN) established in 1967 and the Caribbean Free Trade Association of 1968 form the main instances of this wave in the developing countries. Unfortunately, expectations of economic development through regional economic integration were not realized, and two decades later virtually all regional arrangements among developing countries were judged as failures or moribund. Thus, despite high hopes, this first round of regionalism did not flourish, except for the original European Community and EFTA. The primary motive behind regionalism in the developing countries was industrialization through import substitution. It was thought that infant industries could first learn to export within a protected regional market – and then face world competition. But, as de Melo and Panagariya have recently argued, for the same reason that 'import substitution failed in the countries, it also failed in the regions'.[2] Although at first intra-regional trade increased in some trading groups, it remained a rather modest share of total trade and had the tendency to decline in the 1970s, and stagnated in most of the 1980s. In addition, ambitious plans for joint industrialization could not be implemented.

THE SECOND WAVE OF REGIONALISM

By the mid-1980s, however, a new-found or rediscovered enthusiasm for regional economic integration had been evident in Europe, Africa, and North and South America. Despite generally negative experiences, new approaches to regional cooperation started to re-emerge in recent years. Attempts to revitalize dormant regional groups, to form new blocs and to set partly new priorities are on the increase. Although trade remains the most important element of the new initiatives, fundamental changes have taken place in the assessment of the possibilities and limits of regional integration, as compared with the basic concepts in the 1960s. Briefly stated, therefore, regionalism is back today 'with a vengeance' and, as a recent *World Bank Policy Research*

Bulletin puts it, it is 'here to stay'.[3] Regionalism is once again being viewed as a solution to the major international economic problems of our time.

This has raised a series of intriguing questions. Why, after the mixed experiences with regional cooperation is there such an intense revival of interest in the possibilities that regionalism might have to offer, especially in the developing countries? Is it because other options to achieve development, growth, stability and equity have been tried and failed? Is it because the solidifying of the EU and the emergence of the North American Free Trade Agreement (NAFTA) have driven other countries into a frenzy of fear that unless they too associate in some trade bloc or other, their access to major markets will be impeded and their ability to earn a fair living in the world will be threatened? Is it the violent fragmentation of the world after the end of the Cold War – a process which remains kaleidoscopic with no clear end in sight – that is causing a counter-reaction in more stable states to consolidate and amalgamate? Whatever the reasons, it is inescapable that a new regional dynamic is emerging almost across the globe despite the array of powerful voices and arguments which caution against its less attractive features. On the whole, however, this new regionalism was partly fuelled by the slow progress at the GATT negotiations. Confidence in the GATT process was on the decline, and enthusiasm towards the regional approach on the rise. Put differently, the forces of multilateralism have weakened in recent years, and the attraction towards regionalism has strengthened.

Augusto de la Torre and Margaret Kelly have argued that the GATT's inability to curb rising protectionist pressures since the end of the Tokyo Round 'created frustration with the slowness of the GATT process and raised concerns about its effectiveness and its ability to adapt to the emerging trade issues of the 1990s'[4] (which include problems posed by high-tech industries and by firms engaged in trade and investment in goods and services on a global scale). Thus, doubts had arisen about the political will of the major players to strengthen the GATT's credibility through the Uruguay Round. In this context, regionalism was advocated as an alternative to multilateralism; indeed, regional approaches to liberalization were seen as a response to the regional and global integration of investment and production with which an unwieldy and slow multilateral approach had been unable to keep pace.

Paul Krugman has recently attributed these developments, among other things, to the sheer number of participants in the GATT process which made negotiations difficult and free-rider problem harder to handle.[5] Besides, the changing character of trade restrictions made monitoring increasingly difficult. More significantly, too, conditions had changed. The decline in the relative dominance of the United States had made it more difficult to run the GATT system. The United States is no longer the leader it was in the 1950s and 1960s when it accounted for close to half of global gross domestic product (GDP). It can no longer generate large benefits for the world economy by freeing up its trade. Neither can it take on the promotion of the cause of free trade, as it did in the decades immediately after World War II, when it supplied such international public goods as the Marshall Plan and the various rounds of the GATT negotiations. Japan and the East Asian newly industrializing countries (NICs), hardly significant players in the world economy in the early years after World War II, have emerged. The United States is now what Jagdish Bhagwati calls a 'diminished giant' unable to be an effective leader in multilateral trade talks.

Furthermore, institutional differences among major countries had made GATT negotiations more difficult. While GATT negotiations had been relatively unsuccessful in tackling non-tariff barriers (NTBs) to trade, it was argued that within a more homogeneous regional group, liberalization of NTBs could progress faster and indeed this was the focus of the European Community's Single European Market (SEM) programme. Whether this represents a stepping stone to global liberalization, however, is more debatable, as critics of regionalism, as Robert Hine recently put it, 'see a number of damaging consequences for global trade liberalization'.[6] It has been pointed out, for instance, that preoccupation with regional matters may distract policy makers from multilateral activities. A case in point was the European Community concerns over the SEM and a common currency which might have diverted attention from the Uruguay Round negotiations. Besides, the recent regional initiatives are not wholly outward-looking. In North America, as Hine observes, US arrangements have 'exclusionary provisions against third parties, particularly through local content requirements and strict application of rules of origin'.[7] Despite such critical observations, it is on the whole generally felt that regional trading arrangements offer an opportunity to reconstitute the bargaining process at a level where all of these problems can be diminished. Compared to the difficulty of reforming the GATT a regional trading bloc appeared to be a quick and easy solution to international trade problems.

Besides the difficulties of the GATT system, the emergence of the new regionalism is also partly attributable to the European Community's own initiatives aimed at establishing SEM and an economic and monetary union, and the perceptions and responses of other countries – notably the United States – to those developments. 'Europe 1992' and the impending integration of Eastern Europe into the European Union reinforced, as the formation of the Common Market did with many three decades ago, those in North America who felt that a countervailing bloc must be formed there as well.

Bollard and Mayes have also stressed that, to some extent, regional interests in the Pacific Rim have been fostered by the pursuit of self-interest in Europe. The process of integration in Europe stimulated a response that if linkages were being increased in such a major part of the trading world there ought to be an offsetting accretion of bargaining power for those whose position had become relatively weaker. The second response was that if the process of integration appeared to have the benefits put forward for it in Europe then there might be opportunities for some similar benefits in the Pacific.[8]

Not surprisingly, therefore, the second wave of regionalism has engulfed all major players in the world economy. Canada, Mexico and the United States signed the North American Free Trade Agreement on 17 December 1992, which entered into force on 1 January 1994. The United States has also launched the Enterprise for the Americas Initiative (EAI), whose ultimate goal is a hemispheric free trade area. In Europe, the European Community had launched the 'Europe 1992' initiative to create a single, internal market, while the queue of countries desiring to join the European Union continues to lengthen. January 1995 saw the accession to the European Union, the world's biggest trading bloc, of Austria, Finland and Sweden. There is a growing concern that, *de facto*, a trading bloc is forming in East Asia under the leadership of Japan. And since 1985, 'six substantive regional agreements and innumerable proclamations of intent to integrate' have been signed.[9] More ambitious still are the plans of the Asia-Pacific Economic Cooperation (APEC) forum. This diverse group, which includes America, Japan, China, Taiwan, Malaysia, Australia and a dozen other countries with Pacific coastlines, has pledged itself to internal free trade by 2020, with the richer countries getting there by 2010. The members have not yet decided whether to create a formal FTA.

Hence today, there is a distinct possibility that regionalism will divide the developed world into three trading blocs: Europe, the Americas, and East Asia, which was never an issue in the first round of regionalism. This has brought the global aspect of regionalism to the forefront of the policy debate and divided more sharply than ever the defenders of the multilateral process and the devotees of regionalism.

The second wave differs sharply from the first in the following respects. First, whereas past arrangements were generally viewed as either benign (pacts among developing countries) or complementary (the EU) to multilateralism, there is much evidence to suggest that the new regionalism might work at cross-purposes with the more traditional multilateral approach. Second, the United States is no longer exclusively committed to multilateralism and is actively pursuing regionalism. Third, today, regionalism is being pursued on a much larger scale. And finally, there are now far fewer trade restrictions in developing countries.[10]

The new regionalism has recently been defined by Björn Hettne as a multidimensional process of regional integration which includes economic, political, social and cultural aspects.[11] His stress is much more on the non-economic, on the political and security dimensions of regional integration. Hettne sees regional integration as a package rather than a single policy, whether concerned with economics or foreign policy. The concept, as defined by Hettne, goes well beyond notions of free trade areas and market integration, that is, the linking of several national markets into one functional economic unit. Political ambitions of creating territorial identity, political convergence, collective security and regional coherence now seem to be the primary, neo-mercantilist goals of the new regionalism. One other difference with the old regionalism, according to Hettne, is that the new regionalism is spontaneous and from below (firm, market and consumer driven), whereas the old type was imposed from above (bureaucratically fiat driven) and was therefore more limited and more prone to failure of the kind that grand designs invariably suffer.

On the other hand, the World Bank, in a recent study authored by Carlos Braga,[12] while overtly recognizing the importance of non-economic considerations in driving the new regionalism, still chooses to treat the new regionalism as an economically enhanced free trade concept. The enhancements are essentially the following: liberalization of trade in services, liberalization in movements of capital and labour; harmonization of regulatory regimes; and the emergence of North–South regional arrangements which are now becoming the rule rather than the exception. Braga recognizes that there is a clear shift of inward-looking emphasis in South–South arrangements, from being closed and aimed at the wrong objectives (protectionist), to being open and aimed at the right ones (outward-oriented and competitive). Finally, Braga points to one key feature of the new regionalism: that is, that it underlines non-exclusivity, or more accurately, inclusivity as opposed to a regionalism which once used to be defined in terms mainly of which barriers members of a regional group could erect to thwart non-members, and how high these barriers were to be.[13]

From the specific viewpoint of developing countries, the new regionalism differs from the old regionalism of the 1960s in two important respects. First, the old regionalism represented an extension of the import-substitution industrialization strategy from the national to the regional level and was therefore inward-looking. By contrast the second wave is taking place in an environment of outward-oriented policies.[14] Second, whereas, in the 1960s, developing countries pursued regional integration exclusively with other developing countries, today, as indicated above, in a dramatic shift, developing countries are seeking partnerships with developed countries rather than solely with each other.

This is particularly the case in Latin America, where regional arrangements are being contemplated with the United States with a view to deriving some potential gains. As de Melo and Panagariya note, a free trade agreement (FTA) with the United States is the most effective instrument for ensuring that hard-fought policy reforms are not reversed by weaker (or more protectionist) future governments. An international treaty with a large and rich neighbour 'is much harder to repudiate than national legislation'.[15] Briefly, Mexico wishes to use a trade agreement to underpin domestic policy reform so as to attract inward foreign investment and to use treaties as a way of locking in prior domestic policy reforms.[16] Besides, with the rise of non-tariff barriers in a period when the EU is becoming increasingly inaccessible to those outside it, an FTA with the United States offers Latin American countries guaranteed access to a large market. From Mexico's viewpoint, therefore, a primary motive behind NAFTA is to secure better access to the US market, especially with respect to non-tariff barriers and safeguards.

For developing countries generally, and for the African countries in particular, access to developed country markets is vital. This means that the recent move towards a tripolar world and the difficulties of gaining further market access through multilateral trade talks raise the spectre of isolation for those that do not belong to a bloc. Given the consensus that regionalism is here to stay, what can be done to ensure an open trading system that will protect the interests of the smaller nations, particularly African countries?

AFRICA AND THE BRAVE NEW WORLD OF REGIONALISM

Evidently, as noted above, the formation of new, powerful economic and trading blocs, such as the single market of the European Union, the US–Canada–Mexico NAFTA, initiatives in the Pacific basin, and the transition to market economies in Central (and perhaps Eastern) Europe, seem to foster trends towards a new regionalism in the world economy. This trend has grown side by side with the globalization of world production, and rapid trade expansion and increasing interlinkages among the world's industrialized and rapidly growing regions. Because of the extensive linkages among these dynamic regions, it is unlikely that regionalism will have as much impact on their trade as on that of the late-comers – Africa and Latin America – which are now struggling to join the bandwagon of globalization.

The implication of this world of trading blocs is that whatever the terms of recent agreement of the Uruguay Round trade negotiations under the GATT, these trading blocs will take advantage of their stronger position as integrative groups and derive benefits from the emerging international economic system. Thus, with the approach of the twenty-first century, Europe is increasingly looking to Europe, America to America, Asia to Asia with the ultimate objective of establishing a unified and integrated market, capable of fostering production and trade, in a coordinated approach. The main objective of this regional and global strategy is primarily for individual countries in Europe, the Americas or Asia to avoid marginalization in international affairs and collectively to effect changes which will ensure an adequate balance of political and economic powers to sustain political independence and economic development through collective efforts.[17]

These developments have presented an extraordinary challenge to Africa, which has the greater cause for anxiety than Latin America, and raised some searching questions. How, for example, will Africa, saddled with a proliferation of customs unions and intergovernmental organizations (IGOs), fare in this new world of trading blocs? Will African leaders and governments continue with the business-as-usual policy? Or will they initiate and engineer developments of sufficient impact to enable the continent to achieve an economic turnaround and become an active participant in the historic changes that are bound to occur during the 1990s and beyond? Will the recently created World Trade Organization (WTO) and the international trading system sufficiently protect African countries which have been left out of the blocs? Will the creation of a Single European Market be to the benefit of Africa? Or will the single market turn out to be a 'fortress, more protectionist, inward-looking, and less sympathetic to the exporting needs of its developing African partners'? And will the interest of European business in investing in Africa now wane as a result of the prospects offered by the single market? And finally, what, then, are the implications of the world of trading blocs for the process of regionalism in Africa and the future of African development?

As noted in a recent study,[18] expanding regionalism may substantially narrow down the chances for late-coming sub-Saharan Africa to diversify its regional patterns of trade and investment relations in future, if this region finds itself, *vis-à-vis* largely integrated production and investment systems, extending to the whole of the American and East Asian/Pacific regions, while it will also have to face much tougher internal competition in a European free trade zone stretching from Ireland to Russia and from Sweden to Morocco and Turkey. With this prospect, the African continent, already largely marginalized in world economy, now runs the great risk of being swept completely aside by the fast moving current of world growth and structural transformation.

African countries are now compelled to face these realities and develop urgent responses to the great challenge posed by current global developments. It is only thus that they can reverse the present adverse trends and emerge as one of the dynamic development poles in the next century. Unlike Latin America which is being gradually drawn into the NAFTA orbit, and may become, along with the US and Canada, part of the Free Trade Area of the Americas (FTAA) by the year 2005,[19] Africa has to face the realities of the new regionalism at a time that its links with Europe, which accounts for more than two-thirds of its trade, and a substantial proportion of its inflow of financial resources, are weakening rather than strengthening.

Based on the author's many years of research in the field of economic cooperation and integration and practical knowledge of the operations of the existing economic community schemes in Africa, this book attempts a critical review of the process of regionalism in Africa. It highlights, among other things, the experiences, interlocking problems and prospects of economic integration in Africa and the way forward to enable Africa to meet the challenges of the brave new world of regionalism, the rise of market economies and the advance of political pluralism. It is based on the premise that a continent with over 600 million inhabitants scattered over 50 fragmented, balkanized, independent and sovereign entities cannot be taken seriously as an important and effective partner in the global economy of the twenty-first century with its set of international regulations. The volume therefore focuses special attention on the neglected aspects in the management of regionalism in Africa and provides a new direction to the current integration process on the continent.

As economic integration touches ever more areas of society, more and more people are confronted by the bewildering complexity of the functioning of the African economic integration schemes, and look for a systematic analysis. This book attempts to come to their aid by offering a text that aims to (i) explain the logic of the dynamic processes; (ii) foster understanding of economic integration as a key element of African development; (iii) enhance readers' appreciation of economic integration as *sine qua non* for the achievement of national, subregional and regional socio-economic goals; (iv) increase awareness of the interlocking challenges in the international and regional environments and to assist African policy makers in formulating and implementing appropriate policies to respond to them; and (v) provide readers with comparative experiences in operating integration schemes in other parts of the world, as a basis for coming up with solutions to problems encountered in African integration.

There are cogent reasons why a reassessment of regional integration in Africa is opportune. Apart from the fact that hope exists, at least in policy making circles, for the contribution which integration can make towards economic development, major developments have recently taken place which will reinforce the attention given to regional integration. Among these are the dramatic and profound changes taking place in many regions of the world and the formidable challenges they pose to the process of African economic cooperation and integration. There is first, as noted above, the emergence of trading blocs, in particular, 'Fortress Europe', which threatens to marginalize Africa, which adds considerable force to the economic arguments in favour of regional solidarity. Second, the rapid changes in technology have brought about profound changes in the organization of world production and significantly altered the environment for competition. Today, a worldwide market for goods and services is rapidly replacing a world economy composed of relatively isolated national markets. Domestic financial markets have been integrated into a truly global system, and the multinational corporation is becoming a principal mechanism for allocating investment capital and determining the location of production sites throughout much of the world. The attainment of a high level of productivity now requires, even more than before, the organization of production across national borders. In short, the internationalization of production has become an indispensable basis for maintaining competitiveness in international markets.

Third, the conclusion of the Uruguay Round Agreements, the establishment of the World Trade Organization and the further advances in information science pose new challenges to Africa's trading position in the world and the continent's relations with the other trading blocs, especially as African countries do not yet have the capacity to take advantage of new opportunities under the agreements. The developments have been buttressed by the dominance of the free market economic system based on competition, efficiency and productivity. And fourth, developments in Eastern Europe, where the rebirth of democracy has captured the imagination and compassion of the governments and peoples of the Western world, have led to increasing indifference or withdrawal, if not abandonment, on the part of the industrialized countries towards Africa. Consequently, Africa must take new steps to ensure that it becomes an active partner in the world economic system. The changing international relations have given added relevance to the efforts of African countries to maximize their collective efforts through economic cooperation and integration.

At the level of the continent itself, the adoption of the *African Charter for Popular Participation in Development*[20] and the emergence of multiparty democracies, coupled with the timely publication of the United Nations

Development Programme's seminal *Human Development Report* series,[21] which has given full rein to the importance of the human factor and democracy in development – all have necessitated the need for a reappraisal of the strategy of economic cooperation and integration in Africa. Furthermore, the impact of the World Bank/International Monetary Fund (IMF) structural adjustment programmes (SAPs) on the process of regionalism in Africa has raised a disturbing question about whether, as Jean-Claude Boidin puts it, the orthodox SAPs constitute 'a plus or risk' for economic integration in Africa.[22] Similarly, the incompatibility of the Lomé Convention (particularly with the emergence of 'Europe 1992') on the promotion of regionalism in Africa, especially Lomé IV, which is tied to SAPs, needs urgent review in order to expunge aspects that conflict with the process of economic integration in Africa. This has become particularly important, following the recent ratification of the Abuja Treaty establishing the African Economic Community, which constitutes Africa's collective response to the unfolding new world of trading blocs and its strategy for ensuring that the continent should not remain marginalized and exploited.[23]

Another most prominent event has been the transition to an inclusive democracy in South Africa, Africa's largest and most sophisticated economy. While the major economies of North, West and East Africa – Algeria, Nigeria and Kenya – remain bogged down in autocratic governance, Southern Africa can look forward to the closer integration of the dominant economy of the subcontinent into the economic and political structures of the region. Besides, the unprecedented development crisis has led to the recognition that many development issues transcend national boundaries and should, therefore, be tackled at the subregional and regional levels. These challenges have made the subject of economic integration one of the most discussed issues in Africa today. It has come into sharp focus, as part of the overall interest in the problem of African recovery, development and transformation.

Against this broad background, following this introductory chapter, this book is divided into two parts. The first part covers the process of regionalism in Africa from the modest beginnings of the 1960s to the period of euphoria for economic cooperation and integration in the 1970s and 1980s. The second part devotes attention to the renewed interest in regionalism since the mid-1980s, the new initiatives and challenges, highlighting in particular the problems and prospects of the African Economic Community. It provides policy measures towards a new direction.

This book addresses primarily two groups of readers. First, it addresses the increasing number of students in the higher forms of training colleges and high schools and especially the growing number of university students who are following interdisciplinary courses in which an understanding of the issues of economic integration and African development is important.

Second, it is written for all those interested in African economic integration in practice, including the increasing number of people (researchers, consultants, journalists), particularly those in the African public and private sectors, who in their professional activities are faced with questions as to the organization, functioning and management of economic integration schemes at the national, subregional and regional levels. To facilitate their access to the material, the book has been written in such a way that only a basic knowledge of economics is needed. It is written in a manner intended to encourage wide readership, most importantly by politicians and other decision makers who may not be familiar with economic theory, but in whose hands economic progress in sub-Saharan Africa largely lies. Also, the need for this book is of paramount importance because it may promote further research in the field of African economic cooperation and integration. It would thereby contribute to enlarging regional understanding, stimulating thought, clarifying objectives, and promoting a sense of technocratic *esprit de corps*, thereby creating an atmosphere propitious to integrating moves in Africa.

Part I

Regionalism in Africa: The First Phase

2 Regionalism as a Key Element of African Development Strategy

A key aspect of the development strategy, shared by many policy makers and economists today, is the recognition of the dynamic potential of regional cooperation and integration whereby developing countries can break out of their narrow national markets and form regional groupings as an instrument of economic decolonization. They tend to attribute the causes of failure of different development policies in the developing world to the series of independent efforts carried out in isolated compartments. In their view, developing countries have inadequate resources or the technical capacity to compete with the relatively more developed ones in the same underdeveloped regions, much less with the developed areas. Consequently, it is necessary to establish a gradual process of economic integration, as Raul Prebisch, for example, puts it, 'to settle the balance-of-payments deficit, overcoming difficulties arising from the size of national markets, raising productivity and efficient use of regional resources, and also by serving as a strong stimulus for the incorporation of technical progress and many other objectives in international policy'.[1] It is to this end that regional economic integration has emerged, in the post-war era, as one of the main developmental choices adopted by the developing countries.

It is within this context that this chapter devotes attention to the concept of regional cooperation and integration as a significant aspect of African development strategy over the years. As a necessary background, the chapter provides a brief overview of the basic concepts and structures relating to the term 'economic integration', and the theoretical foundations on which the recent drive towards regionalism has been based. Such an overview will enable us to have a proper understanding of the meaning of the term as well as the details of the process of economic integration. This is followed, first, by a review of the rationale for economic cooperation and integration in Africa, and second, establishment of the pre-1990 regional economic integration schemes.

THE TERM 'ECONOMIC INTEGRATION'

Although 'international economic integration' is one aspect of 'international economics' which has been growing in importance in the past three decades or so, the common usage of the term 'integration' is often confusing. I find some unanimity, a fair amount of consensus, but also much divergence among its users. The term has been used imprecisely in common parlance. So far no single definition of 'integration' has gained widespread acceptance among integration theorists. The concept has therefore provoked considerable discussion and debate in economic and political literature.[2]

The word 'integration', taken from the Latin, is of course, very old. In Latin, *integration* was mostly used in the sense of 'renovation'. The *Oxford English Dictionary* gives 1620 as the date for the first use in print of integration in the sense of 'combining parts into a whole', which leaves open a wide range of ambiguity. In economics, as Machlup notes, the word was first employed in industrial organization to refer to 'combinations of business firms' through agreements, cartels, concerns, trusts and mergers – horizontal integration referring to combinations of competitors, vertical integration to combinations of suppliers with customers.[3] Some authors include social integration in the concept, others subsume different forms of international cooperation under this heading. For example, a large family of words – ranging from economic *rapprochement* via cooperation and solidarity, to federation, amalgamation, fusion, and unification – had been given a new name: economic integration. But who did it? Who were the terminological innovators?

Machlup was unable to find a single instance of its use prior to 1942.[4] Since then the term has been used at various times to refer to practically any area of international economic relations. Users are, however, virtually unanimous on one question: that integration can be understood either as a process or as a state of affairs reached by that process. Whether that state has to be the terminal point or an intermediate point in the process is not always clear, but this ambiguity can be taken care of by distinguishing between 'complete' and 'incomplete' integration. More difficult is the question of what it is that is to be integrated: people, areas, markets, production, goods, resources, policies, or what? The most important questions, however, to ask are (i), what is the substance, what are the essential criteria of such integration?; and (ii) by what indications or symptoms can one decide whether there is or is not a process at work, or a state of affairs attained? These are very different questions. Users of the term may agree on what the substance is and yet disagree on how one can find out or what one should observe; conversely, some might agree on possible indicators without agreeing on the essentials, or what it is all about.

Nevertheless, despite this array of uncertainty, by 1950, the term had been given a specific definition by economists specialising in international trade to denote, as indicated above, a state of affairs or a process involving the combination of separate economies into larger economic regions. Defined as a process, it includes all measures that aim at abolishing discrimination between economic units from different countries. It can also be considered as a state of affairs characterized by the absence of various forms of discrimination between countries. This definition is quite close to what John Pinder, with reference to the European Economic Community, has termed as the twin processes involving both *negative* and *positive* aspects of integration. While negative integration is that aspect of economic integration that consists in the elimination of discrimination against participating members, positive integration symbolizes the formation and application of coordinated and common policies in order to fulfil economic and welfare objectives other than the mere removal of discrimination.[5] It should be noted that the term 'negative integration' to imply the taking away of barriers was coined by Tinbergen.[6]

The term 'economic integration' can also be interpreted in two senses. In a dynamic sense, it is the process whereby 'economic frontiers between member states are gradually eliminated' (that is to say, whereby national discrimination is abolished), with the formerly separate national economic entities gradually merging into a larger whole. In a static sense, Molle refers to a situation in which 'national components of a larger economy are no longer separated by economic frontiers but function together as an entity'.[7] The dynamic interpretation is the more usual, and the one used today. On the whole, a wide consensus exists on three issues: (i) that economic integration refers basically to division of labour; (ii) that it involves mobility of goods or factors or both; and (iii) that it is related to discrimination or non-discrimination in the treatment of goods and factors, as for example, with regard to origin or destination. It must be stressed, also, that economic integration is not an *objective* in itself, but serves higher objectives, both of an economic and of a political nature.

Since it is of some consequence for the argument presented in this book, it is essential at this juncture to examine briefly the meaning of economic integration in light of African conditions. In this connection, we may rely on the analysis of Bingu Mutharika who has warned that the peculiarity of the characteristics of the African economies and the evolution of political and other institutions 'make it unrealistic to apply the term in the same sense as used in the developed countries'.[8] It is necessary therefore to paint boldly and to fix firmly in our minds the economic and political realities of Africa in any discussion of African economic integration. The term may thus be defined as a process whereby two or more countries in a particular area voluntarily join together to pursue common policies and objectives in matters of general economic development or in a particular economic field of common interest to the mutual advantage of all the participating states.[9] The essence of this definition is that any scheme of economic integration must be voluntary and that each state must demonstrate its willingness to pursue certain policies in close consultation with the other states. Significantly, too, economic integration in Africa will have to be broadly based and wide in its application, at least in the initial stages, and sufficiently flexible in its practical form to embody social, cultural, political, and economic considerations.

It is pertinent to stress, too, that economic integration, as defined above, is used in this book not with reference to national integration in respect of the subsistence sector or to the divisions and weaknesses of dual economies in plural societies. Rather, integration refers here to international (that is, continental or regional or subregional) economic cooperation (coordination or association as the case may be) in one form or another. It is worth noting, also, that when the term regional integration is applied to Africa in the scholarly literature it almost always assumes that 'region' refers not to the entire continent but to subregions thereof.

'REGIONAL COOPERATION' AND 'REGIONAL INTEGRATION'

Since in this book we have been tempted to use the two competing terms, 'regional cooperation' and 'regional integration', interchangeably, it might be useful to differentiate between them. While, as noted above, the term regional integration has acquired several quite technical definitions, regional cooperation is a vague concept, applicable to any interstate activity with less than universal participation designed to meet some commonly experienced need. In recent years, Ernst Haas, a central figure in the neo-functionalist school of regional integration theorists, has attempted to limit the semantic confusion arising from the term integration. Basing his early work on an analysis of Europe, Haas has argued that the study of regional integration is not the same as the study of regional cooperation. The former, in his view, is concerned with explanations of how and why states cease to be wholly sovereign, how and why they voluntarily mingle, merge, and mix with their neighbours so as to lose the factual attributes of sovereignty while acquiring new techniques for resolving conflict between themselves. The latter, on the other hand, is concerned with the process of getting there. In other words, regional cooperation may help describe steps along the way to regional integration.[10]

In this sense, therefore, the term integration may be treated as the terminal or resulting condition, the end state, or outcomes or consequences of regional cooperation activities. Hence the study of regional cooperation may be considered as a part of the study of regional integration or as a separate interest. However, the point to emphasize here is that states will either way eventually come to share individual authority with a collective mechanism or entity. I thus agree with Isebill Gruhn that whether the integration process is perceived of as leading to the goal or as constituting the goal itself, the same consequences can result.[11] In this book, therefore, I have been tempted to regard regional integration both as a process and as a terminal condition. In other words, the cooperation of African countries in various fields of economic activity may lead to partial or complete economic integration at either subregional or regional levels.

STAGES OR DIFFERENT FORMS OF INTEGRATION

Considering the main elements in the stages of integration, Molle has identified two distinct areas. There is, first, the integration of the *markets,* of goods and services, on the one hand, and of production factors (labour, capital, entrepreneurship) on the other. And there is, second, the integration of economic policy.[12] The integration of markets and the integration of different areas of economic policy follow in practice a sequence through a hierarchy of forms as described below.

In terms of integration of the markets (specifically, goods and services), there is, first, the free trade area (FTA) where the member states remove all trade impediments such as import duties and quantitative restrictions among themselves. Internal goods traffic is then free, but each country can apply its own customs tariff with respect to third countries. The European Free Trade Association (EFTA), the Latin American Free Trade Association (LAFTA) and the North American Free Trade Agreement (NAFTA) are examples of FTAs.

There is, second, the customs union in which, as in the free trade area, obstacles to the free traffic of goods among partner countries are removed, except that these countries must conduct and pursue common external commercial relations, for instance they must implement a common external tariff on imports from non-participants as is the case in the European Union.

As regards integration of the markets with specific reference to production factors, there is the common market, which consists of (i) an internal market:

that is, fully free internal movement of products (goods and services) and of production factors (labour and capital); and (ii) common external regulation for both products and production factors so this definition encompasses a customs union such as the former European Common Market and the Common Market for Eastern and Southern Africa (COMESA) established in 1994.

In the case of integration of economic policy, there is the economic union, which is a common market that asks for a high degree of coordination or even unification of the most important areas of economic policy. As a minimum these comprise those that are associated with the common market, such as market regulation, competition and industrial structure; next come those that are related to the monetary union, such as macro-economic and monetary policies; and finally there are those that refer to the more social aspects, like redistribution policies and social and environmental policies. Towards third countries common policies are pursued on trade, production factors, economic sectors, monetary stability and so on. A central authority is introduced to exercise control over these matters so that existing member states effectively become regions of one nation.

One other aspect of integration policy is related to a complete political union in which integration is extended beyond the realm of economics to encompass such fields as anti-crime policy (police) and foreign policy, eventually including security policy. It also implies the complete unification of the economies involved, and a common policy on many important matters such as, for example, social security and income tax; macro-economic and stabilization policy. The situation is then virtually the same as that within one country.

It is significant to stress that each of these forms of economic integration can be introduced in its own right: they should not be confused with stages in a process which eventually leads to complete political integration.[13] A case in point was the transformation of the Preferential Trade Area (PTA) for Eastern and Southern African States to a Common Market for Eastern and Southern Africa (COMESA) without necessarily going through the process of a customs union. It should also be noted that within each scheme there may be sectoral integration in particular areas of the economy, for example, the Common Agricultural Policy (CAP) of the European Union. Of course, sectoral integration can be introduced as an aim in itself as was the case in the European Coal and Steel Community (ECSC), but sectoral integration is a form of 'cooperation' since it is not consistent with the accepted definition of international economic integration.

THEORETICAL BACKGROUND

Although most cases of regional economic integration are among Third World countries, research in this field has been dominated by the orthodox theories based on the European experience. The EEC has thus become, in the words of Frankel, 'a living laboratory for the integration theory'.[14] The orthodox theory on which the arguments of such economists as Viner and Lipsey[15] are based was evolved with the developed countries of Europe in mind and expressly for the purpose of throwing light on the problems of integration in Western Europe. The theory is concerned with the gains that may be derived from changes in the existing pattern of trade. Full employment and given inputs of resources are assumed; and apart from the tariff, domestic prices are assumed to reflect opportunity costs, so that the chief domestic grounds for interference with the market allocation of resources do not arise. This argument is based upon the concepts of trade creation and trade diversion.

Given the arguments on which the orthodox theory is based, it is natural to ask how far, if at all, is this theory also relevant to the rather different circumstances of developing countries like those of Africa? This poses a consideration of two vital issues: first, to what extent do the characteristics of developing countries favour trade creation?; and second, is trade creation the significant criterion for evaluating customs unions among such countries?

Viner defines trade creation as a shift in trade from high-cost to low-cost sources of supply within the integration area, and trade diversion as a shift from a low-cost source of supply outside the integration area to a high-cost producer within it. Since trade diversion (at least in the short run) will obviously prevail over trade creation in Third World customs union as the members shift from low-cost producers in the developed world to high-cost producers among their neighbours, Viner and Lipsey are opposed to the creation of customs unions among developing countries. In other words, the conditions that are favourable to trade creation are precisely the opposite of those typically found in developing countries, whose existing external trade is usually large relative to their domestic production and whose intra-group trade is a minor component of their total trade.

However, in recent years there has been a growing criticism about applying Viner's criteria and Lipsey's general conclusions to the possible effects of customs unions among developing countries.[16] Most writers concerned with the problems of Third World countries have rejected neo-classical customs union theory and argued that the problems of economic integration among peripheral countries should be analysed within the context of development economies rather than as a branch of tariff theory.

This argument is based on the fact that conditions in the developing countries are strikingly different from those that exist in the developed world on which the established theoretical framework for economic integration has been based. The critical factors on which Viner's criteria and Lipsey's conclusions were based are among the ones the developing countries, such as those in Africa, are desirous of changing through economic integration. In effect, remarked Onitiri, 'the under-developed areas are involved in a huge effort to alter the structure of their economy and to integrate their foreign trade more closely with it than before'.[17] In other words, these countries aim at changing the structure of production and trade, and then at evolving a new trade mechanism based on regional specialization. These changes are not marginal but structural. Their net effect will not be felt over a short period of time. Attention, therefore, has to be paid to the long-run effects which economic integration is likely to have. Thus, in evaluating the desirability of economic integration among developing countries, the emphasis should be placed on dynamic rather than static effects. More specifically, we should be concerned with the dynamics of economic growth and stress positive effects in the creation of regional markets on the developmental pace of member countries. Consequently, the utilization of deliberate methods to enhance the impact of dynamic factors has taken on increasing importance as the process of integration among developing countries expands into its long-term dimensions.

Briefly, then, economic integration in the case of developing countries should be treated as an approach to economic development rather than a tariff issue. Accordingly, it combines various aspects that could improve the international trade position as well as raise the level of economic development of developing countries. Thus it is only when we look beyond the neo-classical theory of economic integration that we can appreciate the benefits expected to be derived from such efforts. These considerations seem to be of overriding importance in the decision to integrate the economies of the African countries on attaining independence. For while there could not be sufficient justification on a 'purely static analysis basis' for the creation of customs unions in Africa, the contrary is the case when based on dynamic grounds.

On the whole, then, regional economic integration in a developing area such as Africa is in many respects a very different phenomenon than in an economically advanced area such as Europe. Granted many features are the same; but many other features – important ones – are different. First, for example, we may readily point to important differences in infrastructure, market mechanisms, external dependence, administrative resources, political group structure, interdependence of social sectors, national consciousness, and ideology. Amitai Etzioni has thus argued that limited horizons, lack of administrative and political skills, and preoccupation with problems of domestic modernization all present major barriers to successful integration efforts in the developing world.[18]

Second, European nations could afford to treat economic integration as 'a matter of welfare politics' without foreclosing their 'high politics' option because each started from a relatively industrialized base. The base is quite different in the developing region of the world.[19] As Nye has pointed out, integration involving developing countries seems to produce not 'gradual politicization' but 'over-politicization'. Such premature politicization of economic issues greatly reduces the scope for bureaucratic initiatives and quietly arranged package deals.[20] Thus conditions that may be termed requisite for successful economic integration in the developed areas cannot reasonably be applied to the developing areas. The same criteria for judging the success or failure of an integrative process cannot be applied to efforts in both the developed and developing areas. Besides, to some extent, the integrative process itself is different in developed and developing areas.

More significantly, the objectives of economic integration in developing areas are different than they are in developed areas. In the latter the overall or general objective of regional economic integration is to maintain and enhance an already existing sustained economic growth. Hence the principal economic goal is to aid the development of already established industries in highly industrialized countries through trade expansion and increased competition. In the case of developing countries, we would venture to redefine the goal of economic integration. Here, the ultimate purpose of economic integration is either to achieve an acceleration of economic growth in the partner countries, given the limited amount of scarce resources available, or alternatively, to maintain the same rate of growth as before integration, but at lower cost in terms of the use of scarce resources. Put differently, regional economic integration in developing countries is seen primarily as a means of contributing to economic development. The consequences of integration are thus evaluated for their contribution to development and not necessarily to greater efficiency. To this extent, therefore, regional economic integration in developing countries may more properly be called developmental regionalism, or an instrument of collective betterment, because it is designed not only to expand trade but also to encourage new industries, to help diversify national economies, and to increase the region's bargaining power with the developed nations.

POLITICS, ECONOMICS AND REGIONALISM

Although in theory, economics and politics ought to be distinguished as separate disciplines, in practice, however, they cannot be kept separate in any economic integration movement on account of the complex ramifications of individual and state activities involved. To a great extent, integration is political as well as economic in both its objectives and procedures. On the other hand, economic changes made to satisfy the requirements of an extended market can create a need for political union, although they cannot of themselves effect such a union. Haas contends that: 'The decision to proceed with integration or to oppose it rests on the part of existing political actors.'[21] On the other hand, many economic problems involved in integration can be solved only through political measures. The development and orientation of regional trade; the maintenance of full employment; the regulation of cartels and monopolies; the prevention of depression and inflation; and the coordination of regional economic plans – all this necessarily requires legal provisions, executive decisions, and administrative harmony which fall within the responsibility of the highest spheres of government. As Felippe Herrera warned a few years ago:

> We have a long way to travel and all the longer, the more we delay in recognizing that economic integration cannot be attained exclusively through strictly economic measures, that economic integration is not in itself enough to assure the progress and welfare of nations, and that every development progress entails simultaneous struggle on the fronts of technology, law, education, institutions, and fundamentally politics.[22]

To sum up, all of the regional organizations – regardless of whether their purpose is promotion of security, promotion of economic well-being, or promotion of human welfare – are political in nature. Not only do political objectives motivate the establishment of these organizations, political actions also bring them into being, and it is politics that characterizes their functioning, too. As ongoing entities, Cochrane has stated that these organizations are marked by conflict among participant-actors over goals and over the distribution of costs and benefits just as is politics at the national level. 'It is not going too far, then, to say that regional organizations are in reality political systems.'[23]

Thus, whether one follows Lasswell to define politics as the study of who gets what, when and how, or Easton, to define it as the process of making authoritative allocation of values (authoritative in the sense of being binding on the members of the particular community) it follows that in so far as economic integrations set up institutions, or arrangements that are meant either to render a service or to create rules or norms of behaviour, or to adjudicate, conciliate or in any way settle disputes, one cannot avoid talking about politics. As Rothchild notes, organizations that are predominantly economic have significant political dimensions if anything, for the simple reason that 'international organizations are political in their inception, termination, and basic arrangements even if the conflict factor is minimized in their daily operations'.[24]

The involvement of politics in integrative schemes is more pervasive and more divisive in the case of Africa. It has been aptly said that economic integration in Africa must be sufficiently elastic to accommodate political aspirations and that it is important to marry the economic propositions with political dogma.[25] This is essential because it is often difficult in Africa today to consider economic development problems without considering political realities. Experience has shown how in Africa political problems have obstructed implementation of joint development proposals, no matter how plausible. Thus, economic decisions and intra-regional bargaining, which in more developed countries would be left to a much greater extent to technocrats, become of major political consequence. For economics in Africa is indeed high politics. In such circumstances the ability of the technocrat, in whom neo-functionalist theorists of integration placed greater hope, to act independently in the interest of regional cooperation, is severely limited. Economic issues become prematurely politicized.

The main reason for this is that in Africa economic policy is not simply a political concern but a central one, usually second only in priority to internal and external security, and often occupying far more time, resources, and effort than decisions directly connected with security. The process of nation-building and the desire to channel the factors of production into the most advantageous uses have forced many African governments to take control of the machinery for planning for economic development in order to ensure that the benefits of industrial progress, economic advancement, and indeed the fruits of independence are evenly distributed among all the inhabitants of the country. Thus, while the concept of integration may everywhere be the same, the problems of integration are qualitatively different in the African setting.

Against this background of our analysis of the close relationship that exists between politics and economic integration, it is quite evident that, even though perhaps to avoid emotional national conflict, the articles of the treaties establishing the African economic communities do not highlight sufficiently political considerations, the political implications of the schemes cannot be denied. Indeed, the very decision to establish the communities and the framework within which their activities will be performed are the consequences of political bargaining. James Nti drove this point home when he told some newly recruited foreign service officers at Lagos, Nigeria: 'The very decision of sovereign countries to come together to integrate their economies is very much a political matter; one does not need to read about political union before one realizes the political significance of economic integration.'[26]

Almost every detail and degree of African economic integration envisaged in the economic community treaties requires a bold political decision and the coordination of economic and political policies. In Africa, perhaps more than anywhere else, economic integration means more than merely refurbishing an old house; it means jointly building a new and larger house for millions of Africans. Such a larger regional house can only be raised by the cooperation and sacrifices of all participating governments. Indeed, all structural and regional levels required for its growth will, in the final analysis, take place only through the decisions and actions of governments.

THE RATIONALE FOR REGIONALISM IN AFRICA

The major challenge facing Africa in this last decade of the twentieth century is to reverse the trend of economic decline which has afflicted the region since the 1970s and strengthen the capacity of the economies for participation as important and effective partners in the global economy in the next century. One key element in the response to this challenge is the promotion of regional economic integration, which has for long constituted a significant aspect of African development strategy. The myriad regional and subregional organizations testify to the intensive efforts made to harness regional cooperation to the task of African development. Its merits as a desirable strategy for a large number of African states have been well documented in various studies on African development[27] and reflected in virtually all recent internal or external action programmes or guidelines for sub-Saharan Africa.[28] These studies assign a major development role to economic cooperation and integration.

The strategy of regionalism was given a new lease of life with the adoption in April 1980 of the *Lagos Plan of Action (LPA)* and the Final Act of Lagos (FAL) in which African leaders committed themselves to the 'creation, at the national, subregional and regional levels, of a dynamic and interdependent African economy' and thereby pave the way for the essential establishment of an African common market leading to an African economic community.[29] Regionalism, which is discussed in virtually every chapter of the *Plan*, constitutes an integral condition for its implementation. So central is the concept of regionalism to the *Plan*'s prescription of collective self-reliance that, as Browne and Cummings comment, 'without regional integration the *LPA* collapses as a concept' and strategy, 'so no allowance is made for failure in achieving it'.[30]

The case for regional and subregional economic integration and inter-African economic cooperation is indisputable and has long been recognized. Since the massive movement towards independence in the late 1950s and early 1960s, there was immediate recognition that, while independence had been the primary goal, African countries were largely artificial by-products of the colonial scramble of the era of the 1884–5 Berlin Conference. The present fragmentation and small African markets emanate from the specific political and economic conditions in which the continent found itself at independence. Africa has most of the world's mini-states: nine countries with a population of less than one million and thirty-five with a population of less than ten million. Only five African countries – Ethiopia, Egypt, Nigeria, Zaire and South Africa – have a population of more than 30 million. History in the last century and a half indicates that only very large national units have a sufficient resource base, climatic diversity, and population size to afford what Oteiza and Sercovich have termed, 'an autarchic self-reliant model'.[31] As Ruth Morgenthau notes, 'the typical developing African nation has a sparse population, small internal market, limited infrastructure, new and fragile borders, and economies vulnerable to fluctuating world prices'.[32]

Specifically, so many African countries are economically so small, with such small and such poor populations, that production for the domestic markets alone must be extremely restricted. Domestic production for such small markets will be at extremely high cost if economies of scale are of any importance. Without access to the larger market area that could be created by measures of economic integration, it is impossible to see how the economies of these small countries could be developed and diversified. Without access to a larger market for new productive activities, these countries will remain tied to the world economy as producers of primary commodities and importers of manufactures. Indeed, the balkanization of Africa appears to be one of the most enduring of the colonial legacies.

Because of the continent's fragmentation and poverty, economic cooperation is perhaps more relevant to Africa than to any of the developing nations of the world. Using the conventional indicators of economic and social well-being (per capita income, literacy, calorie intake, mortality, and so on), most African countries fall significantly behind Latin American countries and all but a few of the poorest Asian countries.[33] Twenty-eight of the 41 countries designated 'least developed' by the United Nations are in Africa. As Ann Seidman commented a little over a decade ago, what is clear is that, 'despite the independence of over 40 African countries, the majority of African peoples still confront the overriding problem of poverty'. Living on a continent endowed with extensive mineral and agricultural resources, 'they still suffer from among the lowest per capita income and the highest mortality rates in the world'.[34]

In 1989, for example, the gross national product (GNP) of all sub-Saharan African countries, excluding South Africa, put together was approximately equal to that of Belgium.[35] And it is sobering to note that South Africa's gross domestic product (GDP) of US$103 651 million in 1992 – which is approximately three times larger than that of Algeria (the second largest economy in Africa) and three and a half times larger that the Nigerian GDP (the second largest economy in sub-Saharan Africa) – is slightly smaller than the Norwegian GDP of US$112 906 million.[36] In other words, Africa's largest economy by far is approximately the same size, when measured in terms of GDP, as that of a small European economy.

Of considerable significance is the fact that the smallness of the economies in Africa leads to a second perspective: when combined into a larger market behind a common external barrier, the larger, combined market remains small by world standards, and further constrained by high costs of transport and communication. At US$80 000 million, the GDP (1989) of the 16-member Economic Community of West African States (ECOWAS), with a population of 180 million and poor infrastructure, is smaller than that of Denmark with its GDP of US$90 000 million, population of 5.1 million, and integrated, comparatively low-cost transport and communication services. The 20-member Preferential Trade Area (PTA) for Eastern and Southern Africa with a GDP of US$70 000 million and a population of 192 million has an even smaller market than ECOWAS.[37] While the sum of the markets is much larger than the individual markets of the participating economies, thus raising the potential for inward-looking industrial growth to a level which is not possible in the individual states, the combined market is still not large enough to reach high levels of industrial development through import substitution.

Given this background, it is not surprising that economic integration has been seen as a means of helping to overcome the disadvantages of small size, low per capita incomes, small populations, and narrow resources bases, and of making possible a higher rate of economic growth and development. It has also been seen as a means of consolidating the political independence of African countries and thereby strengthening their overall position *vis-à-vis* that of the developed countries, especially the former metropolitan powers. In brief, therefore, economic integration in general is not only desirable, it is necessary if Africa is to industrialize, develop intra-African trade, develop the capacity to participate effectively in the evolving global linkages and interdependence, reduce her vulnerability to fluctuating overseas markets, mobilize and maximize scarce resources of capital and skills, and finally forge the way to effective African unity, both political and economic.

All this has been reinforced by the relatively successful experience of integration among the Western European countries, the United States–Canada Free Trade Agreement and other integration schemes among countries in the Pacific and Asian region. Regional cooperation can help to promote a more complementary and sustained development of African countries, through the reinforcement of the regional infrastructure, more efficient systems of payment, greater access to credit, a more interrelated institutional system, a greater mutual awareness among economic agents operating in the different countries and, above all, through a growing technical complementarity and a greater development and integration of the productive sectors of African countries.

Therefore economic cooperation among African countries, as Adedeji has stressed, 'is a *sine qua non* for the achievement of national socio-economic goals, and not an "extra" to be given thought to after the process of development is well advanced'.[38] For in no area of endeavour – whether it is in the internalization of the development process or international trade negotiations, debt policy, or adjustment with transformation – can much progress be made without cooperation among African countries. As eloquently summed up in the ECA *African Alternative Framework*:

> The political balkanization of the continent into arbitrary nation-states elicits from Africa the understandable impulse to restructure the fragmented region into a more coherent and stronger economic and political entity. The African sense of oneness and solidarity also sparks off natural sentiments for increased socio-economic cooperation. At the economic level, the numerous obstacles to genuine development that individual African countries confront as a result of their limited and fragmented economic space have provided an objective rationale and galvanized the African to resolve to pursue and achieve the goal of collective self-reliance.[39]

It is no wonder therefore that African countries fully accept that they cannot make real progress with economic development without close coordination and harmonization of their sectoral plans and national development policies, and they continue to adopt resolutions and declarations to that effect, as reflected not only in the *LPA* and the Final Act of Lagos, but also in Africa's Declaration on Economic Cooperation and Development (1973), the Monrovia Strategy (1979), Africa's Priority Programme for Economic Recovery (APPER) (1985), Africa's Submission to the Special Session of the United Nations General Assembly on Africa's Economic and Social Crisis (1986), the United Nations Programme of Action for African Economic Recovery and Development 1986–90 (UN-PAAERD) (1986), the United Nations New Agenda for the Development of Africa in the 1990s (UN-NADAF) adopted in 1991 and the Cairo Agenda for Action (1995) – all contain fresh proposals and undertakings about more effective approaches to the goals of economic integration.

In brief, therefore, regional economic integration among a group of small developing countries such as those in Africa, which provides for the pooling of resources and coordinated efforts in the use of the pooled resources, can bring about results in development and enhanced external bargaining power that are greater than the sum of results if each country acted alone. Indeed, in Africa, regional integration is the only viable strategy for optimal development of all the peoples of the region in the contemporary economic and political circumstances in the continent as well as in the world as a whole. It is not surprising that even before the departure of the colonial powers African leaders had realized the significance of establishing economic integration schemes, which are linked to the pan-African movement of the 1950s and 1960s.

PAN-AFRICANISM AND CONTINENTAL ECONOMIC INTEGRATION

Regional cooperation and integration actually started off as aspects of the pan-African movement which aimed at the 'unification of African forces against imperialism and colonial domination'. It was recognized as an essential component of strategies of economic decolonization long before the attainment of political independence.[40] Thus, one of the earliest manifestations of the idea of regional economic integration in Africa was reflected in the resolutions of the famous 1945 Fifth Pan-African Congress held in Manchester, England, under the leadership of Kwame Nkrumah of Ghana and George Padmore of the West Indies.[41] With great foresight, as Adedeji, Executive Secretary of the Economic Commission for Africa (ECA) from 1975 to 1991, reminds us, the Congress recommended the establishment of a West African Economic Union 'as a means of combating the exploitation of the economic resources of the West African territories and for ensuring the participation of the indigenous people in the industrial development of West Africa'.[42] Long before Manchester, similar resolutions had been adopted by the pan-African movement of the 1920s spearheaded by the Congress of British West Africa.[43] Besides, as early as 1942, Kwame Nkrumah, the pace-setter of the independence period, was insisting that all the West African colonies 'must first unite and become a national unity, absolutely free from the encumbrances of foreign rule, before they can assume the aspect of international cooperation on a grand scale'.[44] Thus, pan-Africanism was viewed both 'as an integrative force' and 'as a movement of liberation'.[45]

Because of this link with pan-Africanism, strategies for regional integration adopted in the early post-independence period favoured all-embracing regional or continental organizations. Kwame Nkrumah, the greatest advocate of pan-Africanism, admirably captured the feelings of Africa when he said: 'Indeed, the total integration of the African economy on a continental scale is the only way in which the African states can achieve anything like the levels of industrialized countries.'[46] An Africa divided could never control its own economic destiny and therefore never be genuinely independent, as has been discussed elsewhere and should therefore not detain us here.[47]

It is against this background that the idea of an African common market or an economic community as an approach to integration at the continental level was reflected in the resolutions of the various pan-African conferences held during the early years of African independence. The three historic All-African Peoples Conferences held in 1958, 1960 and 1961 respectively, and the Second Conference of Independence African States held in Addis Ababa in June 1960, advocated the establishment of a broad, continental common market. It was generally felt that an African common market, devoted uniquely to African interests, would more efficaciously promote the true requirements of the African states.

The First Conference of Independent African states, which was held in Ghana, in 1958, resolved to set up an Economic and Research Committee within each country and a Joint Economic and Research Committee composed of representatives of all independent African countries. Their task was 'to consolidate the economic development policies of the states, promote trade and a common industrial policy, and coordinate economic planning among the different states with a view to achieving an all-African economic cooperation arrangement'.[48] Later, in 1960, the independent African states of that time recommended the creation of an African Council for Economic Cooperation, an African Development Bank and an African Commercial Bank. It was recommended that a system of preferential tariff among independent African countries should be established. It was largely as a result of this collective fervour for economic integration that all the early inter-governmental groupings, such as the Casablanca Powers, the Brazzaville Group and the Monrovia Group, aimed at the creation of such African economic institutions as an African Common Market, an African Payments Union and an African Bank for Economic Development.

The continental approach to African development encountered various obstacles. Foremost amongst these was 'newness of the states which made it difficult for national leaders to divest themselves of their newly acquired authority in favour of collective decision-making'.[49] The continental economic integration undoubtedly underestimated the difficulties of welding together largely nationalistic societies differing in size and level of development so soon after independence. There was also the lack of adequate interstate infrastructure, particularly transport and communications links, which circumscribed intra-state trade and movement. One other obstacle arose from the differences in political ideologies adopted by the emergent states. Besides, the strong bilateral links with the former colonial powers continued to militate strongly against horizontal intra-African relations, while strengthening vertical relations with Europe.

Given the environment of the early 1960s, the concept of continental unity of interests was tenuous, despite the common heritage of colonialism in Africa. Indeed, the linkage of the political unity movement with that of a continental common market made those African leaders who were opposed to the former give less than serious attention to the latter. For even though other African governments might accept Nkrumah's analysis, they would not necessarily choose to accept a far-reaching political solution. The threat of neo-colonialism might not have seemed to them to warrant such drastic steps as the derogation of sovereignty to an overall political authority.

Continental economic integration, therefore, remained a 'dream of unity' in the sixties. Neither Nkrumah's enthusiasm for the noble pan-African ideal of political unity and economic continentalism nor Julius Nyerere's preferred incremental regionalism leading eventually towards pan-Africanism went beyond the stage of theoretical discussions. Although, in January 1965, African states glibly mentioned a plan for an African Common Market and large-scale integration of trade and industries,[50] no concrete action was taken to implement it.

Thus, in spite of the optimistic years of the 1960s when the constraints of economic dependence had not yet become apparent, and Africa tended to be treated as 'an homogeneous whole, with a unity of peoples being seen as deriving from a common heritage',[51] affirmed and reflected in some pan-African-conscious institutions or even a union government, an African common market or an economic community eluded the continent and its leaders. The lesson was instructive.

THE 1960–70 PERIOD: MODEST BEGINNINGS OF ECONOMIC INTEGRATION

With the formation of the Organization of African Unity (OAU) and its concentration on the liberation aspects of pan-Africanism, and with the concentration of many independent states on internal developments and on strengthening their ties with their former colonial rulers and, above all, with the overthrow of Nkrumah, the continental integration aspect of pan-Africanism lost its momentum throughout the second half of the 1960s. It was rather replaced by movements for the formation of regional and interstate groupings. According to Adebayo Adedeji, there were by 1977 over 20 intergovernmental multisectoral economic cooperation organizations in Africa and about a hundred single multinational organizations that were meant to promote technical and economic cooperation in Africa.[52] Many of these were established in the 1960s, which were the halcyon years of African integration. But the decade was also characterized by the decline of several regional groupings. By the early 1970s, if not earlier, it was clear that African integration efforts were in serious trouble.

For example, the two initiatives among the French-speaking West African countries, resulting in the successive establishment of the West African Customs Union (UDAO – Union douanière de l'Afrique de l'Ouest) in June 1959 and of the Customs Union of West African States (UDEAO – Union douanière et économique de l'Afrique de l'Ouest) in June 1966, both failed. The Economic Community of West Africa (CEAO – Communauté économique de l'Afrique de l'Ouest), formed in 1973, was the latest of the experiments at regional integration by the majority of the states created out of the former federation of French West Africa (AOF – Afrique occidentale française). Nor did the Customs and Economic Union of Central Africa (UDEAC – Union douanière et économique de l'Afrique Centrale), set up in January 1964, fare any better; restrictions on the opening of markets and non-compliance with its rules have sapped it of most of its energy as an integrative system. Similarly, the Council of the Entente States (Conseil de l'Entente) founded in 1959 through the initiative of President Houphouët-Boigny of Côte d'Ivoire seemed to be diminishing in importance due to the increasing attention being focused on the larger and dynamic grouping, the CEAO. The short-lived (1968–71) Organization of Senegal River States (OERS – Organisation des Etats riverains du Sénégal) was succeeded in 1972 by the Organization for the Development of the Senegal River (OMVS – Organisation pour la mise en valeur du fleuve Sénégal), which has still not been able to establish a workable machinery for cooperation. Also, the cooperation agreements of the nine-member Maghreb Permanent Consultative Committee, formed in November 1965, were never ratified.

In Anglophone Africa, however (apart from East Africa, which attained independence as an economic community), no regional economies were established during the early years of independence. Whereas the Francophone West African countries consistently strove to maintain pre-independence joint institutions and to establish new ones, their Anglophone counterparts, mainly at the insistence of Ghana, disbanded the few joint institutions – the British

West African Currency Board, the West African Court of Appeal, the West African Cocoa Research Institute and the West African Airways Corporation – which the British had established, thus advancing the 'balkanization' of that part of Africa.

More worrying was the East African Community, arguably the most sophisticated regional cooperative arrangement in the Third World at the time, which experienced such acute tensions in the 1960s that by the end of the decade the level of economic integration had declined. The significance of East African integration can best be grasped by reflecting that at independence, external trade, fiscal and monetary policy, transport and communications infra-structures, and university education were all regional rather than national. Subsequently, these links and services were systematically dismantled and all the high hopes that Kenya, Uganda and Tanzania would eventually evolve into full federation under one government evaporated. By June 1977 the whole structure of the East African Community, once regarded as a model for African regional cooperation, had collapsed.

Undeniably, economic integration schemes launched optimistically in the 1960s were largely moribund by the end of the decade. Thus, despite the rhetoric of pan-African solidarity and the paraphernalia of elaborate decision making structures, paradoxically, the period witnessed decline rather than progress in the field of effective regional integration in Africa. No solid foundations for regional groupings were laid, in spite of the countless expressions of fidelity to the principles of pan-Africanism. The question then arises, why so little progress and such faltering steps? Was it because African states failed to see the advantages of regional economic integration and collective self-reliance? Or, were there some undercurrents which rocked the very foundation of cooperation?

The problems and constraints of African regional integration during the early years of independence were many and seemingly intractable. They stemmed from internal as well as external and historical factors. One of these factors was the growth and impact of national consciousness on regional integration. Colonialism not only left behind a patchwork of many sovereign states, but the states spawned by this process were themselves artificial entities. They were, as yet, by no means nations; rather, they represented the shells of territorial independence in which the kernel of national identity had been planted by the independence movements. The major tasks of the new governments was to provide the soil in which the seed could grow. Anxious to encourage national integration, the new leaders were compelled to look inward and to rank as their first priority the political, economic and social developments of their own polities. The immediate concern, then, was to build viable nation-states based on their own traditions and customs, and on the promises which had been held out to the masses. To the extent that national consolidation received high priority, cooperation with other African countries would have to be secondary. Since meaningful cooperation necessarily implied long-term commitment, there was an understandable reluctance to take decisions which restrained national sovereignty in certain key areas, including development-plan formulation. While this did not rule out joint endeavours in some forms of regional integration, it did suggest the existence of very real limits on the extent to which African states were willing to part with or to pool their sovereignty.

Throughout, African states did not display much willingness to sacrifice perceived national interests on the regional altar. They entered into agreement to liberate trade or allocate industries on a regional basis only when these integrative objectives were not in conflict with considerations of national security, prestige, or economic advantage. This tendency was aggravated, among other things, by the different economic groupings within Africa of the pre-Lomé Convention era: the 18 French-speaking associated states with the EEC under the Yaoundé system; the Commonwealth non-associates and Commonwealth associates like Nigeria under a special trade agreement with the EEC signed in January 1966 (but never implemented); and the three East African states of Kenya, Uganda and Tanzania under the September 1969 Arusha Agreement.

From a political economy perspective, too, a variety of factors can be said to have complicated the functioning of schemes for economic cooperation.[53] One such factor was the economic and political heterogeneity of the continent. Countries that followed vastly different development paths would not make good partners in economic cooperation schemes. Indeed, political and ideological cleavages threatened even existing and otherwise viable cooperative arrangements such as the defunct East African Community. Added to all these critical constraints and issues is what Timothy Shaw has termed the intractable problems of politicization of organizations, both of which led to institutional tension and decay.[54] Besides the classic case of the East African Community, was the bewildering frequency of changes in organizations and memberships in Francophone Africa which was partly the result of regional inequalities. Because of such intractable difficulties, the establishment of regional groupings in Africa's first decade of recaptured independence was often no more than a declaration of intent and an indication of continental alignment.

THE 1970s AND 1980s: EUPHORIA FOR ECONOMIC INTEGRATION

Since the mid-1970s, there has been indeed a renewed enthusiasm for pan-Africanism as an integrative force at the regional level. What was the nature of this new interest and how can it be explained? The main reason has been the disappointing African economic performance of the last 25 years. For despite efforts to stimulate industrial growth, to foster agricultural production and to initiate other development programmes to bring about more fundamental changes in the economic situation inherited at independence, today's reality is that the transformation of the continent which was expected to follow closely on the heels of political independence still remains only a hope. There has been no marked improvement in many African economies since 1960. Of the 32 countries identified by the 1974 Sixth Special Session of the United Nations General Assembly as 'most seriously affected' by the 'current economic crisis', 20 are in Africa.

The hopes of African leaders earlier in the 1960s – that a combination of trade with aid from the industrialized nations would provide the necessary resources to satisfy national aspirations for autonomous, self-sustaining development – failed to materialize. The record of the 1960s was therefore most disappointing. Neither the trade nor the aid policies practised by the industrialized nations appeared capable of accelerating economic expansion. Africa thus emerged from the First United Nations Development Decade (1960–70) as the region registering the lowest rate of growth among developing countries – 2 per cent as against Southern Asia (4.1 per cent), East Asia (5.6 per cent), Latin America (4.5 per cent) and the Middle East (7.2 per cent). Initial indications from the Second United Nations Development Decade (1970–80) were that the situation had changed little, if at all. Thus despite its vast natural resources, Africa is unable to point to any significant growth rate or satisfactory index of well-being in the last 25 years.[55]

In spite of exports, many African countries showed throughout the 1970s a pattern of sluggish economic growth, low levels of productivity, a circumscribed and fractured industrial base, high dependence on a vulnerably narrow spectrum of primary export commodities, low levels of life expectancy, and widening deficits on the aggregate current accounts of the balance of payments. Real per capita income declined while the rate of inflation approximately doubled, reaching an average annual rate of over 20 per cent during 1977–9. The combined current account deficit of the balance of payments rose from about US$4 billion in 1974 to close to US$10 billion annually in 1978–9.[56] Above all, between 1970 and 1979 external indebtedness of sub-Saharan Africa rose from US$6 billion to US$32 billion and debt service (for the oil-importing countries) increased from 6 to 12 per cent of export earnings in the same period. The debt burden continued to rise from an estimated US$265 billion in 1989 to US$285 billion in 1993, an amount representing 96 per cent of the combined GDP of the continent.[57] Thus, if Africa's inheritance from colonialism in 1960 was 'inauspicious', to borrow Timothy Shaw's description, by 1980 it had become even less promising.

In the world economy, Africa has always been in a subordinate position, characterized by asymmetrical and unequal economic relationships with the industrialized Western world. Even if one does not accept dependency theory as an accurate description of Africa's economic systems and relations, it is beyond question that the continent's position in the international economic order has been one of inequality. This disturbing condition was aggravated by the impact of the global crises syndrome symbolized by the collapse of the Bretton Woods Agreement, the oil-shocks of the Organization of Petroleum Exporting Countries (OPEC), the energy crunch, and the continuing stagflation of the mid-1970s onwards, which revealed as never before the extreme vulnerability of almost all African countries to external forces. Confronted with this implacable reality, African leaders were forced into a sobering reassessment of what their options were: what is the correct path towards economic development?

Given the imminence of catastrophe and collapse, innovative responses were imperative. For if the deterioration in economic performance was to be halted and reversed, then new directions of policy were required. Africa's hopes, then, lay in a fundamental redirection of national and regional development strategies. The OPEC success crystallized the concepts of strength through collective action and solidarity. It provided a compelling case for collective 'Southern' action in pursuit of counter-dependency ambitions. Such action was seen as vital to the salvation of Africa's economic problems. African states therefore strongly felt that they had to foster mutual cooperation to impart strength to their national endeavours to fortify their independence – for although each individual country might be weak, President Nyerere counselled:

> Together, or even in groups, we are much less weak. We have the capability to help each other in many ways, each gaining in the process. As a combined group we can meet the wealthy nations on very different terms, for though they may not need any one of us for their economic health, they cannot cut themselves off from all of us.[58]

Furthermore, the 1974 resolution of the United Nations General Assembly on the New International Economic Order (NIEO)[59] which drew attention to economic cooperation among developing countries as its key element; and the signing in February 1975 of the celebrated Lomé Convention which groups together the French- and English-speaking African states creating a new political climate and economic structure – all this led to the re-emergence of a rash of regional integration schemes in Africa.

Regional economic integration was seen as more or less explicit challenges to the external domination of the continent inherited from the colonial era. Apart from the more orthodox benefits promised by regional groupings in the shape of expanded trade and investment, economic integration is being vigorously advocated as a means of reducing external vulnerability. This has become increasingly urgent mainly because the dependent relationship does not appear to be lessening; indeed, given the soaring foreign debts of many African states, it is increasing. Hopefully, regional economic integration would break this dependent relationship by helping each member nation to export manufactured goods and eventually capital goods to their neighbours. The underlying premise here is the desire by African states and leaders to determine as far as possible their own economic policies based on their national aspirations, natural resources and political ideologies outside the influence of developed countries. Thus the problems and prospects of recently created regional groupings in the area of dependency reduction merit special attention.

Among the most ambitious and dynamic regional economic integration schemes in Africa is the Economic Community of West African States (ECOWAS for the English-speaking and CEDEAO for the French-speaking), which brings together 16 countries covering an area of 6 million square kilometres stretching from Mauritania in the north-west to Nigeria in the south-east. Established in Lagos, Nigeria, in May 1975, ECOWAS is the first serious attempt at economic cooperation and integration in the West African subregion, cutting across divisions of language, history and existing affiliations and institutions. Of its member states, five are officially Anglophone, eight Francophone, two Lusophone and one Arabic.[60] It constitutes a geographical zone larger than Western Europe and it is the most heavily populated of all the subregions, with a total population of about 180 million.

The advent in 1980 of the *LPA* and the FAL which, as noted already, put forward economic integration as a prime factor of inward-oriented development, saw a spate of proliferation of subregional economic groupings in Africa. Besides ECOWAS, the two first newest initiatives are in Southern Africa. The first is the Southern African Development Coordination Conference (SADCC), which was formally inaugurated in April 1980 by the signing of the Lusaka Declaration on Economic Liberation by the five front-line states (FLS) – Angola, Botswana, Mozambique, Tanzania and Zambia – joined by Lesotho, Malawi, Swaziland and Zimbabwe. The second initiative is the PTA for Eastern and Southern African States, which was concluded in Lusaka in December 1981 by nine out of the potential eighteen states. The PTA was finally launched in Harare in July 1984. Despite its name, the PTA did not confine itself to trade alone. The treaty was much more than an elaborate definition of trading relationships. It addressed itself to virtually every sector relating to the promotion of regional economic integration.

Other manifestations of the concern with regional economic integration in the 1980s were first, the creation in October 1983 of the Economic Community of Central African States (ECCAS), comprising the present members of the Central African Customs and Economic Union (UDEAC – Union douanière et économique de l'Afrique Centrale) and those of the Economic Community of the Great Lakes Countries (CEPGL – Communauté économique des Pays des Grands Lacs). This is intended to be the Central African equivalent of ECOWAS. And, in 1989, the Arab Maghreb Union (UMA) was established in North Africa.

It can be said that by 1990, 49 African states, with a total population of 465 million, had already regrouped themselves in broader subregional economic communities with the result that, apart from Egypt, all African countries are now involved in the process of economic integration. At present, Africa accounts for about half of the 30 or so subregional and regional cooperation and economic integration arrangements existing among developing countries. Table 2.1 below illustrates the African economic integration and cooperation schemes and their membership as of December 1987. However, it remains to be seen exactly how these institutions have achieved their objectives and thus paved the way gradually for the effective take-off of the newly established continental Economic Community.

This chapter has attempted to do two things. First, it has devoted attention to the examination of a few basic concepts and fundamental elements relating to the process of economic integration as the necessary background for a proper understanding of the strategy of economic integration in Africa. Second, it has analysed the significance of this strategy as a key element of the process of African development. It has stressed that regional and subregional economic integration is widely recognized and accepted as a necessary condition for the long-term sustainable and stable development of African countries. There are a number of reasons for this. The single most important one is the acute fragmentation of the African continent. As a consequence of this fragmentation, very few single African countries possess the resources and market size necessary for viable industrialization. Even fewer African countries can participate on their own in the rapid technological and information revolution now sweeping the world. The African countries themselves and the international community, in various convergent policy declarations and statements, have underlined intra-African economic integration and cooperation as indispensable for the socio-economic transformation of African countries.

Table 2.1: African Economic Integration and Cooperation Groupings and their Membership*

Groupings / Countries	UDEAC	CEEAC	ECOWAS	CEPGL	MRU	PTA**	CEAO	SADCC	CPCM	CILSS	LCBC	NBA	OBK	OMVG	OMVS	ALG	SACU
Algeria									X								
Angola								X									
Benin			X				X					X					
Botswana								X									X
Burkina Faso			X				X			X		X				X	
Burundi		X		X		X							X				
Cameroon	X	X									X	X					
Cape Verde			X														
Central African Republic	X	X															
Chad	X	X								X	X	X					
Comoros						X											
Congo	X	X															
Côte d'Ivoire			X				X					X					
Djibouti						X											
Equatorial Guinea	X	X															
Ethiopia						X											
Gabon	X	X															
Gambia			X											X			
Ghana			X														
Guinea			X		X							X		X			
Guinea Bissau			X											X			
Kenya						X											
Lesotho						X		X									X
Liberia			X		X												
Mauritius						X											
Malawi						X		X									
Mali			X				X			X		X			X	X	
Mauritania							X		X	X					X		
Morocco									X								
Mozambique								X									
Niger			X				X			X	X	X				X	
Nigeria			X								X	X					
Rwanda		X		X		X							X				
Sao Tome & Principe		X															
Senegal			X				X							X	X		
Sierra Leone			X		X												

continued

Table 2.1: continued

Groupings Countries	U D E A C	C E E A C	E C O W A S	C E P G L	M R U	P** T A	C E A O	S A D C C	C P C M	C E	C I L S S	L C B C	N B A	O B K	O M V G	O M V S	A L G R	S A C U
Somalia						X												
South Africa																		X
Swaziland						X		X										X
Togo			X							X								
Tunisia									X									
Uganda						X								X				
United Republic of Tanzania						X		X						X				
Zaire		X		X														
Zambia						X		X										
Zimbabwe						X		X										

Notes:
* As of December 1987.
** The PTA agreement is open for signature and ratification by Angola, Botswana, Madagascar, Mozambique, Seychelles.

Frequency of membership: Niger: 7; Burkina Faso, Mali: 6; Chad, Mauritania: 5; Benin, Burundi, Cameroon, Côte d'Ivoire, Guinea, Rwanda, Senegal: 4; Nigeria, United Republic of Tanzania: 3.

Abbreviations (groupings and date of establishment)

UDEAC	Central African Customs and Economic Union founded in 1964 (revised in 1975)
CEEAC	Economic Community of Central African States founded in 1983
ECOWAS	Economic Community of West African States founded in 1975
CEPGL	Economic Community of the Great Lakes Countries founded in 1976
MRU	Mano River Union founded in 1973
PTA	Eastern and Southern Africa Preferential Trade Area founded in 1981
CEAO	West African Economic Community founded in 1973 (but dates to UDAO and UDEAO founded in 1959 and 1966 respectively)
SADCC	Southern African Development Coordination Conference founded in 1980
CPCM	Maghreb Permanent Consultation Committee founded in 1964
CE	Council of the Entente founded in 1959
CILSS	Permanent Inter-State Committee on Drought Control in the Sahel founded in 1973
LCBC	Lake Chad Basic Commission founded in 1964
NBA	Niger Basic Authority founded in 1980 (but dates back to 1963)

OBK	Organization for the Planning and Development of the Kagera River founded in 1977
OMVG	Organization for the Development of the River Gambia founded in 1978
OMVS	Organization for the Development of the Senegal River founded in 1972
ALGR	Authority for the Integrated Development of the Liptako-Gourma Region founded in 1970
SACU	Southern Africa Customs Union founded in 1969 (replacing preceding agreement which dated from 1910)

As a necessary historical background to the study of economic integration in Africa, the chapter has highlighted the linkage between pan-Africanism and economic integration with particular reference to the failure to establish pan-African-conscious continental economic integration schemes, which were being advocated in the late 1950s and 1960s. Closely related to this is a brief assessment of the fluctuating fortunes of the early subregional economic integration schemes.

The chapter, finally, throws some light on the renewed emphasis and interest which has been given to intra-African economic integration and cooperation since the mid-1970s leading to the establishment of the existing regional and subregional economic communities. What is required now is a sober analysis of the basic aims and objectives of these new economic integration schemes and a critical assessment of the extent to which they have achieved their pre-established goals. This constitutes the main focus of the following chapter.

3 Experience of Regionalism in Africa: A Critical Appraisal

The aims and objectives of the economic communities – the PTA, ECOWAS, ECCAS and SADCC – are all embracing and directed towards the eventual establishment of an African Common Market. They all broadly aspire to promote and enhance economic development through close cooperation among the member states in all fields of economic activity. Specifically, the member states undertook, in the treaties establishing their communities, to increase their existing transport and communications links and to create new ones as a means of strengthening the physical integration of the subregional groupings and promoting the movement of persons, goods and services within the communities. In the production sector, the member states declared with regard to industrial development that they would endeavour to promote autonomous industrialization within the communities through the development of the large intermediate and capital foods industries, promotion of the multinational enterprises, and especially development of the strategic natural resources of the subregions by establishing heavy industries, including metallurgical, chemical and petrochemical industries as well as intermediate and secondary industries such as mechanical, electrical and electronic industries. This, with a view to establishing an industrial base to support the development of agriculture and other key sectors. The integration of industry and the other sectors was meant to help trigger off a process of autonomous and self-sustained economic development and internal accumulation and put African economies in a better position to counter international competition.

To stimulate intra-community trade, the states undertook to gradually reduce and then abolish customs duties and the non-tariff barriers, which their trade is currently subject to so as to build up potential markets of between 180 to 200 million consumers in the case of the West African or Eastern and Southern African subregions. They also committed themselves to cooperate in the area of standardization and control of the quality of goods, adopt trade facilitation measures and promote monetary and financial cooperation among themselves, through the establishment of clearing houses, making their national currencies convertible and instituting common monetary zones.

Closely related to this was the undertaking to set up financial institutions and development banks or funds to finance projects aimed at increasing the complementarity of the economies of the member states.

On the whole the economic communities are expected to play a vital role in the socio-economic transformation of the African economies and help alleviate mass poverty through sustained recovery and growth. There are, however, a number of searching questions that force themselves upon us. To what extent, for example, have the African countries been willing to take the measures that will give practical effect to their declared objectives? Why is there this striking contradiction between general emphasis on the need for economic integration in Africa and the scanty evidence of practical success? Or why has the success of African economic groupings so far been rather limited, with little or no impact on the economic growth of the cooperating countries? What have been the challenges, experiences, stresses and strains of these economic community schemes as they strive to translate articulated objectives into concrete results? This chapter attempts a critical assessment of the performance of existing economic communities.

There is no doubt about the difficulty of assessing the costs and benefits of existing arrangements for integration in Africa. Many of the relevant factors cannot be quantified and even for those that can be, there is the difficulty that the costs usually make themselves evident promptly, whereas benefits accrue chiefly in the long term. Nonetheless, it is important to attempt a broad evaluation of existing programmes and strategies in order to determine what weight can realistically be placed on their future contribution and, more importantly, to try to discern what policy reforms or changes in emphasis seem to be indicated if they are to play the role expected of them.

It should, however, be stated at the outset that in Africa, as anywhere else, economic cooperation and integration are not an end in themselves. They are means to an end. The institutional structures and mechanisms put in place should not be confused with the objectives. They are no more than facilitating instruments. The success or failure of a particular economic cooperation arrangement will be measured by the extent to which the intended objectives/targets are achieved within the time-frame set by the participating countries, not by the establishment and maintenance of various institutions or the regularity of technical or policy meetings at which resolutions and declarations are adopted. If the targets are not attained within the set period, the economic grouping will not have been successful even if the institutional structures and mechanisms remain intact and programmes are further elaborated at regular meetings.

BETWEEN STANDSTILL AND PROGRESS?

A critical appraisal of the achievements of the existing economic cooperation arrangements should focus attention on the extent to which they can make a contribution to development. At the purely economic level, the key object of integration is to expand the opportunities for investment that will profit the African peoples, and that will contribute to the mobilization of their underdeveloped resources. To this end, their primary goal should be to reduce the dependence of the members on the outside world and to create conditions that will make self-sustained, autonomous development possible. In the African setting, such development can only come about through the transformation of productive structures. Have ECOWAS, PTA, SADCC or ECCAS contributed to this type of change? Are they the appropriate vehicles for the achievement of collective self-reliance in the African subregions? To what extent have they addressed problems in the right order? Why have they given priority to policy areas which are of little immediate relevance? And what type of cooperation and integration arrangements have they established and with what results?

Not unlike the integration schemes launched in the 1960s, evidence suggests that to date none of the economic groupings established in the 1970s and 1980s has made any appreciable inroads towards the all-engaging objective of creating a subregional economic market, let alone an economic community, despite the human and financial resources deployed. For example, the main objectives set out in the Final Act of Lagos in 1980 in the field of promotion of cooperation at the sectoral level are yet to be achieved. This is particularly true of such a priority sector as agriculture where, as stressed below, not much headway has been made in the setting up of subregional food security arrangements or an African Food Relief Support Scheme, which are intended to assist member countries in times of emergency. Similarly, very little has been accomplished by way of promoting intercountry agronomic research programmes as espoused in the *Lagos Plan of Action*.

EXPERIENCE IN MARKET INTEGRATION

An important segment of the integration process is the issue of commitment to the promotion of trade expansion which, according to the *LPA*, is meant 'to constitute the mainstay for the present [African development] strategy'. Yet, given the North-bound vertical orientation of the African economy, none of the economic integration schemes appears to be meeting this crucial challenge in the area of market integration. There is still a low percentage of intra-subregional trade, the average being below 5 per cent as is reflected in Table 3.1. African trade remains predominantly oriented towards the North, perpetuating the dependence of the continent on exports. Although intra-regional trade, which increased to 8.4 per cent of total trade in 1993, saw a significant improvement over previous years, Africa still trails other regions in this important area: Western Europe (7.2 per cent), Eastern Europe (46 per cent), Asia (48 per cent) and North America (31 per cent). If an interpretation of long-term data is to be trusted, it might also be noted that Africa is the only region which has experienced a consistent decline in this share, from 10 per cent in 1982 to 6 per cent in 1989.

Thus, although almost all the subregional integration groupings have adopted market integration approach, progress towards trade liberalization, which constitutes a significant aspect of this approach, has been painfully slow. This is of major concern because trade liberalization is the first major step towards the formation of free trade areas, customs unions and common markets. A case in point is the ECOWAS trade liberalization scheme which was adopted on 1 January 1990, ten years after the original schedule, the Community having failed to implement the single trade liberalization scheme adopted in May 1983. It must be pointed out that the Single Trade Liberalization Programme optimistically launched in 1990 has still not advanced much beyond ratification of the scheme. Neither has ECOWAS been able to adopt a common external tariff, which is the backbone and distinguishing characteristic of any customs union. Consequently, intra-Community trade has not been stimulated, and has shown a tendency to decline in importance. Nor could ECOWAS have been expected to stimulate trade when its major instrument for this purpose, the liberalization of trade, has made so little progress.[1]

Table 3.1: Intra-regional Trade as a Percentage of Total Exports of Regional Group

	1970	1980	1985	1990	1992
AMU	1.4	0.3	1.0	2.3	3.0
UDEAC	4.9	1.8	1.9	2.4	2.1
ECCAS	2.4	1.6	2.1	2.3	2.1
ECOWAS	2.9	10.1	5.2	8.3	7.8
CEAO	6.6	9.8	8.3	9.9	10.5
Mano River Union	0.2	0.8	0.4	0.3	0.0
Economic Community					
of the Great Lakes	0.4	0.2	0.8	0.3	0.4
PTA	9.6	12.1	5.6	6.6	6.7
SADC	5.2	5.1	4.8	5.2	4.4

Source: UNCTAD, *Handbook of International Trade and Development Statistics* (Geneva: 1993).

Similarly, the Economic Community of the Great Lakes Countries (CEPGL), the Mano River Union (MRU) and the PTA have been attempting to strengthen and consolidate their trade liberalization schemes. The PTA has, however, made some commendable efforts in market integration. It has, for example, among other things, reached an agreement towards the gradual reduction and eventual elimination of customs duties and elimination of non-tariff barriers to trade among the member states, including import restrictions and import licensing. It has adopted trade facilitation and trade promotion measures designed to meet specific interests of member states, including the simplification of import and export procedures as well as customs procedures and documentation. There is also a common method of valuation of goods for customs purposes and classification of goods according to a common tariff nomenclature compatible with GATT and the Customs Cooperation Council.[2]

These measures, however, have not really resulted in considerable trade among the member states, as one would expect, the annual average rate being 8.8 per cent between 1985 and 1991.[3] The figure, however, gives a misleading impression of the extent of integration among the PTA countries, because it is dominated by a few trade flows, mainly from Kenya and Zimbabwe. In any case, a trade liberalization programme as pursued by the PTA, without an appropriate development of transport and communications or the coordination of production, cannot be expected to stimulate a rapid increase in intra-area trade. Not surprisingly, the Eighteenth Meeting of the PTA Council of Ministers held in January 1993, in Lusaka, Zambia, was constrained to express serious concern over the slow growth of intra-PTA trade in spite of the promotion, facilitation and financing mechanisms which the PTA had put in place during the past ten years. The area of tariff reductions continued to experience a backlog of implementation with attendant adverse consequences for the target of reaching zero tariff rates by the year 2000.[4]

On the other hand, ECCAS has yet to launch its trade liberalisation scheme, while AMU only recently approved a programme for intra-regional trade liberalization. The poor record in trade liberalization partly explains the poor intra-trade performance of groupings, especially when viewed in terms of the percentage accounted for by intra-group trade in the group's total exports. This has been so for most groupings, the notable exception being CEAO, as shown in Table 3.1.

A number of conceptual problems have militated against any progress on regional trade liberalization. Among these are: (i) difficulties in standardizing and eventually harmonizing customs documents and tariff schedules; (ii) stringent rules of origin which often disqualified the bulk of manufactured and agricultural products produced by member states from benefiting under the regional trade liberalization programmes; (iii) problems of balancing the distribution of benefits and costs of economic integration, in particular industrial growth, in view of their possible polarization in the more advanced member states; and (iv) the fear, especially on the part of the lesser advanced countries, of loss of fiscal revenue in the event of intra-African trade liberalization, as elaborated below.

Furthermore, the effectiveness of approved trade liberalization programmes of almost all the economic groupings has been constrained by, among other things, low product coverage, low preferential tariff margins and a lack of progress in eliminating non-tariff barriers which are also difficult to define and classify. In addition, the enterprise sector was often not a participant in the drafting of trade liberalization programmes or the corresponding selection of product items for preferential treatment. Consequently, the enterprises were not only unaware, but could not take advantage of the preferences granted. Weakness in production linkages has also hindered intra-regional trade expansion.

Without doubt, intra-regional trade could be an essential vehicle for the promotion of diversification and the establishment of linkages between production units in different African countries. Not only will this contribute to improved productivity and greater competitiveness for African products, it would also provide a stronger basis for an effective participation of the African region in the evolving global linkages and interdependence of production units. Therefore, the present slow progress of the various integration schemes in Africa has not been helpful to the diversification process.

PERFORMANCE IN POSITIVE INTEGRATION/POLICY HARMONIZATION

Besides market integration, ECOWAS, PTA, ECCAS and AMU, have not made much progress in policy integration, that is, in the foreshadowed measures of positive economic integration and policy harmonization. The aim of policy integration, which, as noted above, Timbergen has termed 'positive integration', is the creation of a common policy framework that creates equal conditions for the functioning of the integrated parts of the economy. The harmonization of the economic policies of the member countries is an essential ingredient of an integration scheme. Indeed, it may be seen as one of the features that define integration. The higher the degree of integration, the closer the degree of policy harmonization that is required, and the smaller the scope for independent and divergent policies which could prevent effective integration. Harmonization does not mean the pursuit of identical policies by the various members, but of policies that are compatible with each other and with the aims of integration. The question, then, is, how have the existing economic communities fared in policy harmonization or integration?

So far not much progress has been made on measures leading to industrial and fiscal harmonization, which form such an important ingredient of the treaties establishing the communities. There is generally the lack of harmonization of sectoral policies in agriculture, industry, transport, energy, and so on, and no basic studies for the formulation of such policies. The designing and adoption of agricultural and industrial programming policies have not yet been defined or elaborated in many integration groupings. Common rules governing foreign direct investment such as those concerning investment incentives are matters still under discussion. In effect, the necessary policy guidelines and programmes for subregional industrial development have not been put in place. As a result, most economic communities in Africa have not been able to establish major multinational industrial projects, for example.

In most of the communities, member states have been preoccupied with trade liberalization issues and consequently have paid limited attention to joint agricultural and industrial development cooperation. Hence, these sectors generally remain on the periphery of the process of intra-African economic cooperation. While in the case of ECOWAS, for example, there are timetabled commitments to a tariff standstill, trade liberalization, fiscal harmonization and the introduction of a common external tariff, there are untimetabled obligations to adopt measures of positive economic integration, including industrial cooperation.

Undoubtedly, many economic communities have identified priority objectives for subregional agricultural and industrial development. What is lacking are concrete measures for implementation of these objectives. In the field of cooperation in agricultural development, for instance, the PTA has over the years identified: (i) suitable programmes for increased production of food crops, livestock and fisheries in member countries; (ii) common livestock diseases which hamper the productivity of the sector; (iii) programmes aimed at the reduction of food losses for implementation by member states such as promotion of improved off-farm, on-farm, and national storage facilities; and (iv) programmes to promote agro-industries to the extent of enhancing trade in food and agricultural products and facilitating effective utilization of such products.

However, in almost all these sectors, not much concrete action would seem to have been undertaken by way of implementation. The Twelfth Meeting of the Authority of the PTA held in Kampala, Uganda, in November 1993, only just took note, among other things, of a study on the harmonization of agricultural policies of the PTA member states. A similar note was taken by the Authority of the preparation of a comprehensive PTA Food Security Programme.[5] In the case of cooperation in industrial development, however, the Authority had the pleasure of noting progress on implementation activities in the subsectors of metallurgy, engineering, chemicals, agro-based and building materials industries as well as support programmes on standardization and quality control, energy and environment, and industrial information. It similarly welcomed an integrated industrial development programme prepared to facilitate balanced sectoral and regional industrial development.

On the other hand, a few subregional economic communities have actually undertaken, for example, agricultural cooperation initiatives aimed basically at developing agricultural production and establishing self-sufficiency in food. The SADCC, for example, has implemented activities aimed at the production, processing and marketing of livestock and meat. The experience of SADCC in both agricultural and industrial cooperation is particularly interesting. In agriculture, SADCC's programme relates, first of all, to the problem of food security and, second, to the implementation of a series of national projects with the capability of contributing to the achievement of the region's food security objectives. Several studies have been completed covering, *inter alia*, a Regional Food Security Early Warning System, an inventory of the agricultural resource base, food aid and the need for regional food reserves, food marketing infrastructure, post-harvest food loss and food processing. Initial steps have been taken in some of these areas, such as the installation of additional food storage capacity. A Resources Information System is under active establishment. Some progress has been made in the area of animal disease control, and a number of national projects are under implementation. SADCC has also prepared a large number of industrial projects, including work on a programme for regional cooperation in industrial infrastructural support services – consultancy services, product standardization, research and development of appropriate technology, and so on.

On the whole, then, given the absence of cooperation in agricultural and industrial development, it is perhaps just as well that nothing much has really happened in such major subregional economic communities as ECOWAS, PTA and ECCAS, in the way of 'positive' or 'negative' integration, that is, liberalisation of intra-community trade and harmonisation of sectoral policies. It has been difficult for the member states of these communities to surrender to a regional authority a measure of control over such matters as the structure and content of their development plans, a tax regime with respect to foreign capital, external trade regime, and monetary policies. Equally, it has not been easy for them to consider that such a surrender must be accepted as a trade-off against the benefits that the integration scheme is expected to bring, in particular a more diversified economic structure, an increase in national income and a higher rate of growth.

LIMITED PROGRESS IN INFRASTRUCTURAL INTEGRATION

The success of the efforts to increase production and income growth in Africa is greatly dependent on the efficient performance and effective support of the transport and communications sector. Weaknesses in the transport and communications system greatly constrain economic and social activities as well as efforts towards economic integration and trade. Since the African governments have committed themselves to seeking rapid integration of their economies and expansion of intra-trade as promulgated in the *LPA* and the FAL, there is the great need to develop transport and communications which is the critical support sector for development.

Thus joint infrastructural development has been viewed in the treaties which established the economic communities as a priority area of cooperation. However, not much has been achieved to meet the challenges of the lack or poor quality of regional infrastructure and networks – historically oriented more to developed countries – which have acted as a brake on intra-African trade expansion and industrial growth. Regional transport and communication networks within most subregions of Africa are either obsolete and dilapidated or are virtually non-existent. Yet without adequate and efficient transport and communications infrastructures, full market integration cannot take place in the ECOWAS, PTA or ECCAS subregions. Hence, the strategy for economic integration recognizes the need to develop adequate transport and communications facilities as a *sine qua non* for economic development, in general, and for the expansion of intra-regional trade in particular.

Although this sector is capital-intensive and continues to rely on imported technology, it is possible in the long run to improve its performance through cost-effective measures and better utilization of existing capacities. In most integration groupings there is a need for investment programmes to rehabilitate and upgrade vital components of integrated regional networks and to provide intermodal exchange points, where these are insufficient or missing altogether. Much can be achieved in the long run through rehabilitation, updating and modernization of existing capacities, and in the short run through more efficient exploitation of existing transport modes and communications facilities.

While generally, not much attention has been paid to the challenges of infrastructural integration, there have been some positive developments, mainly in some of the subregional economic communities. This is exemplified most vividly by the experience of SADCC which has been able to secure considerable funds for its projects owing to its emphasis on infrastructure development (rather than on market integration) during its first ten years of existence. SADCC has attained considerable progress in harmonization of programmes in the transport sector. Similarly, it is in the area of physical infrastructure that ECOWAS would seem to have made some commendable impact. It has, for instance, achieved progress towards establishing telecommunications links between all ECOWAS capital cities. In transport and communications, ECOWAS has, on the whole, established the basic structures for the effective harmonization and coordination of some transport modes in the subregion and is in the process of establishing basic structures for other modes. It has also gone a long way in the harmonization of highways legislation. The trans-West African highway network is almost complete, linking all state capitals by road. ECOWAS has prepared the grounds for the establishment of a coastal shipping service and a regional airline by the private sector. Although the PTA has been bogged down in its market integration efforts, it has nevertheless been able to make some headway in the development of physical infrastructure. For example, programmes on transport facilitation have been drawn up, while a Yellow Card Scheme is being implemented and an Advance Cargo Information System established.

Yet, on the whole, the member states have not effectively responded to the undertakings which they have made in the respective treaties to evolve coordinated and complementary transport and communications policies, to improve and expand the existing links and establish new ones as a means of furthering physical cohesion of their countries. Their achievements in this sector are somewhat meagre, despite its significance in the process of economic integration. Indeed, much needs to be done by the subregional groupings, as continental roads, railways, airline and telecommunication facilities linking African countries are still very few. Such important areas as upgrading, maintenance and repairs of roads, railways, airports and harbours to enable them to cope with increased intra-grouping trade have still not been given adequate attention. And thus there is an urgent need to increase telecommunications and postal facilities to facilitate contacts among people in the business community which will enable further exploitation of new market and investment opportunities.

The relative lack of progress in this sector of critical importance points to some of the major weaknesses in the African integration process. First, infrastructural development requires a certain minimum technical capacity to identify and promote specific projects, including the capacity to undertake feasibility studies. Such capacities are severely limited in Africa. Second, the implementation of large-scale infrastructural projects in Africa must depend to an overwhelming extent on external financing. Third, the multinational character of most such projects often requires the constant coordination and political concurrence of member states.

INADEQUATE PERFORMANCE IN MONETARY AND FINANCIAL INTEGRATION

One other area of importance is monetary and financial integration. Although it is widely recognized that monetary and financial cooperation must play a major role in the process of cooperation and of regional integration, and in a more general sense must provide a major contribution to the solution to the African development problematic, the economic communities have not effectively responded to the challenges posed by this sector. Measures have, however, been taken towards clearing arrangements. In 1976, for example, ECOWAS established the West African Clearing House (WACH) in an attempt to mitigate payments difficulties. The PTA Clearing House (PTACH) was established in 1984 for Eastern and Southern African States.

So far, experience with these payments arrangements has been mixed. In the WACH, there has been a tendency towards accumulation of credits by countries with relatively strong currencies and corresponding increases in the debits of countries with relatively weak currencies. Transactions costs have also tended to be high and the time required to go through the payments procedure usually long. As a result, only a small part of the official regional trade now passes through the WACH. The share of intra-regional trade passing through WACH 'decreased from about 40 per cent in 1983 to almost zero in 1990'.

Conversely, the use of the PTA Clearing House increased steadily from its inception in 1984 up to 1989 when total transactions through it reached Unit of Account of the Preferential Trade Area for Eastern and Southern Africa (UAPTA) 441 million or about 56 per cent of total intra-PTA trade. However, as a recent study has noted, since 1990, there has been a persistent decline in the use of the Clearing House and only 136.5 million of intra-PTA trade was settled through the clearing facility in 1994, which is less than 20 per cent of total intra-PTA trade.[6] From January to August 1995, the transactions dropped significantly to only UAPTA 27.6 million. According to this study, at this rate, the PTA Clearing House may close shop sooner rather than later as the volume of transactions through it would not be sufficient to justify its existence. It was not surprising therefore that at its meeting held in Lusaka, Zambia, in April 1996, the Common Market for Eastern and Southern Africa

(COMESA) Council of Ministers expressed serious concern about the inadequate utilization of the Clearing House and the UAPTA Travellers Cheques. Consequently, in a subsequent resolution adopted by the Council, member states of COMESA were urged to make 'full use of the Clearing House facility which they voluntarily created'.[7]

Several factors have been instrumental in limiting the operations of the clearing arrangements established by ECOWAS and PTA respectively. Chief among them are: (i) weaknesses in the intra-trade of the integration groupings; (ii) imbalances in the trade exchanges of member states which fostered persistent debtor–creditor patterns; (iii) restrictions on the types of goods for which transactions could be cleared through the clearing arrangements; (iv) the avoidance of the clearing system by member countries on account of foreign exchange problems; (v) policies associated with economic liberalization in member states; (vi) indifference of the banking sector including the Central Banks; (vii) delays in settlement of payments; (viii) length of settlement period; and (ix) exposure to interest as well as foreign exchange risks – these are the main reasons responsible for the low volume of transactions and the decline in the use of the clearing houses.

POOR IMPLEMENTATION RECORD

One other issue worth considering in this general appraisal of the performance of the economic communities, particularly in the area of market integration, is their poor implementation record compared to that of the regional integration arrangements among industrialized countries. Whereas the European Union, for example, formally removed intra-union tariff and quota restrictions and established the common external tariff by July 1968, one and a half years ahead of the original deadline,[8] contrary has been the case with regard to the African economic community schemes. Again, in the case of the recently established Australia–New Zealand Closer Economic Relations Trade Agreement (ANZCERTA), all tariffs, quantitative restrictions, and export subsidies on trans-Tasman trade in goods were fully phased out as of July 1990, five years ahead of the original deadline. And in the case of 'Europe 1992', about 70 per cent of the 282 proposals submitted by the EU Commission were approved by the EU Council by mid-1991.[9]

On the other hand, in most cases in Africa, initial deadlines for the removal of barriers to intra-subregional trade were postponed, often several times. In a number of cases (for example, the PTA) delays in liberalizing intra-regional trade reflected a lack of automaticity in implementation timetables, with reciprocal tariff reductions made subject to periodic negotiation rounds and consensus, either on a product-by-product basis or on a request-and-offer basis. In addition, in many cases (for example, the CEAO and PTA), reductions in trade barriers were not based on across-the-board reductions in tariff and non-tariff barriers but on a system of positive 'lists' that gave participating countries considerable latitude to exclude sensitive products from the set of items subject to reciprocal trade concessions, and biased the selection of products in favour of those with limited potential for intra-regional trade.

The low degree of implementation of intra-regional liberalization programmes in Africa is quite spectacular even compared to the record of regional economic communities in the developing countries in Latin America and Asia. For instance, implementation was fairly successful in the case of the Central American Common Market (CACM), which broadly adhered to the original liberalization timetable, and maintained a substantially unrestricted intra-regional trading environment throughout most of the 1960s and 1970s. At the other extreme are some sub-Saharan African groupings (for example, the ECOWAS and UDEAC), that are characterized by an almost complete non-implementation of intra-regional liberalization. In most other cases, implementation has been partial, and initial liberalization has often been followed by impasses, delays, and sometimes reversals – the latter frequently taking the form of erosion of previously granted trade preferences because of exchange and trade restrictions introduced in response to balance of payments difficulties.

A comparison between the basic documents prepared by various pre-1990 African subregional communities and those elaborated by the EU, or the most recent free trade agreement between the US, Canada and Mexico, reveals striking differences. First, while the US–Canada–Mexico trade agreement contains an extremely detailed description of mutual commitments, the documents establishing the subregional economic groupings in Africa are a summary of 'loosely-formulated general proposals, without quantitative projections or an accurately-detailed legal and institutional framework'.[10] Thus, the effective impact on the member countries cannot be properly assessed, nor can member countries be compelled to observe fundamental commitments made. Second, the objectives of the African subregional groupings try to cover almost all areas of potential cooperation, rather than concentrating on one or a limited number of priorities. Third, developed market economies are prodded into regional integration by major economic participants. Only then do the governments or other institutions involved in the integration respond with adequate policy measures.[11] In contrast, in Africa, integration schemes are essentially derived from political concepts and efforts. While, in the developed market economies, development is organic, from bottom to top, from economic realities towards political decision making, in the African economic groupings, the opposite occurs and politically generated agreements are imposed on economically insufficiently prepared national economies.

To some extent, therefore, implementation problems also account for the failure of African regional integration schemes to raise intra-regional trade in line with initial expectations. For while many integration arrangements in Africa were ostensibly modelled on the European Union, most lacked the necessary institutional mechanisms to achieve their objectives. This was evident in inconsistencies between national legislation and integration commitments, the absence of strong enforcement mechanisms and ineffective dispute settlement procedures, and lack of compensation mechanisms to address distributional concerns.

The analysis to this point has shown that regional economic integration in Africa has fundamentally failed to achieve its pre-established goals. It has also revealed that it was primarily in the 'hard core' areas of economic integration that the record of achievements has been meagre despite the panoply on institutional structures and cooperation programmes in place. Thus, on the whole, despite great expectations, the existing economic integration communities have so far been unable to generate massive support among the African peoples for the objectives of economic integration, to proceed to the necessary structural transformations, to bring about an increase in agricultural and industrial production or to gradually redistribute income from economic activity. In short, they have not been able to show evidence of movement towards economic independence of the member states through subregional integration. Africa is hesitating to take the decisive step towards economic integration; the member states are dilly-dallying about adjusting their national policies in line with the objectives of subregional economic integration, about giving priority to relations with other member states and attaching secondary importance to their relations with non-African countries, so as to boost intra-community trade at the expense of foreign trade.

The clearest proof of the failure of regional integration in Africa is provided by the abysmal growth performance of Africa as a whole. As reflected in the *LPA*, economic integration was supposed to promote 'self-sustaining development and economic growth'. Instead, in the past decade, as Foroutan has recently highlighted, Africa as a whole has registered 'the worst economic results of its post-independence history by seeing real incomes of individuals falling at a sustained pace',[12] as illustrated in Table 3.2 below, in lieu of growing. It may be argued that the disappointing results could partially be attributed to the structural weakness of the economies of sub-Saharan African countries and outside events, especially the collapse of world commodity prices in the 1980s. It remains true, however, that despite great expectations, economic integration was unable to bring any structural changes to the economies of Africa that might have lessened their vulnerability to commodity price fluctuations.

Table 3.2: Some Economic Indicators for Sub-Saharan Africa
(1989 unless otherwise indicated)

	GDP		Population		GNP per Capita	
	US$ million	Annual growth rate 1980–9 (%)	1000	Annual growth rate 1980–9 (%)	US$	Annual growth rate 1980–9 (%)
West Africa						
ECOWAS						
CEAO						
Benin	1600	1.8	4593	3.2	380	1.8
Burkina Faso	2460	5.0	8776	2.6	310	2.3
Côte d'Ivoire	7170	1.2	11713	4.0	790	−3.0
Mali	2080	3.8	8212	2.5	260	1.0
Mauritania	910	1.4	1954	2.6	490	−2.2
Niger	2040	−1.6	7479	3.5	290	−5.0
The Senegal	4660	3.1	7211	3.0	650	0.0
MRU						
Guinea	2750	–	5547	2.5	430	–
Liberia	–	–	2475	3.1	–	–
Sierra Leone	890	0.6	4040	2.4	200	−3.2
Other ECOWAS						
Cape Verde	281	5.8	369	2.5	760	3.2
Gambia	196	2.2	848	3.3	230	−1.0
The Ghana	5260	2.8	14425	3.4	380	0.8
Guinea Bissau	173	3.4	960	1.9	180	1.5
Nigeria	28920	−0.4	113665	3.3	250	−3.6
Togo	1340	1.4	3507	3.5	390	−2.4
Central Africa						
UDEAC						
Cameroon	11080	3.2	11554	3.2	1010	0.7
CAR	1050	1.4	2951	2.7	390	−1.5
Chad	1020	6.5	5537	2.4	190	3.9
Congo	2270	3.9	2208	3.4	930	0.1
Equatorial Guinea	149	–	334	5.1	430	–
Gabon	3060	1.0	1105	3.7	2770	−2.6
CEPGL						
Burundi	960	4.3	5299	2.9	220	1.6
Rwanda	2170	1.5	6893	3.3	310	−1.9
Zaire	9610	1.9	34442	3.1	260	−1.6
Other Central Africa						
Sao Tomé & Principe	43	−2.8	122	3.0	360	−5.7
East and Southern Africa						
PTA						
Angola	7720	–	9694	2.5	620	–

continued

Table 3.2 continued

	GDP		Population		GNP per Capita	
	US$ million	Annual growth rate 1980–9 (%)	1000	Annual growth rate 1980–9 (%)	US$	Annual growth rate 1980–9 (%)
Burundi	960	4.3	5299	2.9	220	1.6
Comoros	209	3.1	459	3.7	460	–0.6
Djibouti	–	–	410	3.5	n.a	n.a.
Ethiopia	5420	1.9	48861	2.9	120	–1.1
Kenya	7130	4.1	23277	3.8	380	0.4
Lesotho	340	3.7	1722	2.7	470	–0.5
Malawi	1410	2.7	8230	3.4	180	–0.1
Mauritius	1740	5.9	1062	1.0	1950	5.3
Mozambique	1100	–1.4	15357	2.7	80	–6.0
Rwanda	2170	1.5	6893	3.3	310	–1.9
Swaziland	683	4.1	761	3.4	900	–0.6
Somalia	1090	3.0	6089	3.0	170	–1.3
Sudan	–	1.1	24423	3.0	–	–1.8
Uganda	4460	2.5	16772	3.2	250	–1.0
Tanzania	2540	2.6	25627	3.5	120	–1.6
Zambia	4700	0.8	7837	3.7	390	–3.8
Zimbabwe	5250	2.7	9567	3.6	640	–0.8
SADCC						
Angola	7720	–	9694	2.5	620	–
Botswana	2500	11.3	1217	3.4	1600	6.7
Lesotho	340	3.7	1722	2.7	470	–0.5
Malawi	1410	2.7	8230	3.4	180	–0.1
Mozambique	1100	–1.4	15357	2.7	80	–6.0
Namibia	–	–	–	–	–	–
Swaziland	683	4.1	761	3.4	900	0.6
Tanzania	2540	2.6	25627	3.5	120	–1.6
Zambia	4700	0.8	7837	3.7	390	–3.8
Zimbabwe	5250	2.7	9567	3.6	640	–0.8
SACU						
Botswana	2500	11.3	1217	3.4	1600	6.7
Lesotho	340	3.7	1722	2.7	470	–0.5
Namibia	–	–	–	–	–	–
Swaziland	683	4.1	761	3.4	900	0.6
South Africa	80370	1.5	34925	2.4	2460	–0.8
Other East & South Africa						
Madagascar	2280	0.8	11174	2.8	230	–2.6
Seychelles	285	2.5	68	0.9	4170	1.7
Total SSA	171K	2.1	480K	3.2	340	–1.2

Note: SSA is uniformly defined to exclude South Africa.
Source: World Bank: *World Development Report* (1991) and *World Bank Atlas* (1990).

All this raises some disturbing questions. Why so little progress? Why have African states not taken advantage of regional economic integration or collective self-reliance? What are the underlying factors which have rocked the very foundation of cooperation? Does the failure to date imply that regional economic integration as a model of development is harmful or infeasible and should be abandoned altogether? What has, in short, gone wrong? These critical issues are examined in the following chapter.

4 Interlocking Problems of African Regionalism

Disappointment with the achievements of integration in Africa is as widespread as the continued belief in its virtues and importance. It would be no exaggeration to say that Africa's experience with integration schemes over the last quarter of a century has been the experience of failure, and that the achievements of integration have been slight or non-existent.

It has become necessary therefore to find out the reasons for the wide consensus over the disappointing results of the process of economic integration in Africa, despite the continuous rhetoric about the need for regional cooperation and integration. The complexity and sensitivity of the subject does not appear to allow for simple explanations. A multiplicity of factors have played a role in the poor record. This chapter attempts to analyse the various factors that have hampered economic integration in Africa, highlighting, in particular, the challenges of the approach to African economic integration, which do not seem to have received much attention in the extensive literature on the subject.

IS MARKET INTEGRATION APPROPRIATE?

The focus of the majority of regional integration groupings in Africa has been on market integration or, specifically, liberalization of trade relations with a view to quickly establishing preferential and free trade areas, customs unions and common markets. This approach to economic integration has raised some crucial questions and provoked debates and exchanges on regionalism in Africa. How appropriate, for example, is the market approach to economic integration in the developing areas, especially Africa? How valid is the traditional treatment of trade as central and of other areas of cooperation as either trade-facilitating or secondary? Even if it is valid with respect to industrial economies, is it with respect to sub-Saharan Africa, where structural changes and qualitative development in production, not just marginal changes in output patterns and sustained growth within only gradually changing production structures are required? Where are the commodities in which African states are to conduct trade? In other words, since all the African states have primary products to offer with no complementarity between them and since there are no manufacturing or processing industries in Africa to absorb the raw materials, will the mere formation of a payments union or a common market necessarily enhance the flow of trade in Africa? Is economic regionalism in Africa best analysed as a branch of applied international trade theory or as an extension of applied national development theory? Is the model of market integration the most appropriate means to effect development and growth in a regional setting in Africa? What kind of approach to the process of integration will be most effective in realizing the potential of the African region for the benefit of its populations?

It is generally agreed among economists, Africans and non-Africans alike, that the major cause of the poor return on economic integration efforts in Africa over the past 30 years has to do with the integration approach adopted by African economic groupings. Almost all of them have been modelled on the classical EU prototype, which is designed for developed countries. The model's underlying assumptions, as Ahmad Aly has recently stressed, 'are far from relevant in the African context'.[1]

A realistic approach to economic integration in Africa must start with the recognition that African countries lack most of the prerequisites that are considered necessary for successful economic integration to take place. But most of those prerequisites were developed in the context of the industrialized world, and most in fact, were derived from the experience of the European Union. In Europe, the formation of the EU and EFTA were intended to increase trade among the European nations, but the situation in Europe is entirely different from that of Africa. The rate of industrialization and the rate of economic development are high in most of the countries of Europe, and the creation of the EU merely catered to trade in the existing products. The EU nations are able to offer products for mutual exchange. Furthermore, it is possible for the EU nations to switch their markets to the partner countries in substitution for the loss of outside markets. Since a common market has the effect of trade diversion, the initial steps taken by the EU are to fill up the gaps in trade with the goods from the member countries. This cannot be done in Africa, since the African countries must first create an economic base on which the other institutions can be built.

Furthermore, past experience with successful market integration in Western-type economies suggests, first, economic homogeneity, that is the lack of strong subregional disparities; second, national economic performance, that is sustained economic growth on a national level to help to contain domestic opposition to exposing domestic industries to regional competition, and, third, political commitment in a legally binding way underlying the irreversibility of intra-regional liberalization and making economic integration credible. These are major shaping factors in the formation of free trade areas or customs unions. Sub-Saharan Africa has never enjoyed the privileges of these three factors.

It is quite evident, therefore, that none of the preconditions are sufficiently present in the regional integration process among African countries. As a consequence, ECOWAS, PTA and other subregional economic schemes, which have adopted the market integration approach, operate in an environment quite different from that of Western Europe, and it could very well be that the dynamics of the integration process will be quite different.

Specifically, in Africa, the low levels of development and the limited possibilities for profitable intra-subregional exchange simply do not provide the basis for integration at the present time. As the perquisites for integration do not presently exist, subregional or regional cooperation must start from the premise that these perquisites must *be created*. This is in contrast to the dominant approach of the existing economic communities which tended to entertain the belief that integration in Africa could be legislated from above, *ex nihilo*. There is little purpose in liberalizing trade when the parties have nothing to exchange: regional cooperation, *inter alia*, must create the basis for trade. Otherwise, market integration in Africa will merely be for promoting non-African goods and services.

Hence the continuing emphasis of the economic schemes in Africa on customs unions based on the European experience of market integration is entirely inappropriate for such an underdeveloped region as that of Africa where the problems are non-orthodox, that is, where the principal need is not for the consolidation and rationalization of existing production according to comparative advantage, but to promote development by employing previously non-utilized factors of production.

Given this background, it is evident that the main thrust of the integration strategies of the subregional economic communities in Africa has not been helpful. The accent has been on integration of markets and much valuable time has been spent on measures at liberalization of trade with little or no impact on the volume of intra-subregional or even interstate official trade. The whole debate on regionalism in Africa has generally taken for granted the validity of the market approach and incrementalism. This is evident in the concept of regional cooperation as a process and discussion of its major stages or forms beginning with a free trade area or the liberalization of the movement of goods regionally produced, to be followed by the establishment of a customs union and so on. The framework of ECOWAS, PTA and ECCAS, for example, was therefore largely influenced by approaches to apparently similar problems in Western Europe. The fields of cooperation covered by the schemes accordingly corresponded to the trade preoccupations of organizations such as the European Free Trade Association and the EU, where the existence of mature economies was an established feature, rather than to a context in which the structural transformation of economies was the overall goal.

While the European countries needed a wider market to increase the competitiveness of their established industrial structure, African countries are faced with the problem of developing on a collective basis a viable industrial structure that they could not develop individually because of their small size and poor economic and social infrastructure. It need hardly be stressed then, that in Africa, as in other developing countries, economic cooperation in whatever form – customs union, common market or economic community – has little chance of contributing effectively to economic development and structural change without the concerted effort of the participating countries to coordinate their sectoral plans and programmes, most especially in agriculture, industry, transport and communications and energy production and utilization, as well as their overall development strategies and perspectives.

It is worth stressing here, at the risk of digression, that market integration as a process towards the building of viable communities is not easy to achieve. Even in Europe, despite the over 30 years period of operation of the Treaty of Rome, the creation of a unified internal market is yet to be attained. As a recent study by the European Institute of Public Administration has shown, although the EEC Treaty is based on the idea of a common market, there is as yet 'no such thing as a common market in the EC'. It turned out that the constraint of tariff-free intra-EC trade 'was really a minor one, in the light of an armoury of other instruments that could be employed'.[2] For notwithstanding the rapid expansion of trade, there are a number of factors that have prevented the emergence of a fully developed internal market. These include 'differences in customs formalities and differences in health and safety requirements'; such practices introduce price differences for the same goods in so far as imports from their countries are concerned.[3] It is as recent as 1985 that an important step towards the creation of a unified internal market was taken by the Heads of State of the member countries who endorsed the recommendations put forward by the European Commission for the completion of the internal market to be implemented by 1992. Thus, not even the considerable force of the geopolitical considerations generated by the Cold War and the need for economic recovery – with integration meant to speed up post-war recovery and the creation of European unity against the Soviet Union – could prevent the incremental development of a common market from being spread over four decades. Indeed if the post-war experience with integration in Europe and North America is anything to go by, market integration is a process that moves at a slow pace over a long period. The NAFTA, which as a free trade area is a less-intensive form of market integration, was ratified in 1994 after decades of incremental integration arrangements between Canada and the United States and Mexico.

This brief reference to the European experience with market integration might perhaps constitute an important lesson for the cooperation and integration decision makers of Africa. The continuing emphasis on customs unions and import-substituting manufacturing, important as they are, does involve too narrow a view of the purpose of economic integration and cooperation between the countries of Africa, of its potentialities and of the ways to achieve it. A programme for collective self-reliance that rests primarily on the establishment of a preferential trading area through the removal of the formal constraints on trade, is inadequate, for one reason, because the beneficial effect of the potential enlargement of the market is likely to be felt only in the long term. The effect overnight of the removal of tariffs, quantitative restrictions, and monetary constraints on trade between the members may not be great.[4]

The major reason why trade might not rapidly increase is the lack of very much to trade, particularly once the unrecorded trade (smuggling) is totally ignored. It is basically the low level of production that would be tradable in African markets that accounts for the small volume of intra-African trade and the likelihood that the mere removal of trade barriers would not produce a rapid expansion of such trade. Undoubtedly, trade has a role to play in making available products to where demand exists. But, if supply, that is, production and infrastructure for the transportation of goods, does not exist or not at the appropriate level, trade facilitation mechanisms will function in a vacuum as is presently the case. As Hazlewood stressed many years ago:

> ... integration is not simply a matter of lowering tariffs. The existence of tariffs is not the sole, or even the primary impediment to trade between the countries of Africa. The main reason for the low level of trade is to be found in the economic structure of the countries [and in] ... the fact that the 'infrastructure' for intra-African trade is generally lacking.[5]

Moreover, as noted above, in these integration schemes, subregional industrial and development studies and programmes have not yet been designed or launched to promote the development of regional complementary structures of production. Serious efforts are thus needed regarding the formulation and implementation of joint industrial and agricultural development policies.

The lack of progress of ECOWAS, PTA or ECCAS is also the reflection of the discontent of participating governments with the design and results of the subregional market integration schemes, as has been analysed elsewhere.[6] Suffice it to say that these schemes do not provide demonstrable benefits to the participants. While they impose maximum constraints on decision making autonomy they offer minimal prospects for the realization of immediate benefits. A case in point is the loss of revenue derived from indirect taxes – mainly import and export duties as a consequence of the removal of barriers and tariff harmonization. And while the impact of tariff harmonization on revenue would be felt immediately the expected benefits might be of a long-term nature and less certain. Hence, tariff harmonization, a crucial aspect of market integration which entails the removal of tariffs in intra-regional trade, may not appeal to the political leaders, particularly in view of the perceived inability to recoup the resultant loss of revenue from the expected long-term benefits of enhanced regional integration.[7] Moreover, so far, none of the schemes has devised measures of 'positive integration' to effect the loss of tariff revenues.

This last point is worth elaborating. A characteristic feature of the majority of the member states of the subregional economic communities is that a significant proportion of their revenue is derived from indirect taxes – mainly import and export duties. Consequently, a great deal of importance is attached to customs duties in their countries as a share in their foreign trade and GDP as well as their share in total government revenue. United Nations sources for 1973 indicate large variations in the degree of dependence of many African countries on customs duties as a source of government incomes.[8]

Given the widespread financial crisis in the continent and the high share of custom duties as public revenues in most countries, African governments find it difficult to abolish tariffs altogether. They either show outright reluctance to reduce, let alone eliminate tariffs, or they try to get around relevant provisions by levying other charges that have an equivalent effect. Table 4.1 below shows that four of the thirty-nine listed sub-Saharan African countries derive about three-quarters of their revenue from customs duties, and nine obtain more than two-thirds of their income from this source. Nineteen countries receive more than half of their income from customs duties, and thirty-six more than one-quarter.[9]

The situation is compounded by the inability of the compensatory arrangements to compensate member countries for revenue losses. The solidarity funds, in the case of ECOWAS, the compensation fund, that lack their own resource depend instead on contributions by member countries, which in most cases are 'virtually unable to honour their obligations, given their worsening financial positions'.[10] Indeed, attempts to integrate regions, especially in the developing world, will need to include much more effective arrangements for *equalizing* the gains from regionalization to secure the continued commitment of the smaller, less developed economies to a regional market for sufficiently long for the gains from credible integration to emerge,

Table 4.1: Customs Duties as Percentage of Total Tax Revenue
in Sub-Saharan Africa, 1969 and 1980

Country	Import Duties 1969	Import Duties 1980	Export Duties 1969	Export Duties 1980	Total 1969	Total 1980
Benin	56.3	62.6	5.1	1.9	61.4	64.5
Botswana	65.1	56.4	3.4	0.5	68.5	56.9
Burkina Faso	53.1	48.5	2.9	3.7	56.0	52.2
Burundi	23.5	21.3	17.9	31.5	41.4	52.8
Cameroon	38.0	48.9	16.6	3.8	54.6	52.7
Cape Verde	24.0	24.6	0.1	0.2	24.1	24.8
Central African Republic	38.1	33.9	3.8	9.4	41.9	43.3
Chad	39.7	51.8	8.0	10.0	47.7	61.8
Comoros	56.5	58.9	20.2	14.0	76.7	72.9
Congo	30.0	36.4	5.7	0.4	35.7	36.8
Ethiopia	28.5	28.3	8.1	26.1	36.6	54.4
The Gambia	70.8	66.7	17.0	10.2	87.8	76.9
Ghana	16.1	19.3	29.8	23.7	45.9	43.0
Guinea	34.8	20.1	3.0	–	37.8	20.1
Guinea-Bissau	25.7	24.1	5.6	4.3	31.3	28.4
Côte d'Ivoire	36.9	37.7	19.4	12.3	56.3	50.0
Kenya	29.5	20.0	0.4	–	29.9	20.0
Lesotho	74.1	70.8	3.5	0.7	77.6	71.5
Liberia	32.1	40.1	0.9	0.6	33.0	40.7
Madagascar	26.6	34.1	6.8	9.0	33.4	43.1
Malawi	26.3	21.2	–	–	26.3	21.2
Mali	38.4	32.3	7.1	4.1	45.5	36.4
Mauritania	36.1	45.5	1.1	0.7	37.2	46.2
Mauritius	34.2	37.2	9.6	12.6	43.8	49.8
Niger	15.6	15.6	4.8	4.8	20.4	20.4
Nigeria	19.9	17.1	0.2	0.1	20.1	17.2
Rwanda	23.2	33.7	22.1	19.8	45.3	53.5
Sao Tomé & Principe	10.7	11.6	18.0	35.6	28.7	27.2
Senegal	39.1	43.6	2.8	1.8	41.9	45.4
Seychelles	63.5	47.7	2.1	0.4	65.6	48.1
Sierra Leone	36.6	38.0	10.5	17.4	47.1	55.4
Somalia	48.5	50.9	4.2	1.9	52.7	52.8
Sudan	41.9	45.5	6.2	4.0	48.1	49.5
Swaziland	25.6	52.3	0.1	11.1	25.7	53.4
Tanzania	23.6	16.3	3.1	7.8	26.7	24.1
Togo	57.3	30.6	6.9	9.8	64.2	40.4
Uganda	19.6	3.6	19.3	70.4	38.9	74.0
Zaire	29.5	17.8	21.8	11.6	51.3	29.4
Zambia	17.0	6.5	–	–	17.0	6.5

Note: I have tried in vain to update this table. The situation seems to have worsened, or, in the best of circumstances, remained unchanged throughout the 1980s.
Source: IMF, *Taxation in Sub-Saharan Africa*, 1981.

as alluded to above. To maintain momentum in favour of economic cooperation and integration, its future thrust has to have built-in mechanisms for redistributing regional benefits more equitably to other partners in ways that accelerate their levels of overall development.

Although regional integration should result in substantial benefits – economic, political and security-related – there is legitimate concern in many developing regions, especially Africa, that the gains from market integration would accrue mainly to the larger or more industrially developed member countries which are in the most advantageous position to capture immediately the additional income benefits from an open accessible regional market. Asymmetries in the relative economic weight and capability of regional partners has contributed in the past to the disintegration of many regional arrangements in the developing world despite specifically designed measures to redistribute some of the gains captured. Such problems have been encountered in the Andean Pact countries and have slowed down the process of closer integrations in ASEAN. Other cases in point, in Africa, are the respective experiences of the defunct EAC, the UDAO, UDEAO and the withdrawal of Chad in 1968 from the membership of UDEAC. The PTA has similarly been confronted with the problem of inequitable distribution of costs and benefits of integration. Countries like Rwanda, Djibouti and Comoros have argued that because of their low level of development, their structures of production, and commodity composition of exports, if any, they have little to gain from integration.[11] Mauritius even submitted a notice of withdrawal in 1986 (which was subsequently cancelled).

Even if all the long-term potential gains of integration were to be realized their continuing disadvantaged position would still make it impossible for them to derive an equitable share of the benefits to which integration would have given rise. These amply demonstrate that distributional crises cannot be solved through market mechanisms, as for example, fiscal compensation alone, which has proven in various cases to be the least appropriate and politically most unacceptable instrument. This is largely because it fails to address the most fundamental issue of balanced development and the equitable distribution of productive activities: the location of industrial production within the region with its spillover effect on employment, technological transfer and learning-by-doing.

It is no exaggeration to say that the key to the viability of integration schemes in Africa will obviously be their capacity to balance the benefits of common market operations in a manner acceptable to their members. The point worth emphasizing here is that no government can be expected to justify its participation in a grouping to its people by saying that their interests should legitimately be sacrificed to those of the group as a whole. Although the less favoured countries might still expect to benefit in the long term from cooperation, no African government can afford to adopt this time horizon. Perceptions that neighbouring countries have gained a disproportionate share of the benefits from integration usually lead to moves that have the consequences, whether intended or not, of restricting the scope of regional cooperation. Arthur Hazlewood has driven home this important aspect of the integration process in a recent study:

> The case for integration, for a particular country's participation in an integration scheme, rests on the benefits that country itself will obtain from integration. The case of integration is not a case for helping others; it is a case for helping oneself. However, it must be appreciated that integration will not benefit one country, or at any rate not for long, unless it also benefits the others; the case for integration arises from self-interest, but the pursuit of self-interest requires the interest of others to be simultaneously served. Integration will not succeed unless every partner benefits, because any who think they will not benefit will not participate, and there will then be no integration. The benefit is for everyone or no one.[12]

Thus, even if the political rhetoric were to indicate that some member states see ECOWAS, PTA or ECCAS primarily or solely as a step towards the eventual political union or an African economic community, these schemes will command the loyal support of all their members and succeed only if each member is likely to be better off inside the community than it would have been outside it. They would be attractive and receive support only if they could show demonstrable benefits to their participants, and the arrangements for cooperative action provide good reason to believe that such benefits can be realized. Indeed, unless governments can be convinced that economic cooperation and, eventually, integration will strengthen their capacity to cope with urgent domestic problems better than they could on their own, they will continue to be preoccupied with managing policy issues with a national orientation and lose sight of the significant benefits that regional cooperation can bring.

And finally, market integration which gives no priority to the basic industries, reinforces the position of the foreign private sector in the African countries and increases economic domination from abroad. It creates problems for the participating states with regard to the sharing of gains with transnational corporations (TNCs). There is always the tendency on the part of the TNCs to either become the main beneficiaries of the larger market, to the detriment of the indigenous agents of production and trade, or to fragment the market both at national and subregional levels and entrench external dependence, thus defeating the objectives of subregional economic integration and self-reliance. The analysis by Langdon and Mytelka[13] of UDEAC reinforced by the 1981 ECA evaluation report[14] provides an excellent case study of the way in which TNCs derive benefits from regional economic schemes.

On the whole, while recognizing current integration arrangements in Africa as a *fait accompli*, we should note that experience in Africa and elsewhere in the developing world reveals that market integration is not effective. By and large, diversifying industrial growth, the final goal of the development-oriented market integration model, has not materialized. An important reason for this failure has already been discussed: the model demands unrealistic levels of political commitment and of technical and administrative expertise which are not always available in developing regions such as Africa. Where the creation and strengthening of national identity is strong, as in many African countries, governments are naturally loath to sacrifice national sovereignty. Furthermore, the asymmetry in the size.and levels of development of the participating economies leads to polarized development. Consequently, the distribution of the costs and benefits of integration becomes the focal point of the integration exercise. This gloomy picture about market integration approach adopted by ECOWAS, PTA and ECCAS and the other small communities like CEAO, UDEAC and MRU is compounded by some complex problems relating to the management of economic integration at the national and subregional levels.

MANAGEMENT OF REGIONAL ECONOMIC INTEGRATION

Lack of Commitment of African Governments

By order of priority and responsibility, the African states come first as far as the implementation of the treaties establishing the economic communities are concerned. This is underlined by the *LPA* and the FAL which stipulates that it is the responsibility of the African states to take 'measures to effect the establishment of an African Common Market' that would lead 'to the attainment of the aims and objectives of the African Economic Community'.[15] This is particularly important because, as development studies scholars like Stockwell and Laidlaw have recognized, the role of government in development has risen steadily to a point where successful growth is not really possible without the active support of government.[16] John Lewis has gone so far as to argue that there is 'no substitute for the continuing lead that governments must supply to development-promotion efforts'.[17] It follows that if a government is unwilling or unable to play an active positive role, then the government itself can be considered a barrier to development or a fundamental cause of failure of policy orientation.

This is particularly evident in the case of regional cooperation and integration where the most crucial factor is strong and sustained political commitment to keep to the agreed regional agenda. This makes the African political leaders key figures in cooperation and integration. It is their decision which determines the role of the regional organizations and institutions, as well as that of the private sector. Likewise, it is their decisions and commitment to succeed which determine the response of the international community. Hence the establishment of effective subregional economic schemes crucially depends upon the extent to which the member states have committed themselves to the concept of regionalism in Africa. For while regional policies are formulated at the regional level, responsibility for implementation rests with the various national governments. So far evidence suggests what appears to be a lack of special interest in, support and total commitment on the part of African states to, the cherished goals of the existing economic groupings. In the scheme of things in most African countries matters of economic cooperation are not accorded the same priority in the official mind as primarily national issues. And in most cases, commitment expressed to subregional programmes at community fora becomes very difficult to implement once their practical implications, such as the loss of national control, becomes evident.

This can only be the consequence of two things: first, that African states still believe that they can develop autonomous and self-sustained economies on individual bases; and second, that they do not fully comprehend the link between national interest and community interest. However, we believe that in the long term there is more harmony between national interests and community interests in Africa than anywhere else in the world. This is because African economies with their very limited markets cannot individually form autonomous production systems, capable of bringing about self-sustained economic development. This is why in African countries, the long-term national interest should necessarily aim at the economic integration of Africa. When this vision of integration is missing from national policy then it is either because certain groups of individuals have disregarded the real national interest or that these politicians have misinterpreted the national interest because of short-term gains. Unfortunately, this lack of political vision is apparent in some African countries.

Indeed, the gravity of the economic crisis clearly shows that African economies cannot constitute viable production systems. They do not have the capacity to counter adverse circumstances. First of all, there is no interaction between the various branches of the economy, particularly between industry and the other priority sectors, and second, there is no adjustment between production and consumption structures. The African economies are integrated to the national systems of the dominant economies, consequently their resources are drained to the outside world. A new fact is emerging, which is that the developed countries have undertaken to reduce their relations with African countries while the African countries are increasing their dependence on the dominant economies. The result of this phenomenon is that economic growth is occurring in full force in Europe: adoption of a new generation of advanced technology, establishment of a single European market, and so on, while the economic crisis in African countries is worsening. It appears, therefore, that this other manifestation of the unequal exchange is intensifying.

The lack of commitment to regionalism has manifested itself in member countries independently developing their own strategies, plans and priorities, with regional cooperation hardly reflected in them. Although African countries continue to speak of collective action for regional integration, no single state has as yet designed its national plans to be consistent with the promotion of effective integration for development. As discussed below, most have not even developed a national apparatus for monitoring and coordinating their involvement in the different intergovernmental organizations.[18] The lack of commitment has also been reflected in tardy payment of budgetary contributions and a low level of participation in meetings, as well as in the fact that not all member states have ratified and implemented the protocols, acts and decisions of the groupings. As at the end of March 1992, the total arrears owed to the Executive Secretariat of ECOWAS alone stood at ECOWAS Unit of Account (UA) 21.5 million, equivalent to over US$30 million.[19]

In addition, African leaders have not been able 'to distinguish between long-term development requisites and short-term political tactics, a situation responsible for the frequent rise and fall of subregional groupings'.[20] There has been evidence of collapse of numerous subregional economic schemes while many others were created not with regard to their economic viability or technical soundness, but merely for the sake of political alliances and friendship. The history of economic cooperation in Africa provides ample evidence. A recent case in point was the establishment of the Senegambia Federation in 1981, after Senegalese troops had thwarted a *coup d'état* in the Gambia. A few years later, in 1989, the presidents of the two countries essentially dismantled it. In East Africa, the same political factors contributed to the collapse in 1977 of the EAC. The situation in North Africa was no better. Political factors contributed in no small measure to the delay in establishing an all-embracing cooperation arrangement in the subregion. Even the Maghreb Permanent Consultative Council, the only multilateral scheme in the subregion, was brought to a standstill by the political conflict between Algeria and Morocco over the Sahara crisis, as well as by the earlier withdrawal of Libya in 1970.[21]

Lack of Adequate Institutional Mechanisms at the National Level

Adequate and viable institutions have not been established for management of economic cooperation process at the national level. While the literature on regional cooperation in Africa largely focuses on enhancing the role and functions of regional institutions, far less attention is being paid to the institutions required at the national level to manage regional cooperation processes. This has particularly been the case as the 'rush since independence to create new institutions at the regional level to promote increased cooperation has diverted attention from national level requirements for cooperation'.[22] Hence decisions at the regional level by Heads of State and Government and by ministers have seldom been reflected in decisions at the national level in the form of legislation and regulations. In fact, these national decisions are often taken without reference to regional decisions.

Thus although integration organizations have been duly established in all the subregions, as envisaged in the Final Act of Lagos, cooperation agreements have not been internalized in national administrations and development plans. In most African countries, cooperation does not go far beyond the signing of treaties and protocols. The objectives of the treaties are not integrated in national development plans or in the sectoral programmes of appropriate substantive ministries. The officials and ministers who participate at intergovernmental meetings on the implementation of the treaty of cooperation generally come to the meetings without the mandate of their cabinet colleagues and, on returning to their respective capitals, they do not brief their colleagues on the proceedings and decisions taken at the meetings. What seems to be the practice is that the reports of the meetings are shelved and gather dust until the next round of meetings.

Not surprisingly, therefore, there is the lack of effective coordination linkage and channels of communication at the national and the subregional levels. Some of the constraints at the interface level are: lack of internal consultation between officials and ministers on the proceedings and decisions taken at regional meetings; representation in regional meetings by officials who have not the appropriate expertise for the issues to be discussed or who have only an indirect relationship with the matters under discussion; and lack of involvement of sectoral ministries in the follow-up of decisions taken at the regional meetings by Heads of State.

Not only does this appear to reflect a lack of political commitment to decisions taken at the regional level but also a failure to develop the institutional measures which are required to follow up and manage these regional decisions. Almost no African state has the essential well-structured or strong institutions and managerial skills at the national level for the implementation of the large and increasingly diverse number of conclusions and recommendations formulated within regional cooperation and integration schemes. Consultation and coordination machinery at the governmental level as well as between the government and the private sector and other societal groups are generally weak and ineffective. There is no relevant institutional machinery in place to enable the people, the business community, the private sector or agents of socio-economic activity and their organized associations, like the chambers of commerce and industry and professional associations, to find appropriate and adequate channels of participation in economic development activities at the subregional and regional levels.

What progress, then, can be expected in this context of weak and ineffective policy instruments and institutions? Even with the necessary political commitment the results of regional cooperation efforts will remain poor if the institutional machinery is not in place. To be sure, unless these issues are addressed, the frequently asserted objective of closer regional cooperation and integration will remain exactly that – an assertion without implementation. In other words, unless national institutions and administrative processes are adapted to ensure that regional policies and programmes are integrated into national decision making, little or no substantial progress can be achieved in the process of African regionalism.

Whatever policy is decided on regional cooperation will need a strong institutional set-up, which is indispensable for the implementation of the large and increasingly diverse number of conclusions and recommendations formulated within cooperation and integration schemes at both the regional and continental levels. Indeed, it would be virtually fruitless to attempt to improve or build regional or continental administrative and management structures without ensuring strong mechanisms at the national level, and promoting intense awareness at the level of the role that regional and continental integration can make to the attainment of national economic and social objectives.

Deficiencies of Community Institutions

The situation at the subregional or community level is no better. Although the institutional deficiencies of the regional economic communities to formulate and carry out policy making functions effectively have long been recognized as a critical factor, not much reference is made to this aspect of the management of economic cooperation and integration in Africa. Yet, the secretariats of almost all the existing communities suffer from a lack of real decision making process, and their resources are totally inadequate for independent, practical cooperation and integration activities. Their development is blocked by the marked dominance of nation-state interests, allowing genuinely supranational regional development policies only within a narrow framework. This situation is compounded by first, the lack of clarity of the tasks and objectives of the institutions and flexibility in the programme implementation; and second, the problems relating to the ability of the institutions to reconcile national and multinational interests in the implementation of programmes.

In general, the operations of community institutions are at a standstill, which means that progress towards subregional integration is blocked. It has become evident that discussions of the committee of experts or of the Council of Ministers or even those of the summits of Heads of State and Government of the African communities do nothing but reiterate the viewpoints or positions of the member states. The secretariats of the communities, composed of international civil servants who have sworn to be faithful to the treaty but who are answerable to the Council of Ministers, made up of incumbent ministers and member states, are too weak to enforce the community viewpoint.[23]

Closely related to this is the inability of the Council of Ministers in solving community problems at its level, systematically referring technical issues to the Heads of State and Government. These leaders, overburdened with the magnitude of problems, which, needless to say, are contrary to the principle of a supranational institution, hide their hesitation and their indecision behind the unanimity rule. Major decisions systematically come up against the veto based on the principle of unanimity of the states.

In sum, it can be said that the existing institutional framework for subregional communities is not operational. Community issues are entrusted only to intergovernmental machineries: government committees of civil servants, councils of ministers, and summits of Heads of State and Government. The civil society, as indicated below, is not involved in the economic integration process. Decisions are taken by these intergovernmental organs but they are not put into operation because individual governments do not have to report to national institutions or to any subregional parliaments. The economic integration experience of many subregional economic groupings is a succession of meetings of intergovernmental organs. However, as noted already, each country continues to pursue individual national development policies. This experience of economic integration, therefore, has no impact on the lives of the population and does not improve the economic performance of member states.

The functioning of African economic communities is also put to the test by their meagre financial resources. Their source of revenue is essentially contributions of member states, the majority of whom do not pay such contributions. Some member states have accumulated considerable arrears in their financial contributions. For example, in ECOWAS as of December 1990, most of the member states had accumulated arrears amounting to over four years of contributions.[24] The communities are thus not only deprived of the resources for implementing their programmes but they are also unable to meet their current expenditures: salaries of employees, electricity and water costs and other overheads. This notwithstanding, the policy making organs request the secretariats to conduct numerous studies each year.

The economic communities can only count on assistance from the outside world to finance their key programmes. Similarly, they rely solely on external assistance to execute their programme of subregional integration. A case in point was the mobilization of as much as nearly US$61 million by the PTA as external assistance for 48 projects during 1992–3. Similarly, ECOWAS managed to mobilize about US$12 million from external donor agencies for eight projects between January and October 1990. Foreign donors, of course, finance projects which conform to their priorities and thereby impose their economic integration approach on the countries. This is why very little progress has been made in the development of hydro-power, the promotion of basic industries and in the development of a heavy transport system, without which African economies cannot be modernized.

Another cause of the deficient functioning of the economic communities is the poor choice of personnel of the secretariats by the member states. Both in qualitative and quantitative terms most economic groupings in Africa are inadequately staffed. It is a fact that the institutions of the European Union are served by first-class European personalities such as Gaston Thorn, Jacques Delors, and Raymond Barre, former Prime Minister of France. On the other hand, in the case of the African economic communities, the quality of staff is low, largely because most of the executive and professional positions are usually filled on political and geographical representation grounds rather than on experience, technical and administrative competence. Invariably, member governments put their own narrow national interest above those of the communities by insisting on politically desirable appointees to head multilateral organizations. The political appointees at the head of the economic communities do not always fully comprehend the problems of economic integration. Some of the executives, therefore, lack conviction and the determination to promote subregional economic integration because they themselves do not know what direction the communities should take. With no vision for the future, they content themselves with the day-to-day running of their secretariats. Evidence from all African subregions suggests that inexperienced leadership has largely contributed to the paralysis or poor performance of quite a number of regional groupings. The situation is aggravated by the lack of grassroots support at the national level or credible genuinely effective regional or subregional lobby in the individual countries.

Lack of Participation of Interest Groups/Private Sector

A significant aspect of the African economic integration scheme is the apparent lack of a forum created for exchange of views with interest groups such as civil societies, employers associations, trade unions, market women associations, who are directly interested in and likely to be directly affected by many of the provisions of the treaties establishing the various economic groupings. To what extent, for example, do the broad masses of the people participate in or influence the decision making process of the African economic integration groups? Or is the idea of economic integration normally 'sold' to a reluctant, uncommitted and sceptical working population? This extremely important aspect of the strategy of developmental regionalism in Africa has so far not received adequate attention.[25]

Theoretically, the importance of the role of interest groups in promoting integration has been stressed *ad nauseam* by neo-functionalist scholars like Haas and Lindberg.[26] According to such neo-functionalist theorists, by participating in the policy making process, interest groups are likely to develop a stake in promoting further integration in order to acquire economic payoffs and additional benefits from maintaining and stimulating the organization through which certain demands can be articulated and goals attained. This implies that in the integration process interest groups can play an instrumental role in the maintenance of the integrative system. Through their involvement in the policy making process of an integrating community, these groups will 'learn' about the rewards of such involvement and undergo attitudinal changes inclining them favourably towards the system. The result of this process is quite significant for the growth of the integrating community. For while the interest groups would be interested in working steadily towards the perpetuation of the system, the decision makers would in turn develop an interest in being responsive to demands of these groups. Through this process, the supportive clientele of the integrating community, which is of paramount importance for its growth and operation, would be wide and considerable. Thus the interest groups can enhance the position of responsive institutions.

Given the importance neo-functionalists attach to the role of interest groups in promoting integration, it is not surprising that discussions leading up to the establishment of the EEC considered the formal involvement of economic and social groups in the policy making process. Hence within the European Union channels have been developed through which economic and social interests participate in discussions, although it is far less clear what influence they can exert on the outcome. The main formal channel provided for under the Rome Treaty is the Economic and Social Committee (ESC) set up under Articles 193–198. According to Article 193 the ESC shall consist of representatives of the various categories of economic and social life, in particular, representatives of producers, agriculturists, transport operators, workers, merchants, artisans, liberal professions, and the general interest. In practice, about one-third of the members are trade unionists. It was thought that this body would provide a stimulus to interest groups to participate directly in Community discussion, from which support for policy proposal would flow. But the ESC has not developed as an institutional resource for mobilizing opinion at the supranational level to respond to interest group demands. Consequently, recent commentators, like Lodge and Herman, do not assign any great weight to its role in the EU decision making process, yet this does not entirely diminish the significance of its existence as a forum for the articulation of interest group positions.[27] It is worth noting that neo-functionalist premises have been realized for the EU outside of ESC, that is, through channels other than the ESC. By 1965 there were 231 regional offices of business and trade associations and 117 regional agricultural associations with offices in Brussels.[28]

This experience of the EU is not reflected in the institutional structure of African economic communities. Indeed, these can rightly be criticized for not having any popular roots, and because the personalities and institutions controlling them have little contact or involvement with the man in the street. The whole institutional structure can be described as the brainchild of an elite, and there is no organ through which interest groups can bridge, as neo-functionalists suggest, the elite–mass gap. Being intergovernmental in nature, key decision makers are generally the top-level political elites and bureaucrats. Participation in the decision making process by the staff of the executive secretariats is minimal while the various bodies play, if at all, a very peripheral role. Not only is the bulk of the people virtually ignored but also, and perhaps more importantly, organizations representing business interest – employers' associations or chambers of commerce – are not included on a regular and formal basis even though they do make their presence felt individually, indirectly, and informally.

Indeed, in general, participants in the decision making process within African regional organizations are the political elite, the bureaucratic elite, and representatives of foreign interests. Hence the broad mass of the people are excluded from effective participation in the economy as both producers and consumers. This low level of economic mobilization of the broad masses of the people means that they are unlikely to be involved in regional integration efforts based on functionalist strategies. This implies, therefore, that regional groupings in Africa will be between only a tiny fraction of the population of the states concerned.[29] The leadership fails to explain fully to the people the reasons for participating (or joining) in the arrangements and what advantages will accrue to the majority. The treaties or articles of association become the private property of a few politicians and civil servants. Nobody else reads or knows of them. To the extent that cooperation arrangements are (or were) forged without the full participation and knowledge of the population, their stability and the implementation of their programmes cannot be guaranteed. Indeed, it has to be admitted that if an integration process remains a bureaucratic affair and the people are not really convinced of its usefulness, it is unlikely to succeed.

ECOWAS, UDEAC, and especially the defunct EAC, did not establish any forms of consultation with interest groups; therefore they did not in principle, associate persons other than official experts with their work. These three groupings have no organs whose membership consists of representatives of the economic and social sectors. Put differently, neither ECOWAS, the EAC nor UDEAC provided for a separate and continuous committee of experts or for the formal involvement of private individuals or groups in the decision making process. Indeed, at the meeting of heads of state and government of UDEAC held in Yaoundé in January 1967, it was firmly resolved that UDEAC decisions must be made entirely at the intergovernmental level, thus closing the door to business groups within the region to have any right to participate formally in UDEAC decision making.[30]

By contrast, however, the association of independent or private experts and representatives of professional organizations or the private sector with the preparation and implementation of decisions, through advisory bodies or *ad hoc* groups, are to be found, with some variations, in all the Latin American groupings. In the case of the Central American Common Market (CACM), for example, the private sector is closely associated with the activities of its institutions through various working parties. However, it is perhaps with the Andean Group that consultation through such bodies as the Consultative Committee and the Economic and Social Advisory Committee has been firmly institutionalized and formalized. For although the erstwhile Latin American Free Trade Agreement (LAFTA) allowed for private sector consultation through various advisory committees, consultative committees and sectorial meetings, that consultation was not formalized as it is in the Andean Common Market.[31]

Interest groups, however, need not necessarily be in favour of the integration process. In general, many of these groups remain a weak force, as Werner Feld concluded in his study of European interest groups.[32] In many cases the types of interest that are aggregated at the regional level tend to be very general, with more specific interests and structures remaining at the national level. For instance, as Nye has emphasized, 'despite the existence of regional trade union secretariats in Brussels, the idea of collective bargaining at the European level in response to the creation of a European market has not taken hold – in part because of divisions in the labour movement but also because of the importance of national governmental power in collective bargaining'.[33] Besides, many interest groups could conveniently be opposed to it. A characteristic case in point was the opposition mounted by the Venezuelan private sector against the country's entry into the Andean Common Market. The private sector was extremely effective in turning its interests into government policy. Specifically, Federation de Camaras (Federation of Chambers), the best organized pressure group in Latin America representing 168 Venezuelan trade associations and federations, stoutly opposed its country's membership in the Andean Group. Consequently, although the Andean Pact was signed in 1969, Venezuela did not join the Andean Common Market until 1973.[34]

In spite of these observations, the argument favouring the importance of interest groups or the private sector as relevant actors in promoting integration remains valid. These groups, lacking in authoritative decision making capacity, should not lead to the interpretation that they are unimportant. They may prove to be very significant. By building in the involvement and collaboration of the private sector, these groups may well play a vital role, as they have done, in the case of the European Union. In his examination of the role of the trade unions as an interest group in the European Union, Colin Beever has come to the conclusion that, as far as general community policy is concerned, the unions in the EU countries, with the exception of the World Federation of Trade Unions (WFTU), have almost unreservedly supported the principles of European integration and the Common Market itself 'and have pressed for more progress and a greater degree of supranational power to be given to the Community institutions'. They claim that they are the true defenders of the principles of the Rome Treaty, and have never wavered in this belief.[35] Similarly, in the 1969 crisis of CACM, for example, it was the Federation of Chambers of Commerce and Industry of Central America which issued a statement defending the Common Market.

Furthermore, in addition to representing a shift of political activity towards the regional level and a potential source of regional pressure on national governments these non-governmental groupings themselves have elite socialization effects.[36]

In this regard, the failure to involve the interest groups in decision-making processes of the African economic communities appears to be more serious than may readily be appreciated. This apparent lack of popular participation in the regional cooperation and integration process in Africa is one of the main causes of the ineffectiveness of the present economic groupings. For in the final analysis, cooperation among African countries is not or rather should not be just the concern of governments. If the political will to cooperate, to pool sovereignty is the 'subsoil in which we must nurture the tree of collective self-reliance', the intellectual inputs in terms of ideas and especially the sustained pressure of the working population and organized opinion on their government to push ahead 'is the water which must continually nurture the growth of the tree'.[37]

This chapter has devoted considerable attention to the reasons for the limited progress made and faltering steps. In this connection, the chapter questions the appropriateness of the market integration approach which has been adopted by almost all the subregional economic integration schemes in Africa, highlighting the complex problems generated by this approach as for example, loss of government revenue, distributional crises, and the adverse impact of the role of TNCs on the economic communities. Indeed, in a context of underdevelopment, trade must not be treated as a priority objective as the major problems are elsewhere, that is, in lack of complementarity of industrial products, deficiency of the means of transport and communications, absence of adequate means of payment for trade exchanges, obsession with unequal development in less developed member countries, fear of budgetary losses where carriage charges constitute the bulk of the resources of states, and so on.

The chapter has also highlighted the poor management of economic cooperation and integration in Africa at both the national and subregional levels stressing, among other things, the lack of commitment of African ruling classes to regionalism as a strategy for development; the equal lack of adequate and viable institutions; the meagre financial resources; inadequate staffing both qualitatively and quantitatively; and finally, the limited role of the private sector and interest groups.

On the whole, management of economic integration in Africa constitutes a permanent challenge to the most elementary principles of 'economic calculation'. Instead of being a factor for development, African integration tends to become a hindrance, owing to the financing burden that it imposes on the budgets of member states without any significant results. However, by the early 1990s, there has been a renewed interest in economic integration, which is once again at the centre of policy agenda in almost all the subregions of Africa. Hence the post-1990 regional initiatives and challenges constitute the focus of the second part of this volume.

Part II

Into the 1990s:
The New Phase of
Regionalism in Africa

5 New Regional Initiatives in Africa

As noted in the introductory chapter, since the beginning of the 1990s, the trend towards regionalism in world trade has gathered momentum at a time when other profound changes are taking place in the world economy. All over the world, the pace of regionalism has accelerated and the division of the world into three trading blocs based on Europe, the Americas and East Asia has become a serious possibility. This has created a renewed interest within Africa in revitalising and resuscitating regional groupings. Recognizing the sheer enormity of the changes now taking place, African countries have called for a re-examination of present policies and strategies regarding regionalism and the adoption of new initiatives that will respond effectively to the challenges. There is the fear that the position of Africa in the world economy will be weakened further if the continent does not strengthen the institutional and managerial capacity of its existing subregional economic schemes. This has been prompted by the fact that, given the changes in the world economy, a failure to overcome, or reduce, the costs of market fragmentation in regions whose countries have not yet begun to cooperate will mean that those regions, as a whole, will be less well placed in the future to attract the foreign investment, technology and know-how on which they will have to depend for their future growth. Besides, developments in the rest of the world have forced African countries to take a serious look at their efforts at regional integration. The experience of Europe and developments in North America suggest that there are gains to be derived from integration and that these gains are beyond the static welfare effects.

It was against this background that the all-important Abuja Treaty was adopted in June 1991 establishing the African Economic Community (AEC). This inspired the launching of numerous subregional initiatives of different types. In Eastern and Southern Africa, the PTA was transformed into the Common Market for Eastern and Southern Africa (COMESA) in 1994 with a view to attaining, among other things, sustainable growth and development of the member states by promoting a more balanced and harmonious development of its production and marketing structures. The SADCC was similarly transformed in August 1992 into the Southern African Development Community (SADC) to attain a higher level of cooperation that would enable the countries of the region to address problems of national development, and cope with the challenges posed by a changing, and increasingly complex, regional and global environment more effectively.

In 1993, an agreement on East African Cooperation was signed by the three Heads of State of Kenya, Tanzania and Uganda which led to the relaunch of the old East African Community in March 1996 as a way of boosting external investment, local manufacturing and trade between the three countries. The Cross-Border Initiative (CBI), sponsored by the World Bank, the International Monetary Fund (IMF), the Commission of the European Communities and the African Development Bank (ADB), was launched in early 1992 to promote private investment, trade and payments in Eastern and Southern Africa and the Indian Ocean. The Indian Ocean Island States also launched a programme to promote closer integration between them. In particular, more recently, following President Nelson Mandela of South Africa's visit to India in January 1995, another regional initiative emerged – the Indian Ocean Rim Association (IORA) – which aimed, most basically, at promoting trade and investment within the Indian Ocean Rim. Its membership includes such countries as Australia, Singapore, Oman, Malaysia Kenya, South Africa and Mauritius.

In West Africa, the Authority of Heads of State and Government of ECOWAS adopted a decision at its Thirteenth Ordinary Session held in Banjul, the Gambia, on 30 May 1990, to set up a Committee of Eminent Persons under the chairmanship of General Yakubu Gowan, former Head of State of the Federal Republic of Nigeria, to undertake a review of the 1975 ECOWAS Treaty to enable the Community to adjust itself to the rapidly changing economic landscape in different parts of the world, the ongoing democratization process in many regions of the world, coupled with the widespread emphasis on the free market economy. The Committee was mandated to expand the coverage of the 1975 ECOWAS Treaty and modify its strategies in order to accelerate the integration process and contribute effectively to West African development. It was felt that ECOWAS must now see itself within the context of similar economic blocs in the world and, nearer home, of the other regional economic groupings in Africa being established in the 1990s. The revised ECOWAS Treaty was adopted in 1993.

While the ECOWAS Treaty was being revitalized, the French-speaking countries of the subregion created in 1994 the Union économique et monétaire ouest-africaine (UEMOA), an economic and monetary union which aims at producing a more rational and dynamic way of approaching the integration of the Franc Zone countries of the area. Similarly, in Central Africa, the Heads of State of the UDEAC formulated a new treaty for the creation of the Communauté économique et monétaire de l'Afrique Centrale (CEMAC), with the aim of attaining a transition from a Customs Union under UDEAC to an Economic and Monetary Union.

These post-1990 regional initiatives in Africa and elsewhere are based on the precepts of economic openness and marked efficiency. They embrace different principles for achieving progressive economic cohesion than their fiat-driven predecessors which were based on protectionist, closed-economy policies of the kind which typically pervaded development thinking particularly in Africa, for more than three decades. Not only do the new groupings in Africa reflect respect for and observance of certain fundamental principles and basic undertakings, they have shifted the exclusive focus on government to government, to involving the people, non-governmental organizations (NGOs), the civil society and the private sector. This chapter attempts a brief review of these new regional initiatives with particular reference to the African Economic Community, the Cross-Border Initiative and the French-sponsored vertical integration approach as reflected in the UEMOA and CEMAC, which have hitherto not received adequate attention in the literature on integration.

AFRICAN ECONOMIC COMMUNITY: A NEW HOPE FOR AFRICA?

The adoption of the Abuja Treaty on 3 June 1991 by 48 member states of the Organization of African Unity (OAU) at its Twenty-seventh summit establishing a timetable towards the creation of an African Economic Community by the year 2025 is a major historic undertaking which must be seen as vital for Africa's economic survival, in the face of its economic crisis and growing marginalization in world affairs.[1] It is a giant step towards Africa's long-cherished goal of unifying the continent's fragmented and vulnerable national economies into a single, more powerful economic bloc with a view to translating into reality the dream of pan-Africanism and continental integration advocated by Kwame Nkrumah of Ghana and other founding fathers of Africa's independence movement.[2] It is also the realization of Article 11(2) of the Charter which established the OAU itself on 25 May 1963. Above all, Abuja is Africa's response to the challenges posed by the regionalist fever which has spread rapidly all over the globe: the US–Canada–Mexico Free Trade Agreement, the Australia–New Zealand Free Trade Area, the new economic bloc in Asia and the Far East, the recently inaugurated Asia Pacific Economic Cooperation Agreement and, especially, the single European Market or 'Fortress Europe' 1992 – all of which threaten to isolate Africa from world markets.[3]

At the African continental level, by signing the Abuja Treaty the member states of the OAU have at last taken the bold and courageous step of establishing a legal framework for the realization of the economic integration of Africa. History will no doubt record this achievement as a step in the right direction along the long and arduous path leading to the economic emancipation of Africa. Abuja represents a decisive shift in African political thinking on the 'extremely sensitive and controversial subject of African unity'. The treaty, in historical perspective, is a culmination of the collective vision of some of the greatest architects of African nationalism, independence and solidarity. Looked at idealistically, it is a major accomplishment on the part of the member states of the OAU to conclude a treaty on such delicate matters as economic integration and articulate principles and objectives relating thereto. Their ability to prescribe institutions and mechanisms for implementation is equally significant. Realistically, however, the crux of the matter in every collective economic integration venture is whether the member governments possess the political will to operationalize within their national domain decisions of regional authorities with supranational jurisdiction assigned specific tasks in the sphere of economic integration.

Significantly, too, the Abuja Treaty poses a new challenge to the process of regionalism in Africa and gives a new lease of life to the existing subregional economic communities – ECOWAS, COMESA, ECCAS, SADC, AMU – which hold a special place in the progressive establishment of the new pan-African community. It has thrown up new challenges which demand that these economic communities should make more progress in the realization of their stated objectives apart from consolidating their achievements within a specific geographic area. So central is the role of the subregional economic communities in the attainment of the community objectives as executing instruments of AEC programmes at the national and subregional levels that without them the new pan-African Economic Community collapses as a strategy for African development.

All this tends to raise a number of crucial questions about the prospects of the AEC in realizing the objectives of African economic integration and meeting the challenges of the emerging new world of regionalism. To what extent, for example, can the AEC be realistically described as a new hope for Africa, particularly in the process of African development? How different is the Abuja Treaty from the treaties that created the subregional economic communities of the 1970s and 1980s? How far has Abuja responded to the various challenges and deficiencies of the pre-1990 economic communities such as ECCAS, AMU, PTA or SADCC? This section of the chapter seeks to examine critically the substantive provisions of the Abuja Treaty in the light of the experience of the pre-1990 subregional economic communities.

It will also highlight the challenges of implementation of the treaty and evaluate its potential for creating a vibrant community.

Background

The Abuja Treaty is the mature outcome of a long process and not an isolated act. The preamble to the treaty sets landmarks for the 28-year journey which may be described as the key sources of inspiration for the collective wisdom of the member states of the OAU.[4] First, the adoption of the OAU Charter in 1963 of which the treaty itself is an integrated part; second, the decisions, resolutions and declarations adopted at the Algiers summit in September 1968, and the Addis Ababa summits of August 1970 and May 1973 which made economic integration an essential condition for the achievement of OAU objectives; third, the Libreville summit of 1977 endorsing the Kinshasa Declaration of 1976 on the establishment of an African economic community; fourth, the Monrovia summit of 1979 at which was adopted the Monrovia Declaration of Commitment to the Guidelines and Measures to be taken to achieve national and collective self-sufficiency in economic and social development with a view to establishing a new international economic order and which, among other things, called for the establishment of an African common market as a prelude to the creation of an African economic community; fifth, the source of inspiration is reflected in the *Lagos Plan of Action* and the Final Act of Lagos (1980) reaffirming the commitment to establish an African Common Market by the year 2000; and finally, the OAU Declaration reaffirming the commitment and determination to accelerate the establishment of the proposed African Economic Community.

The implication here is that these regional instruments have been the major catalysts for Africa's new treaty on economic cooperation. It is significant, therefore, that in the preamble to the treaty, the member states of the OAU thought it proper to place on record that the 'efforts already made in subregional and regional sectoral economic cooperation are encouraging and justify a larger and fuller economic integration'. It would, however, be unrealistic to deny, as a secondary source of inspiration, the effects of the external stimuli emanating from the emerging world of trading blocs to which attention has already been drawn.

THE ABUJA TREATY: PRINCIPLES, INSTITUTIONS AND DECISION MAKING PROCESSES

The Abuja Treaty is remarkably significant and, to a large extent, different from the treaties that established the subregional economic schemes of the

1970s and 1980s in terms of institutional and decision making process, as well as approach and orientation.[5] It is comprehensive in scope containing 106 articles arranged into 22 chapters and incorporating not only the substantive development sectors highlighted in the *Lagos Plan* but also many other strictly non-economic aspects of cooperation. Hence it reflects admirably the holistic view of the concept of development which links the so-called objective and quantitative factors of production on the one hand, and the so-called non-economic factors – political, social, cultural, environmental and institutional – on the other. In particular, Abuja reflects the essential elements of a democratic framework or the importance of popular democracy in the development process as ingredients *par excellence* of sustainable development.

Unlike the 1975 ECOWAS and the 1981 PTA treaties, Abuja provides an instructive preface of a set of fundamental principles which breath through the operative chapters of the treaty. Among them is the strict adherence to the principles of equality and interdependence of member states; 'solidarity and collective self-reliance'; promotion of 'interstate cooperation, harmonization of policies and integration of programmes', as well as 'harmonious development of economic activities among member states'. Other principles relate to the 'promotion of a peaceful environment' as prerequisite for Africa's successful economic development. Linked to this is the emphasis placed on 'the respect, promotion and protection of human and peoples' rights', in accordance with the provisions of the African Charter on Human and Peoples' Rights adopted by the OAU in 1981. Abuja also commits African states to the promotion of accountability, economic justice and popular participation in development.[6] Consequently, the Community seeks the cooperation of African NGOs in order to involve peoples of Africa in the process of economic integration and to mobilise their skills and financial support. Abuja therefore reflects what has been forcefully articulated in the UNDP *Human Development Report* series and the ECA *African Charter for Popular Participation in Development and Transformation*.[7]

These are the strategic principles derived from the adoption of an endogenous development model which constitute the framework of the treaty. They reflect much insight and perception of the OAU member states, recalling the post-independence records of many African governments of lack of respect for the Rule of Law and the principle of legality, disregard for the international legal norm enjoining sovereign states to settle their differences peacefully, violation of human and people's rights, and non-application of the doctrine of democratic accountability.

Besides the principles are the specific general undertakings which are critical, as they focus on key obstacles that have stood in the way of constructive and effective process of economic integration at the subregional level. To this end, Abuja commits the member states to undertake to create favourable conditions for the development of the Community and the attainment of its objectives, particularly by harmonizing their strategies and policies, and to 'refrain from any unilateral action that may hinder the attainment of the said objectives'. Furthermore, each member state should pledge, 'in accordance with its constitutional procedures' to 'take all necessary measures to ensure the enactment and dissemination of such legislation as may be necessary for the implementation of the provisions of this Treaty'.[8] To some extent, this approach is based on hindsight. Experience has shown that one major legal impediment to economic integration derives from dissimilarities and divergencies in national laws and policies of member states regulating key areas of cooperation, for example, industrial and trade laws (notably investment incentive laws and policies), customs and excise laws, exchange control laws and policies, and taxation legislation.

In terms of Community objectives, the treaties establishing the pre-1990 subregional economic groupings do not seem to have much to learn from Abuja, as they all reflect the standard provisions of African economic cooperation and integration schemes. The AEC Treaty, however, defines with much more clarity and specificity, the need for promoting 'economic, social and cultural development and the integration of African economies in order to increase economic self-reliance and promote an endogenous and self-sustained development', which are the two main principles underlying the *Lagos Plan of Action*. To achieve a self-reliant development, Abuja aims at establishing, on a continental scale, 'a framework for the development, mobilization and utilization of the human and material resources of Africa'.[9] Article 4(2) particularizes in 16 paragraphs the measures to be adopted by member states to implement the Community's objectives.

Another area of significance relates to the institutions of the Community. The process of integration necessitates creation of suitable institutions to deal with the complex problem of linking the economic destinies of several nations. Indeed much of the success of the European Union is attributable to the wide range of institutions which have been instrumental in translating its programmes and policies into action. The Treaty of Rome established clear provisions not only for setting up the organs of the Union, but for a gradual transfer of initiative from member states to these supranational entities. A significant result of these built-in provisions is that integration among the member states of the Union has become a 'continuous process, whose scope is expanding along a previously determined time path'.[10]

While the institutions of the AEC are not so elaborate, the Abuja Treaty recognizes the development of adequate institutional machinery as an essential condition for successful coordination of development policies. Its provision for an African Parliament breaks entirely new ground, as this has not been the case with the subregional economic community treaties of the 1970s and 1980s. The African Parliament would ensure the involvement of the people in the 'development and integration process of the continent'.[11] Abuja, therefore, once again, responds to the current concern about the role of the people and the democratic imperative in the process of integration. In this regard, the treaty is in accord not only with the May 1990 decision of the Andean Group Heads of State summit to create a directly elected Andean Parliament to promote popular participation in the integration process, but also with the undertaking by the Tenth Conference of Heads of Government of the Caribbean Common Market (CARICOM) held in July 1989 to establish an Assembly of Caribbean Parliamentarians to act as an important instrument for popular participation in the integration process.[12] Three key issues likely to arise in creating such a forum are, first, whether or not it should be a directly elected body of members representing the peoples of the member states; second, whether its powers are to be legislative, consultative, advisory or supervisory; and third, whether the members of such a body should sit in political groups reflecting their political affiliations or their nationality.

One other institutional novelty is the Economic and Social Commission (Article 15), composed of Ministers responsible for economic development, planning and integration in member states. They may be assisted as and when necessary, by other Ministers. Representatives of regional economic communities have a right of participation in meetings of the Commission and its subsidiary organs. The modalities and conditions for such participation are to be the subject of a protocol. It shall meet at least once a year in ordinary session and may be convened in extraordinary session on its own initiative or at the request of the Assembly or the Council.

Specifically, the Commission is mandated to carry out the following functions:

(i)   prepare, in accordance with the *Lagos Plan of Action* and the Final Act of Lagos, programmes, policies and strategies for cooperation in the fields of economic and social development among African countries on the one hand, and between Africa and the international community on the other, and make appropriate recommendations to Assembly, through the Council;

(ii) coordinate, harmonise, supervise and follow up the economic, social, cultural, scientific and technical activities of the Secretariat of the Committees and any other subsidiary body;

(iii) examine the reports and recommendations of the Committees and submit the same, together with its observations and recommendations to the Assembly, through the Council and ensure their follow-up;

(iv) make recommendations to the Assembly, through the Council with a view of coordinating and harmonising the activities of the different regional economic communities;

(v) supervise the preparation of international negotiations, assess the results thereof and report thereon to the Assembly through the Council; and

(vi) carry out all other functions assigned thereto by the Assembly or the Council.[13]

These functions of the Commission are central to the Community's objectives. Together with the Specialized Technical Committees, the Commission will provide a rich pool of professionalism, expertise and specialization in the appropriate fields of knowledge. It is from these resources that the Community will draw upon for the accomplishment of its objectives. This will be critical for the existence and survival of the Community. In brief, the institutional implications of the Abuja Treaty are impressive. The politico-administrative machinery to be created is almost a copy of the institutional framework of the European Community with a Council of Ministers, Economic and Social Committee, Court of Justice, and a pan-African Parliament.

In terms of powers and functions of both the Assembly of the Heads of State and Government and the Council of Ministers, the Abuja Treaty is significantly different from the provisions provided to these important organs under the treaties establishing the old subregional economic communities, in particular the ECOWAS. Article 8(3) of the treaty confers on the supreme organ of the Community, that is, the Assembly of Heads of State and Government, the power to 'give directives, coordinate and harmonise the economic, scientific, technical, cultural and social policies of member states'. Similarly, in the treaty establishing the EU, the Council is endowed with authority to 'ensure coordination of the general policies of the member states' (Article 145 of the Rome Treaty). A transparent organic link is thus established between the supreme institution of the Community and the member states. In contrast, the Council of Ministers established under the 1975 ECOWAS Treaty, for example, has neither original nor delegated powers to give directives in connection with the crucial task of the Community which is the coordination and harmonization of the socio-economic policies and activities of member states. Specifically, it has no original power to give directives to member states nor can the Authority of ECOWAS confer such powers on it.[14]

As regards the binding force of Community decisions, Abuja breaks more new ground by making the decisions of the Assembly and the regulations of the Council binding on member states as well as the subordinate institutions (Article 10(1) and Article 13(2)). Similarly, under the Rome Treaty establishing the EU, a Council regulation 'shall have general application' and 'shall be binding in its entirety and directly applicable in all member states' (Article 189). On the other hand, under the 1981 PTA Treaty and the 1975 ECOWAS Treaty, there is the striking absence of any power to bind member states. With the exception of the decisions of the Court of Justice (Article 56), and the provisions of Article 54(3) on sanctions for non-payment of budgetary contributions, not even the decisions of the highest organ of ECOWAS – the Authority of Heads of State and Government – are binding on member states. Such decisions and directives are binding only on the 'institutions of the Community' (Article 5(3)). Similarly, the decisions and directives of the ECOWAS Council of Ministers are 'binding on all subordinate institutions of the Community' (Article 6(3)).[15]

As Wilmot rightly remarks, the difference between the provisions of the old ECOWAS Treaty on the one hand, and those of the AEC and EU Treaties on the other, in relation to the binding force of decisions, 'is one of substance, touching on the fundamental issue of supranationality'. In this context, supranationality refers to a situation 'where an international institution is endowed with powers to take decisions binding on sovereign states either generally or in specific areas of state activity'.[16] Thus, whereas it is clear that the provisions of the AEC and EU Treaties envisaged the establishment of supranational institutions to oversee their integration process, the 1975 ECOWAS Treaty did not contemplate any such institutions.

It is interesting to note that following the example of the Abuja Treaty, the framers of the revised Treaty of ECOWAS (1993), the SADC Treaty (1992, Article 19(8)) and COMESA Treaty (1994, Article 8(3)) have endowed the new and/or transformed subregional communities with supranational powers as an indispensable instrument for effective integration. Since these communities are the pillars or building blocks in the construction of the AEC, it became necessary that each of them should be endowed with similar powers to ensure their effectiveness and viability. Indeed, having conceded the principle of supranationality to the AEC, it was not difficult for the member states of the SADC, COMESA and ECOWAS to accept the same in the context of their subregional economic communities.

Abuja also puts the African Community in a slightly different setting in the area of decision making process. In the case of ECOWAS, for example, there is no prescribed procedure for arriving at decisions, no clear indication as to whether decisions are to be reached by unanimity, consensus or by majority vote and, if the latter, whether by simple or qualified majority. In practice, however, the ECOWAS Authority has, since its inception, taken all its decisions by unanimity or consensus. Similarly, in the PTA Treaty, provision is made for adopting decisions by consensus (Article 5), while in the Arab Maghreb Union Treaty, decisions by the Presidential Council are to be taken unanimously (Article 6). Indeed, in most regional groupings of the developing countries, unanimity is required for all important decisions, although in some cases, majority decision is prescribed at certain levels. Thus, in both the Central American Common Market (CACM) and the Andean Common Market, the Executive Council and Commission respectively take clear decisions by majority vote, while all decisions in the Economic Council must be taken unanimously. Again, the unanimity rule prevailed in the defunct East African Community while it features in the treaty establishing UDEAC.

No doubt a decision arrived at unanimously has the advantage of accommodating the vital interests and concerns of all the parties. A decision by consensus reconciles the interests and concerns of all parties, in circumstances where the small minority is willing not to insist on its objections and is prepared to go along with the majority. In either case, the willing cooperation of all parties in the implementation of the decision can reasonably be assumed. A decision by unanimity or consensus is also conducive to the promotion of a congenial atmosphere and harmonious working relationship, as no party has any reasonable cause to feel aggrieved that its vital interests are being trampled upon.[17]

On the other hand, experience has shown how decision making restricted to consensus or unanimity only can become a major obstacle to positive action by an organization. The constant need for complicated deals, and the arduous efforts to arrive at a compromise indispensable for decision, often lead to immobility and obscure the text or resolutions. Thus a compromise is often reached at the expense of precision. Generally, also, the consensus requirement renders the decision making process a slow and inadequate one.[18] Furthermore, it creates the irritating and inequitable situation where the minority may hold the majority to ransom by its negative posture, retarding overall progress. The current difficulties posed by the British in the decision making process of the European Union on such issues as monetary and political union are a case in point.

The Abuja Treaty is quite explicit in stating that decisions of the Assembly and the regulations of the Council of the Community are, as a rule, to be taken by consensus. However, an alternative of a two-thirds majority vote of member states is provided in cases of failure to reach a consensus, unless otherwise specified in the Treaty (Articles 10(4) and 13(4)). In the light of experience of decision making solely by consensus or unanimity, the importance of having this alternative provision in the Abuja Treaty cannot be overemphasized. It is reassuring that the revised ECOWAS Treaty and, in particular, the new COMESA Treaty, make a special provision for the Council of Ministers to take decisions by consensus; failing which, by two-thirds majority of the members of the Council (Article 9(6) of the COMESA Treaty). On the other hand, the new SADC Treaty maintains that decisions of the Council of Ministers 'shall be by consensus' (Article 11(6)) only.

APPROACH AND NEW ISSUES FACED BY ABUJA

Of particular importance is the approach which the African Economic Community has adopted with a view to realizing the potential of the African region for the benefit of its populations. Unlike ECOWAS, PTA or ECCAS which, as noted above, have focused attention for more than a decade on market integration, the new Community is based on a certain number of key sectors with a great capacity for integration, notably industry, agriculture, transport and communications, energy, science and technology, trade, money and finance. Thus primarily, Abuja adopts a production-focused approach or, specifically, collaboration for expansion and diversification of material production. This is an approach that emphasizes broadening the regional production base and that gives priority to deliberate measures for increasing industrial and agricultural production in the framework of a variety of cooperative schemes and arrangements.

The approach of Abuja is based on the premise that expansion of mutual trade can take place only if the African countries are able to produce the desired merchandise in sufficient quantities to meet each other's demand. The possibility of increases in mutual trade is a crucial incentive to expansion of production, but it cannot be taken for granted that the desired expansion will automatically follow. Gradual harmonization of industrial and agricultural policies and joint industrial and agricultural planning and production are complementary to market integration.

Another significant element of the Abuja Treaty is the emphasis placed on environment (Article 58), which has become a major developmental challenge in Africa and indeed, a global concern compelling the Forty-fifth session of the General Assembly to create a US$1.5 billion environmental fund.[19] Future prospects for development depend on maintaining healthy environments, and on rehabilitating degraded ones. Consequently, Abuja stresses the need for promotion of healthy environments by adopting not only national, but more importantly, subregional and continental policies, strategies and programmes, since a substantial number of African environmental problems – desertification and river basin development, for example, – go beyond the limits of national borders.

One other distinguishing feature of Abuja is its response to the rapid changes in scientific and technological developments which have generated a new industrial revolution whose consequences for Africa are enormous. To meet this challenge, the treaty commits Community members to strengthen their scientific and technological capabilities in order, *inter alia*, to bring about the socio-economic transformation required for improvement of the quality of life of their populations; to reduce their dependence and promote their individual and collective technological self-reliance (Article 51). This is reflected in the 1995 *Cairo Agenda for Action*, adopted by the Council of Ministers of the OAU, which recognized that 'Africa's low science and technology base is highly inadequate for the requirements of modern development processes such as agriculture, health, etc.' There is therefore the urgent need to build up and strengthen Africa's capacity in the field of science and technology, if Africa is to be efficient and competitive in its production and thus participate in the increased flows of advanced technologies and globalization of production processes. It therefore urged African governments to give high priority to building national and regional capacities in the areas of science and technology as the basis and means of all development activities, and to 'formulate effective national policies for education and training in science and technology for development'.[20]

A closely related aspect is the importance which the Abuja Treaty attaches to education, training, research and culture, thus reflecting the fact that economic development, or any kind of economic change, does not occur in isolation but is part of a much larger and more general cultural transformation. African states are therefore called upon to 'strengthen cooperation in the field of education and training, coordinate and harmonize their policies in this field' with a view to 'training persons capable of fostering the changes necessary for enhancing social progress and the development of the continent' (Article 68). Regional approaches to education, training and research have a positive long-term effect on economic and political cooperation in the African region. They enable institutions to be built that are more indigenous, economical and better suited to local conditions.

Acquiring technical skills is costly. No African country can afford all the higher-level institutions required for training, research, and development. Centres of excellence in various fields are needed in Africa, and they can be most efficiently established and operated on a regional basis. And because technical training and research are specialized, regional cooperation yields significant economies of scale. Quality is also enhanced because regional institutions can achieve a critical mass in staffing and justify the provision of facilities and equipment (such as libraries and laboratories) that smaller institutions cannot afford; this enables them to set higher standards. And by mixing students and staff from several countries, they broaden perceptions and foster human and institutional links across borders. By creating regional centres of excellence based on national institutions that take students from several countries, the sending country avoids creating and running expensive institutions, while the host country can reduce its unit costs by optimizing the scale of its facilities.

And to consolidate their cultural identity, Abuja commits African states to pursue not only the objectives of the Cultural Charter of Africa but also to ensure that 'development policies adequately reflect their socio-cultural values' (Article 69). In this respect, Abuja responds meaningfully to the cultural reality of developing societies as recently analysed respectively by development scholars like Dube[21] and Thierry Verhelst[22] and underscored and promoted by the proceedings of several regional and international conferences organized by UNESCO on the theme 'The Cultural Dimension of Development', within the framework of the World Decade for Cultural Development (1988–97), proclaimed by the United Nations General Assembly in resolution 41/187 of 8 December 1986. Indeed, the increasing calls on African countries to take ownership and control of their development process confirms the criticism that much too often in the past the indigenous cultural factor was either completely ignored or assumed to be neutral in the success or failure of development programmes and projects, whether sponsored exclusively by governments themselves or in collaboration with their external partners. Emphasis was on the economic and technical feasibility of projects and not on their socio-cultural relevance, feasibility and sustainability.

Another significant novelty is Abuja's stress on the need for strengthening the private sector participation in regional industrialization and development effort. There are provisions for the coordinated establishment of stock markets and for the free movement of capital within the Community. Freeing labour and capital flows within Africa would improve growth prospects by creating conditions – through increased competition and wider market access – for mergers, acquisitions, joint ventures, and other forms of horizontal and vertical integration.

Finally, it is evident from the Abuja Treaty, that the concept of the African Economic Community, its take-off and its progressive establishment is closely related to the process of economic cooperation and integration at the subregional level. The Community, designed according to a system of concentric circles, will have as subfoundations the subregional economic communities. These federative poles will, within the space of 25 years, move the continent into a Customs Union, a Common Market and finally the African Economic Community in line with Article 6 of the Abuja Treaty. Therefore, it is of overriding importance that the subregional economic communities be viable by providing them with the human and financial resources required and ensuring the centralization of all subregional economic cooperation and integration activities. They should be provided with effective operational basis for the AEC in the implementation of programmes at the Africa level. First, ECOWAS, COMESA, SADC and other subregional economic groupings are the operational arms of the AEC in the implementation of programmes at the subregional level. Second, policies adopted at the subregional level are to be channelled upwards to the continental level. Third, in all the six stages constituting the transitional period leading to the establishment of the AEC, the subregional groupings are assigned contributory tasks, either explicitly or implicitly. And fourth, the institutional set-up at the AEC level provides for representation of the subregional groupings. In these and other ways the place of the subregional groupings in integrative programmes and actions in the continent as a whole becomes both crucial and critical.

On the other hand, the AEC is expected to contribute to the strengthening of the existing subregional economic communities, partly by encouraging them to rationalize their IGOs. It is therefore expected that it will have a positive impact in two ways. The first is in the context of the provisions on the Community's role in the coordination, harmonization, evaluation and integration of the activities of the subregional groupings; in particular that part of Article 6 of the treaty in which member states commit themselves to strengthen the subregional economic communities. The second is in the context of the possible harmonizing impact that the texts establishing the subregional economic communities, as well as their protocols, may have on the Abuja Treaty and the protocols of the AEC. For example, the AEC protocols on trade and customs might well provide valuable guidelines for the harmonization of activities in these areas in the subregions. This will be important especially on those issues, such as rules of origin, where differences in the legal provisions of the different IGOs have retarded progress towards harmonized subregional programmes.[23]

There are, however, some disturbing questions which are likely to raise a set of institutional, legal, technical and even political problems that might impede the take-off of the Community. There is first, the merging of the OAU and the Community into a single organization with a single secretariat. Questions may be raised about the implications for such a merger. As a result of this merger, the pan-African Community has no such thing as a Secretary-General of its own with the requisite qualifications and experience to carry out independently the functions prescribed for it under Article 22 of the treaty. It is headed by one of the five political appointee Assistant Secretaries-General of the OAU. Put differently, unlike the COMESA or ECOWAS, the all-important African Economic Community has no special or independent secretariat of its own and not even a letterhead. In fact, it has no identity, and its functions are completely dominated by those of the politically oriented OAU secretariat, as is evident in the deliberations of the annual summits of the OAU. The AEC has no special summits of Heads of State and Government or meetings of a Council of Ministers of its own devoted entirely to economic cooperation and integration issues as is the case with ECOWAS, COMESA and SADC.

It is not surprising, therefore that the officials of the subregional economic communities have not been as cooperative with the OAU/AEC secretariat, as could be expected. There is the concern that the AEC does not have a clear identify within the OAU secretariat, which would have made it possible to draw a clearer distinction between relations of the subregional community schemes with the AEC and relations with the OAU. There are lingering doubts about the positive benefits that the ECOWAS, COMESA, SADC or ECCAS can expect from the AEC in the implementation of the latter's mandate to 'strengthen existing regional economic communities'. Indeed, there are doubts about the possible contribution that the OAU/AEC secretariat can make to these subregional communities, arising in particular from the perception of the OAU as a political organization, with no track record of handling economic matters.

The question that forces itself upon us is: to what extent would such a merger provide the AEC with the much-needed free hand for the implementation of community decisions, since, as noted above, politics cannot be so easily disassociated from economics especially in integrative schemes, as highlighted by Bergsten, Keohane and Nye in their illuminating study?[24] Unless these delicate and sensitive issues are adequately resolved, the take-off of the Community might be unduly delayed, if it takes off at all. An all-important continental economic community like the EU, has, in Africa, become just a division of a continental political institution (the OAU) which is dominated almost entirely by political issues. It is not surprising, then, that while the Twenty-fourth edition of *Africa South of the Sahara 1995* covers in detail all the regional organizations active in Africa just a footnote is made to the AEC under the extensive coverage of the OAU.[25]

Linked to this, is the composition of the Council of Ministers of the Community who shall be the same Council of Ministers of the OAU, and therefore ministers of foreign affairs, many of whom might not have the requisite knowledge and competency in handling effectively and meaningfully issues of economic development, let alone appreciate the intricacy of the process of economic integration. How can the Council rewardingly assess the programmes, policies and strategies for cooperation in the fields of economic and social development which, under Article 16(a) of the treaty, would be presented to it by the Economic and Social Commission composed of Ministers of Economic Development, Planning and Integration? Or would the Council, in matters of economic integration, serve merely as 'post office' for the Assembly of the Community?

One other potential problem stems from the sequencing of activities. The AEC is to be established by a process running through six stages; the completion of one stage is the start of the next one and so on, forming a chain. However, if one or more of the subregional groupings is not able to meet the conditions of say, the third stage, then the whole process is likely to be blocked. The idea of sequencing reflects the expectation that all members of subregional groupings would simultaneously attain the objectives of each stage, and preferably as rapidly as possible within the time frame accorded. Progress towards the formation of the AEC could very well depend on the speed at which the slowest grouping moved towards attainment of the basic objectives marking each stage.

Experience has so far shown that this principle of 'unison in movement' in the shortest period possible has been difficult to apply in practice because of differences among member states at different development stages, with disparate trade and tariff structures and macro-economic policies. Consequently, the timetables have not been kept. The pace of the regional integration process has consequently been determined by the country with the slowest rate of implementation. If this problem is not averted, then it is very likely that the take-off of the AEC and its progress would once again be disturbingly delayed.

There is, also, the question about publicity, the need to explain to the people of Africa why an African Economic Community is necessary and how it would benefit them. This is necessary, if the experience of the *Lagos Plan*, which remained a 'scarce commodity' unknown to the broad masses of the people, were to be avoided. In this era of *perestroika* and popular participation in development, one of the priority tasks of the OAU is to mount a sustained campaign to raise awareness of the African Economic Community and give wide currency to the concept of the Community. This is particularly important as ignorance and unawareness of the merits of the treaty will constitute a great challenge. And unless appropriate action is undertaken, this ignorance could degenerate into suspicion and ultimate rejection. No doubt the AEC will be seen in different ways by different countries, especially outside the African continent. While some may half-heartedly tolerate it on the platform of old political or commercial links, others will readily consider it a monstrous foetus which must be aborted to make sure it is not born. Therefore, the priority consideration is for Africa and Africans to understand and accept the AEC as a veritable and inevitable means to an end, which is ultimate freedom from the oppressive and exploitative lopsidedness of the current international economic order.

THE ABUJA TREATY: ISSUES OF IMPLEMENTATION

The biggest challenge arising from the Abuja Treaty is to move from talk and prescription to action and to change the assumption that once goals for regional cooperation have been set, implementation will automatically follow. Conviction and recommendations must be matched by commitment to implementation. One of the most crucial and urgent questions now is how the new Community's machinery will be gradually established. This machinery is needed to take the important decisions and, when taken, to implement them without delay or dilution. The treaty provides little operational guidance on how the declarations of intent can be implemented, and what is required to make them effective. How can Africa bridge the implementation gap and move from words to deeds?

The Abuja Treaty establishing the AEC entered into force on 12 May 1994 thus paving the way for its implementation. This poses a great challenge to African organizations – perhaps the greatest challenge that they have faced since the dawn of independence. Embracing, as it does, all aspects of African economic and social life, it provides a framework for re-examining the roles of myriads of African organizations and institutions, streamlining their activities and mobilizing them more purposefully to address the pressing problems of African economic and social development. Meeting this challenge will not be easy. In the African context, experience suggests that reforming, restructuring or rationalizing institutions is an extremely difficult task. And yet, in the context of the African Economic Community, it is a task that has to be accomplished if the Community is to face up to the challenges of a rapidly changing world.[26]

One thing is, however, clear. The primary role of establishing and operationalizing the African Economic Community belongs to member states of the OAU whose secretariat has an obvious coordinating role to play both through the Permanent Steering Committee and within the framework of the Joint OAU/ECA/ADB Secretariat. The Joint Secretariat is entrusted with the responsibility of providing the necessary political, technical and financial drive for the operationalization of the Abuja Treaty. The Heads of State and

Government have therefore always been aware that the magnitude of the task and the diversity of actions required call for team work. National, subregional and regional institutions have to move in unison, each in its area of competence. The synergy of all these actions rather than duplications will eventually lead to the effective implementation of the treaty.

Meanwhile, Article 6 of the treaty lays down the modalities for the establishment of the Community. The first stage of the implementation of the treaty is to be devoted, among other things, to the strengthening of existing regional economic communities (RECs). To this end, the protocol on 'Relations Between the African Economic Community and the Regional Economic Communities' commits the AEC and the member states of each regional economic community to strengthen the regional economic communities, through appropriate financial, technical and institutional support, in order to enable them to realize the tasks assigned to them under Article 6 of the treaty. In meeting this challenge, the main strategies should include the following:

(i)   preparation of comprehensive and up-to-date information on what programmes the RECs have established in all the areas for priority action, what progress has been made, what problems have impeded implementation and in what ways the AEC can contribute to speeding up the implementation of the programmes;

(ii) elaboration of measures to expand relations among the RECs and to promote coordination and harmonization among them;

(iii) measures to strengthen effectively sectoral integration, particularly in the fields of food and agriculture, transport and communications, industry and energy;

(iv) measures to promote the harmonization of strategies, policies and programmes within and among the RECs; and

(v)   elaboration of strategies in collaboration with the ABD and the African, Caribbean and Pacific (ACP), to encourage joint projects, particularly in food and agriculture, transport and communications, industry and energy.

In furtherance of the above objectives, the AEC should establish as early as possible the following Specialized Committees provided for under Article 25 of the Treaty:

(i)   The Committee on Rural Economy and Agricultural Matters;

(ii) The Committee on Monetary and Financial Affairs;

(iii) The Committee on Trade, Customs and Immigration Matters;

(iv) The Committee on Industry, Science and Technology, Energy, Natural Resources and Environment;

(v)   The Committee on Transport, Communications and Tourism;

(vi) The Committee on Health, Labour and Social Affairs; and

(vii) The Committee on Education, Culture and Human Resources.

Article 26 of the Treaty requires them to undertake the following functions:

(i)   prepare projects and programmes of the Community and submit them to the Commission;

(ii) ensure the supervision, follow-up and the evaluation of implementation of decisions taken by the organs of the Community;

(iii) ensure the coordination and harmonization of projects and programmes of the Community;

(iv) submit to the Commission, either on its own initiative or at the request of the Commission, reports and recommendations on the implementation of the provision of this Treaty; and

(v)   carry out any other functions assigned to it for the purpose of ensuring the implementation of the provisions of this Treaty.

The Specialized Committees will obviously be very important Committees for sectoral as well as macro-economic coordination. Therefore, they should be established within the early years of the ratification of the treaty. Their establishment needs not be delayed until the relevant protocols have been approved. In fact, the Committees themselves could be involved in the finalization of the protocols pertaining to their further functions.

The goals of the second stage as provided for under Article 6 are: first, to stabilize then begin to reduce, at the subregional community level, internal and intra-AEC tariffs and non-tariff trade barriers and to harmonize customs duties to non-AEC states; second, to strengthen sectoral integration at the subregional and continental levels, especially in priority areas such as agriculture, transport and communications, energy, money and finance and industry; and third, to coordinate and harmonize economic policies and development activities among members of subregional communities.

To meet the challenge of the process of establishing the Community during its first ten years, both the subregional communities and the AEC secretariat are to undertake certain specific functions. On the one hand, the subregional economic schemes are expected to implement a three-pronged strategy providing for: first, the extension of vital physical infrastructure and associated services throughout their spaces; second, the integrated development of productive capacities in agriculture and basic industries, with the aim of laying the foundation for equitable distribution of the industrial base; and third, the integration of national economies into the subregional market through a programme for trade liberalization.

On the other hand, during this same period, the role of the AEC Secretariat will be to coordinate the subregional communities through inter-subregional integration programmes and projects with synergic potentialities – such as electric energy production and distribution networks, coastal shipping, air transport, satellite communications, continental rail and road projects, continental centres of excellence in science and technology, establishment and maintenance of continental buffer stocks for food security, stabilization of currency exchange rates, formation of pan-African multinational corporations (MNCs) and so on.[27]

One of the urgent issues to which the Economic Commission for Africa (ECA) has drawn attention is the need for the subregional communities to be innovative in the programming of their activities with a view to easing the operations of the AEC.[28] So far the subregional communities have developed their respective programmes with little or no reference to those of similar organizations existing elsewhere in Africa. The implementation of the AEC makes it necessary for the subregional communities to cooperate so as to facilitate the process of harmonization of their respective programmes.

To this end, the subregional communities would need to adopt the same economic integration approach. It would indeed be difficult for these communities to proceed towards the same goal if the existing divergent strategies were persistent with some favouring the market integration approach, while others focus on infrastructure or production sectors. To enable the AEC to move as fast as possible towards its objectives, it would be necessary for the subregional communities to adopt the same approach and strategies towards the common goal. None of the subregional communities deals exclusively with a trade liberalization scheme or infrastructural cum productive integration. However, the stages of integration reached by the various communities are quite different. These discrepancies need to be corrected at an early stage of the functioning of the AEC. It would also require, in some cases, the realignment of the treaties of the subregional communities in order to make them consistent with the objectives and provisions of the Treaty of the AEC just as the revised ECOWAS Treaty and the recently adopted COMESA Treaty have attempted to do.

Another area of priority for the implementation of the treaty relates to measures to demonstrate to the generality of the African population that, far from being a pipe-dream, the AEC is an institution that can have a profound effect on their daily lives. In this connection, it has been pointed out that substantial progress on trade liberalization and free movement of persons, rights of residence and establishment, will be an effective way of sensitizing the African population about the good impact that the AEC might have on their lives and business interests. The report of the consultants on the protocol on free movement revealed that, in many African countries, non-Africans enjoy greater right of movement than Africans themselves. As Onitiri rightly remarks, this is 'obviously a sore point at a time that other countries are tightening immigration rules, and inducing Africans who are already resident in their countries to go back home'.[29]

In terms of programmes, the issue of rationalization of the multiplicity of IGOs, would constitute a disturbing challenge for the AEC. The AEC should be able to make a constructive contribution to the process being made by ECOWAS, in West Africa, and COMESA/SADC, in Eastern and Southern Africa. The Abuja Treaty has provided for this under Chapter XIX as well as under the Protocol on Relations between the AEC and the Regional Economic Communities. In this connection it is noteworthy that under Article 6 of the draft protocol on relations between the AEC and the Regional Economic Communities, member states of each Regional Economic Community undertake to carry out at most five months after the entry into force of the treaty establishing the African Economic Community, the rationalization of the structures, organs and activities of the regional and subregional intergovernmental organizations within the new integration framework of the Regional Economic Communities, with the assistance and support of the AEC.

Besides rationalization, AEC should, in implementation of programmes, also direct efforts towards promotion of joint projects. Since there have been very few successful examples of multinational enterprises, as Onitiri notes, the AEC should give particular attention to this subject.[30] In cooperation with the ADB and the World Bank, it should encourage a major study of the subject which should examine new approaches and modalities. In this connection, all efforts should be made to finalize the protocol on Rules of Origin as soon as possible. Other areas where the AEC should develop specific policies in the early years are, first, trade liberalization; second, free movement of persons; third, coordination of macro-economic policies; fourth, coordination of sectoral policies; and fifth, coordinated approach to international negotiations. Besides the AEC is the second major new regional initiative, that is, the Cross-Border Initiative (CBI).

THE CROSS-BORDER INITIATIVE

Following the launching of the Global Coalition for Africa at the Maastricht Conference on African Development in July 1990, the European Commission undertook to explore ways for the donor community to be more supportive of African regional economic integration. It was this which resulted, amongst other activities, in the Initiative to facilitate Cross-Border Trade, Investment and Payments in Eastern and Southern Africa and the Indian Ocean – the CBI. It involves a series of core measures in the areas of trade, payments and exchange systems and investment. In the trade area, the programme envisages eliminating all tariffs on intra-regional trade and on a reciprocal by 1996 and removing a range of non-tariff barriers on imports from all countries. On payments, the programme aims at 'complete non-discriminatory elimination of all restrictions on current account transactions and relaxation of certain types of capital account transactions'. In the area of investment, the programme envisages harmonization of investment incentives and simplification and liberalization of cross-border investment procedures.

The emphasis of this initiative is on 'unilateral action and self-selection'. Although based on extensive interactions with the PTA and consultations with SADC and the Indian Ocean Commission (IOC), it does not simply seek to reinforce efforts of these organizations, but to encourage a self-selecting group of countries to proceed on a faster track. Goaded by an offer of US$30 million on average, a number of PTA, SADC and IOC member states are reported to be keen to sign on to this new initiative.

The broad objective of the CBI, which is a new initiative on the process of economic integration in Africa, is to help reduce the obstacles to cross-border activity so as to promote efficient patterns of growth with economies of scale and opportunities for vertical and horizontal integration among the participating countries. The CBI, according to its co-sponsors, offers a pragmatic approach to promote regional integration, while also helping the participating countries to gradually integrate their economies into the world economy. The initiative aims to address the regional dimension of structural adjustment while supporting the efforts of the countries of the region to achieve closer economic integration. Moreover, the flexible approach allows countries to implement regional measures on the basis of reciprocity at their own pace (variable geometry). The emphasis on the private sector should facilitate the process of making the economies of the region more competitive within the region and internationally.

Launched in early 1992, the CBI has evolved in four phases. First, a desk study,[31] which was carried out with a view to identifying the constraints on interregional trade, investment and payments in the Eastern and Southern African subregion. Second, the 'Mauritius Initiative' emerging out of the June 1992 workshop in Mauritius. The workshop agreed on the establishment of country specific Technical Working Groups (TWGs) with public and private sector participation. The third phase was initiated in December 1992 with the adoption of a *Concept Paper* at a workshop in Harare, Zimbabwe. The *Concept Paper*, on which the initiative is based, proposed how the interested governments could implement the core measures with donor support. At a ministerial meeting in Kampala in August 1993, the *Concept Paper* was endorsed, paving the way to the current implementation or fourth phase.

The CBI no doubt has some commendable and positive features. For example, it reflects voluntary participation by a willing subset of countries so as to allow the fast adjusters to set the pace of integration. Viewed against the background of the slow process of integration in Africa, this would appear to be a welcome feature of the CBI. The common feature of the existing economic community schemes has been their 'top-down' approach, requiring the members of a subregional organization to participate out of solidarity with the rest of the group. In the absence of real commitment in all of the member countries to remove obstacles to cross-border economic activity, most of the regional integration treaties would continue to be long on declarations and short on implementation. Another special feature is the implementation of reforms based on the principle of reciprocity among the participating countries, thereby encouraging action which countries would likely hesitate to take if they were acting alone. There is, also, harmonization of economic policy reforms across the countries so as to facilitate cross-border economic activity.

The CBI attempts to look for a new practical approach to promoting economic integration that is anchored in outward-oriented adjustment programmes, which could be supported actively by the donor community. The new approach would focus on measures that promote intra-regional mobility of factors, goods and services with relatively low tariff barriers against third parties. It rests on the premise that small, low-income economies such as in the PTA/SADC/IOC subregion, movement towards deeper integration with an outward orientation can confer benefits. The emphasis is on outward orientation because in such economies export-led growth is the only viable option for accelerated and sustained growth.

Therefore, the initiative, which emerges from the neo-liberal or the market-oriented camp, attributes the failure of integration efforts in Africa to their being inward-looking, basing their hopes for growth mainly in increased protection, and on moving import substitution to a regional level. Thus while relevant African intergovernmental organizations, including the African Economic Community, aim at fostering primarily economic links among African countries, the immediate objective of the co-sponsors of the CBI is rather to open up Africa to the world economy, their argument being that any protectionism results in wastage of resources by preventing consumers from having access to best goods and services from the view of price and quality.

It should be noted that the World Bank and the IMF are relatively recent converts to regional integration. Both institutions stood aloof from integration efforts, both in Africa and elsewhere, in the past. The SAPs, adopted by a succession of African countries at the behest of the Bank and the Fund, were partly premised on a view that the fundamental requirement as far as a country's external economic relations was concerned was to undertake 'unilateral trade reform' which would 'open up' the domestic economy, and integrate it more closely with the world economy at large. Regional integration 'was seen as, at best, an irrelevance and, at worst, a diversion from the fundamental goal of lowering tariffs towards the world at large'.[32]

The Bank's shift towards supporting a new round of regional integration efforts in Africa partly derives from the fact that most countries are now following the Bank-supported SAPs, and partly from a perception that an integration programme of a certain type could reinforce efforts to promote unilateral trade reform. In studies undertaken to give substance to the Bank's new-found support for regional integration programmes, a significant attempt to modify the conventional trade integration paradigm to make it compatible with 'unilateral trade reform' is accordingly discernible.

The main argument of the 1991 World Bank study on integration in sub-Saharan Africa[33] is that the Bank should support a new round of integration projects in sub-Saharan Africa, but that these should be 'consistent with an outward-orientated strategy that promotes incentives which are neutral between production for the domestic market and export'. Regional integration should thus not become a means of salvaging failed import substitution industrialization programmes, but should be harmonized with ongoing structural adjustment programmes.

Evidently, the main aim of the World Bank study is to get African economies to open up totally to international trade and investment. It is also clear about where its institutional programmes lie. It notes that since a number of regional economic organizations already exist in Africa, these must be used to implement the Bank's new initiatives. The Bank undoubtedly prefers avoiding inward-looking and protectionist agreements in favour of unilateral liberalization. Viewed against this background, to what extent does the CBI respond positively to the legitimate aspirations of African regionalism?

Critically examined, there is much evidence to suggest that the CBI is problematic, especially when viewed against the processes advocated by the Southern African subregion. In the first place, the relevance of the neo-classical theory of regional economic integration to Third World developmental conditions is questionable. As Saasa[34] rightly remarks, for developing countries, export promotion through trade liberalization does not necessarily lead to growth. It should also be added that economic growth *per se* is no guarantee for economic development to necessarily follow, as generally expressed in the popular phrase 'growth without development'. It would be unwise, as Saasa asserts, to assume that trade and its liberalization should be the driving force behind integration among developing countries. There is the need for increased, planned and coordinated industrial infra-structural development that recognizes the efficiency and developmental roles of industrial complementarity, specialization, external economies and economies of scale.

There are other problems with the CBI which have been highlighted by critics such as Cheru[35] and Keet.[36] In general, the initiative is seen as a disruptive intrusion cutting across complex ongoing processes within the Southern African subregion. A case in point is the current process of renegotiating the Southern African Customs Union agreement. It also effectively sidelines existing subregional organizations and has the potential to reduce the COMESA to a merely advisory body. As van Nieuwkerk concludes:

> Finally, there is a danger that the cross-border initiative could undermine the possibilities for developing regionally balanced investment strategies in Southern Africa. The sweeping liberalization measures being promoted by this initiative are inimical to the regulatory interventions that will be required for the development of regional programmes of co-operation in manufacturing, mining, energy, transport, tourism and much else. Reliance on the operations of competing business interests is totally inadequate to the region's strategic need for consciously structured reconstruction and development programmes.[37]

The question, then, is: is the CBI an appropriate approach to regionalism in Africa? To what extent is it different from the market integration approach discussed above?

The CBI deliberately addressed only one segment of the integration process, that is trade, leaving the others to the market forces. The focus on trade and related issues does not mean that the co-sponsors of the initiative are oblivious of the necessity to deal with the other aspects of regionalism. However, among the major reasons for the limited progress achieved in economic integration in Africa is, as indicated above, the excessive emphasis put on market integration mechanisms, with comparatively little attention paid to production activities and removal of physical barriers to trade.

The recommendations of the *Desk Study* and the *Concept Paper* are more appropriate to the situation prevailing in the Western European countries at the time of signing of the Rome Treaty establishing the European Economic

Community than that of the situation of African countries. As referred to above, Europe had fairly well developed infrastructures and production capacities. What was needed was large markets and free flows of factors to enhance competition and expansion. The national economies in the Eastern and Southern African subregions, with a few exceptions such as South Africa, are not in a position to take full advantage of the kind of trade liberalization which is the thrust of the CBI. The infrastructure links are still weak and so are production capacities in many countries of the subregion. The initiative does not address such critical questions as how to overcome the barriers to integration deriving from underdevelopment, inadequate infrastructure and other deficiencies, or how to empower the most impoverished and least developed partners to become more effective in regional trade.

It is our considered view that trade and investment schemes must take into account differences in levels of development of the participating countries and mitigate the effects of liberalization such as revenue losses through compensatory mechanisms. The initiative takes little heed of, and indeed appears to be relatively indifferent to the potentiality for polarization in *laissez-faire* approaches to integration. The fact that the major benefits of integration were seen to be flowing disproportionately to stronger partners was one of the major reasons for the collapse of several earlier integration schemes in Africa, as noted above. In Southern Africa, with its inherited disparities and a legacy of economic destruction left by apartheid destabilization, achieving an equitable relationship between South Africa, with a GDP three times that of the present SADC member countries combined, will be one of the most complex and difficult issues that will have to be confronted.

Besides, as Davies notes in a recent paper[38] the initiative of the study rests on the notion that successful externally oriented growth strategy requires a prior liberalization of domestic tariff and regulatory regimes. This type of proposition, as Davies rightly points out, flies in the face of the experience of the East Asian Newly Industrializing Countries (NICs), which became world-class competitors through levels of protection in their domestic markets while taking advantage of opportunities made available (for geostrategic reasons) for them to gain easy access to the markets of 'the North'.

More significantly, the CBI does not confront the possible implications of a scenario in which liberalization of trading regimes by the countries of the 'South' proceeds but it is not matched by a corresponding greater 'opening up' of the markets of the North to products, and particularly manufactured goods, from 'the South' as experienced, for example, in the Lomé system. A scenario of this nature, which would seem to be quite possible in the current global climate, would create precisely the opposite conditions from those in which the 'outward-oriented' growth strategies of the NICs achieved their results. Premature unilateral liberalization could, under such circumstances, potentially remove one of the strongest bargaining levers which integration could potentially create for countries of the South, that is, enhanced leverage to bargain against greater access to markets of the North in multilateral or bilateral trade liberalization deals.

Above all, the initiative is obviously in contradiction with recent moves of its initiators in many aspects. First, both the World Bank and the European Commission have recognized the inefficiency of donor-driven programmes and have called for home-grown programmes that put emphasis on 'ownership' as a key element in reform programmes. Second, the initiative is another way of attempting to reintroduce the World Bank/IMF-sponsored national orthodox structural adjustment programmes through the back door at the time when the European Commission is advocating an 'overhaul' of these programmes and the Bank is advocating for home-grown reform programmes. And third, the initiative would seem to give the impression that it is aiming at 'freezing' the integration process in Eastern and Southern Africa and preventing countries in this subregion to build up strong groupings at a time when such groupings are emerging the world over, as highlighted above.

One is tempted to conclude that the CBI is, on the whole, no more than an attempt to set back economic integration process in Africa and reinstate the market integration approach. This could only end up increasing Africa's dependence and impeding efforts to develop production within the continent. In other words, Africa's markets would be integrated for the benefit of TNCs and other foreign agencies.

VERTICAL INTEGRATION SCHEMES

While the CBI is confined to the Eastern and Southern African subregions, the French-sponsored vertical integration approach initiated in 1991 leading to the establishment of the economic and monetary unions in West Africa (UEMOA) and Central Africa (CEMAC) in 1994, is limited to the French-speaking countries of the two subregions. Member countries of UMOA and BEAC envisage that the establishment of these unions would enable them to maximize the advantages inherent in their membership of a single currency zone. The sponsors believe that this will reinforce the economic integration of the member states and arrest the present drift of their economies. They explain the move by drawing attention to historical factors as well as the apparent need to match monetary union with economic integration. In this approach priority is given to the coordination of the banking systems and that of the fiscal and budgetary policies of the participating countries. These

Franc Zone communities are expected to regain the investors' confidence in a new environment of legal security and a tighter monetary control as well as strict monitoring of budget deficits and levels of indebtedness.

The vertical integration is unlike the other brands of integration which are horizontal, so to speak, in the sense that they aim to bring together states and economic agents that are physically close. The new approach aims at closer linkages between an industrialized metropolitan power (France) and its less developed monetary zone associates, with whom it shares language and administrative/legal institutions.

A question that forces itself upon us is this: is the creation of UEMOA and CEMAC really necessary? Is there any crucial difference between UEMOA and ECOWAS, for example? It is interesting to note that the advantages of integration, as reflected in the orientation paper on the establishment of UEMOA, are outlined in much the same way as they were in the basic instruments establishing ECOWAS: the realization of large-scale economies in the larger market to be created; the emergence of community enterprises; improved circulation of goods and persons; and increased collective influence of the integrated market in world affairs. It goes without saying that these advantages are easier to realize in the ECOWAS market than in the narrower UEMOA market. It should not be forgotten that while a common currency is a powerful instrument for economic integration, it is not a sufficient guarantee of rapid economic growth and development.

This French-led vertical integration strategy seems certain to have negative political consequences in the economic cooperation and integration efforts in West and Central Africa. In the first place, stringent monetary and financial policies would foil efforts being made in the West African subregion for the harmonization of economic policies in general and monetary and financial policies in particular. Second, the approach is as divisive as a new brand of neo-colonialism. Both ECOWAS and ECCAS would be 'disjointed' as a result of the establishment of these two monetary and economic unions with the isolation of non-Communauté Financiére Africaine (CFA) Zone members, that is countries that do not use CFA, such as Ghana and Nigeria. Programmes and guiding principles of ECOWAS are at variance or even contradictory to those of the CFA Zone community. This would create insurmountable difficulties to the harmonization process envisaged in the African Economic Community. Given the current trends in the world towards free market policies, the formation of large economic blocs, and the establishment of close interlinkages between production structures in different countries, fragmenting the already tiny markets of West Africa, in particular, will do more harm than good to the whole subregion.

A review of this newest approach to economic integration tends to suggest that it would both at best contribute to West and Central Africa's overdependence on France and subsequently on the European Union and would foil the two subregions' efforts to develop productive structures on the basis of collective self-reliance policies. It would, above all, jeopardize the achievement of West and Central African as well as continental economic integration. The vertical integration approach in general poses a serious challenge to the July 1991 ECOWAS decision reaffirming the sole legitimacy of ECOWAS in integration efforts in West Africa.

This chapter has sought to do two things. First, to review critically the AEC treaty with particular reference to the extent to which, compared with the treaties of the pre-1990 economic communities, it attempts to chart a new path for Africa, break new ground or offer new perspectives. In many respects, the AEC no doubt seeks to project an exciting vision of what Africa must do if it is ever to overcome its excessive dependence on others, raise living standards for its people, and assert its position as a major economic unit within the global economy. The Abuja Treaty, therefore, seems to give cause for optimism, albeit cautious. The treaty is a major breakthrough.

It remains true, however, as always with ventures of this nature, that its success will depend largely on the political will of the member states to translate goals into reality. Considering that ratification of the treaty alone took almost three years, one becomes seriously concerned about how long it would take to implement the treaty to enable the Community to take off. This becomes all the more disturbing when viewed against the background of the AEC's lack of a dynamic, independent and professionally competent secretariat of its own to enable it to create a vibrant Community for the implementation of the Abuja Treaty. Thus, although the African Economic Community has been established, is it not still business as usual for the OAU secretariat? Is the so-called OAU/AEC secretariat in a position to meet the challenges of the implementation of the Abuja Treaty, having regard to the rapid changes taking place in the world, which have already relegated African countries to the periphery of world development? Would it be possible to call for concerted effort to use the AEC, dominated by the politics of the OAU, as a platform to launch new and bold initiatives that can help reverse the present adverse trends and set African countries on the path to sustained growth and development?

Second, the chapter has attempted to shed some considerable light on such comparatively recent initiatives and approaches as the CBI and the vertical integration schemes, both of which would tend to impede the economic integration process in Africa. In particular, such market-led integration and across-the-board trade liberalization advocated by the CBI would not appear to be consistent with the *raison d'être* of the COMESA and SADC, whose integration process it is supposed to support. Similarly, the French-sponsored vertical integration approach which is not very different from the CBI, has the potential for further disintegration of the West and Central African subregions. The next chapter focuses attention on the new challenges to the process of regionalism in Africa.

6 New Challenges to African Regionalism

The changing face of international relations, the technological developments accompanied by changes in the organization of production, together with a trend towards the formation of more integrated trading blocs, have not only revived interest in regionalism in Africa and other regions of the world, they have also posed some formidable challenges to the promotion of regional integration in Africa and, indeed, African development as a whole. In particular, the expanding scope of European Union development cooperation, the impact of the end of Cold War which has made the developing countries no longer of geostrategic interest to opposing factions, the substantial implications of the Uruguay Round, the completion of the Single European Market project, the creation of the European Economic Area, the enlargement of the European Union to include several new members and the ongoing and increasingly wide-ranging dialogue with the economies in transition in Central and Eastern Europe – all these factors have combined to marginalize African interests. They have combined to undermine the basis of Euro-African relations on which Lomé is predicated, making it increasingly irrelevant to the African ACP states.

Besides the challenges which the profound changes on the global level pose to regionalism and Africa's development are certain internal key development issues such as structural adjustment programmes (SAPs) which threaten to challenge and, in some cases, actually impede the process of economic cooperation and integration on the continent. An entirely different and, indeed, welcome challenge to regionalism in Africa is reflected in the emergence of democratic South Africa. This chapter attempts a brief overview of the internal and external challenges to regionalism and Africa's development highlighting, in particular, the impact of trading blocs on Africa.

THE CHALLENGE OF TRADING BLOCS

The increasing tendency towards the establishment of larger, stronger and more cohesive trading and economic blocs, as one of the most striking features of the existing economic relations, either between developed or developing countries of the world, constitutes a major challenge to Africa.

With the approach of the twenty-first century, the trend towards regionalism, together with the globalization of world production, is becoming particularly discernible among the developed countries of the North and the Newly Industrialized Countries (NICs) in South Eastern Asia and the Pacific area.

Although the situation with regionalism is still rather fluid, the main trends are already evident. The EU will be further consolidated and expanded to include several countries in Central and Eastern Europe. The NAFTA will be gradually extended to embrace all or several Latin American countries as the implications of the FTAA gets under way. In the Asia-Pacific region, the 18 members of the Asia-Pacific Economic Cooperation forum (APEC) have committed themselves to creating a free trade area stretching from New York to Bangkok and from Chile to China. How all this will be affected by new plans to breath new life into the Europe–US relationship, with less stress on security and more on economic cooperation, is at present difficult to comprehend, although the thought of a free trade area encompassing the whole of North America and Europe is not being dismissed off-hand.

Where will Africa stand in this tangle of interlocking free trade zones? What will be the implications of the trading blocs for the process of regionalism in Africa? To what extent does this trend towards regional blocs, as reflected in what is now termed revival of regionalism or a 'new regionalism', as Jaime de Mello and Arvind Panagariya[1] would have it described, constitute a major challenge to African regionalism? Generally, African integration schemes seem to be in the least encouraging position and much of the continent seems to be on the losing side in the unfolding of trading blocs. The economic implications of trading blocs, especially 'Europe 1992', for Africa are more crucial and more widely understood. Because of historic, geographic and political reasons, Africa trades far more with Europe than any other area of the world. Therefore, the implications of Europe 1992 for Africa are more significant and more carefully studied than the implications of similar existing or yet to-be-formed trading blocs elsewhere in the world.[2]

'Fortress Europe' and Africa

As the EU accounts for about two-thirds of African trade, Africa's concern about the growing regionalism has been greatest as regards development in Europe: the consolidation of the EU, the progressive enlargement of the Union, and EU's policies towards other developing regions. In 1987, for example, 57.7 per cent of Africa's total exports went to the EU while its imports from the Union were 52 per cent of Africa's total imports. Regarding resource flows, EU's aid to sub-Saharan Africa accounts for more than half of the Union's total aid. In the 1980–1 financial year, EU's aid to sub-Saharan Africa was

60.1 per cent of the Union's total aid and, in 1986–7, the figure was 55 per cent. These figures are of much higher magnitudes than those on aid flows to Africa from the United States and Japan which, in 1986, were respectively 20.1 per cent and 5.4 per cent of Africa's total official development assistance.[3]

The consolidation of the EU is of particular importance to African countries for many reasons. First, as already stated, close to two-thirds of Africa's trade is with Europe. Second, Africa has enjoyed a special relationship with Europe under the Lomé Convention which will now be affected, not only by increasing regionalism, but also by the Uruguay Agreement. Third, the extension of EU membership to several countries in Central and Eastern Europe will lead to profound transformation in the structure and priorities of the EU which will have profound effects on African countries.

Questions that have arisen are whether the creation of the single European market will result in the weakening of the existing ties and, more specifically, whether there will be declines in Africa's exports to the EU and in the Union's aid flows to Africa. Will African interests be protected in the momentous events reshaping the European continent? Will there be exciting opportunities for the African states deriving from dynamic growth and expansion of the newly uniting European economies in the 1990s, as repeatedly proclaimed by the EU Commission officials? How real are these opportunities? Even if they exist, are the African states sufficiently robust to take advantage of them? What is likely to be the impact on their fragile economies, at least in the short term, of incipient diversion of aid, finance, and trade opportunities to other priority regions, not least Eastern Europe? Will Europe's resurrection advance or diminish Africa's prospects for economic development? These are some of the bewildering questions confronting African states, as Europe treads its way towards a tight union.

Given a single European market of some 375 million consumers with a total GDP (1994) of US$8 trillion, exports worth US$680 billion, and imports of US$708 billion – the world's biggest single market – coupled with the considerable importance of the EU in the world economy, there seems to be little doubt that Europe 1992 will create trade opportunities for the EU partners. Unfortunately, however, the structure of and recent trend in African exports to the Union would tend to suggest that Europe 1992 would present the continent with more challenges than opportunities. Despite EU lip-service to its special relationship with the African countries under the Lomé Convention, it is evident that these countries stand to lose most within the framework of Europe 1992.

It is important to recognize that the benefit of a single market will be in direct proportion to the ability offered. For Africa, the economic crisis and the absence of an efficient industrial base would very much militate against or weaken its capacity to compete with the newly industrializing countries like South Korea, Taiwan and the relatively less developed EU members like Portugal and Greece. The end result would be a redirection of trade away from traditional suppliers and towards partner EU members.

As Ravenhill has recently argued, with little prospects of significant reversal of Africa's economic decline in the coming decade, and new opportunities for the EU opening up in Eastern Europe, the African states are likely to continue to decline in significance as economic partners for Western Europe.[4] Although Africa's raw materials will continue to attract some interest, with commodity prices likely to remain low and African supply uncertain, Europe is unlikely to be motivated by fears of raw-materials shortages to provide significantly more assistance to the African states. It must be emphasized that the EU has already declared that the trade preferences of the Lomé Convention are of little importance to the African states and their partners and that they are susceptible to reduction in response to the European objectives in the Uruguay Round. The European Union's enlargement to incorporate Spain and Portugal has admitted countries that not only compete directly with some ACP states in agricultural production but that are keen to improve EU links with non-ACP Southern countries with which they have traditional ties.

Table 6.1 below indicates the overall evolution of ACP–EU trade from 1976 to 1992, comparing the ACP performance with that of other developing countries, principally those in Latin America and Asia. In 1992, the EU imported goods and services from the ACP states worth 18 billion ECUs, compared with 24.8 billion ECUs from Latin American countries, 30.3 billion ECUs from Mediterranean countries and 66.4 billion ECUs from Asian developing countries (that is, Asia excluding Japan and Hong Kong). Over the period 1976–92, the average annual growth in exports to the EU for each of these areas were: ACP, 2.28 per cent; Mediterranean, 5.87 per cent; Latin America, 5.97 per cent; and Asia, 11.7 per cent.[5] This comparison of ACP exports to the EU with those of other developing countries which have enjoyed less preferential access to the European market makes the deterioration in the ACP performance become even more apparent.

The principal source of potential negative impact for Africa is the trade displacement effect. That is, the removal of national restrictions may erode the competitive margin that the African countries enjoy *vis-à-vis* other exporters to the EU as a result of preferential access to certain EU markets. Besides, the range of African exports is far too narrow to allow it to take advantage of EU market potentialities and the level of flexibility of their production system in most cases remains low. As the structurally weakest members of the Third World, African countries, as André Sapir of the

Brussels-based Institute of European Studies concludes, 'will find life in post-1992 Europe harder'.[6] On the other hand, the NICs are expected to be in a better position to compete for and secure access to post-1992 EU markets. Asian nations, unaccustomed to receiving any special EU trade favours, have learnt to market their products in Europe. They are also better placed to profit from the post-1992 boost in demand for manufactured goods and services and will be quick to meet 'the new quantitative and qualitative changes in export demand in Europe', as Jacques Bourrinet of the Aix-Marseille University has stressed in a recent seminar.[7] This contrasts sharply with the position of the African countries *vis-à-vis* the emerging 'regional age', or what some are calling the 'age of a multipolar world economy'.

Table 6.1: Trends in EC Trade with Developing Countries,
1976–92 (in billions of ECUs)

EC Imports from	1976	1980	1985	1990	1992
ACP	10.5	19.4	26.8	21.9	18.0
Asia	6.7	16.0	26.0	50.9	66.4
Latin America	8.3	13.7	25.8	25.7	24.8
Mediterranean	9.6	16.4	32.3	29.8	30.3
Rest of the world	273.5	453.4	717.3	1021.4	1067.7
Total	308.6	518.9	828.2	1127.8	1207.2
ACP	9.6	15.7	17.4	16.6	17.0
Asia	7.5	13.1	29.7	41.0	47.1
Latin America	7.7	12.0	13.5	15.6	20.4
Mediterranean	12.3	19.8	29.8	28.5	28.6
Rest of the world	255.1	414.4	721.4	975.3	1023.9
Total	292.9	475.0	811.8	1077.0	1137.0
ACP–EC Trade balance	1976	1980	1985	1990	1992
Imports–Exports	0.9	3.7	9.4	5.3	1

Source: Eurostat: calculations by CTA Economic and Export Analyst Ltd.

Furthermore, the demand for tropical agricultural products, which constitute the main African exports to the EU, has reached saturation point in the developed market economies. Even in the area of manufactured exports, where the prospects are much brighter than those of tropical agricultural products, the African countries appear to be handicapped by the low industrial capacity and lack of competitiveness of the manufactured products in terms of price, quality, packaging, delivery terms and so on.

On the whole, African individual economies, with their fragility and uncompetitiveness, seem ill-placed to take advantage of any opportunities that Europe 1992 and the other regional economic blocs might offer outsiders. On the contrary, in post-Europe 1992, when present European currencies are merged into one common European currency West and Central Africa in particular might feel the impact of the first serious shock from the European Union through the effects of that currency integration on the CFA Zone as critically analysed by Allechi M'Bet.[8] In these circumstances, delinking or disengagement is no longer an issue for Africa to worry about. The developed world had in certain respects started to delink from the continent.

Besides trade, Europe 1992, coupled especially with the dramatic changes that have taken place in Eastern Europe following a rebirth of democracy, will also have a disturbing impact on foreign investment, as an engine of growth, as well as EU aid flows to the African region. Indeed, it is the fear of commercial and investment exclusion that has dominated Africa's reaction to Europe 1992. Given the opening up of Eastern Europe to trade and investment, as well as the increasing stiff conditionalities, the volume of external resource flows to Africa is fraught with uncertainties.[9] As a result of the growing interest in OECD countries of the need to provide resources to such Eastern European countries as Poland and Hungary, the external resource famine from which Africa is currently suffering may be intensified in the 1990s. This is evident from the European Union's establishment of a Bank for Reconstruction and Development with a US$14 billion initiative which will channel Western financial aid eastward hopefully to turn Eastern Europe's stalled economies in a new direction.[10]

Hence, today, the question is no longer when and how European capital flows to Africa will be channelled and utilized but whether the resources which hitherto have been coming to the continent in a trickle, will continue at all. The infrastructural base for investment in Eastern Europe is better. Proximity and cultural affinity at least for Europe are added incentives. Moreover, given the ties within Europe, Western European governments' aid to Eastern Europe is likely to be politically more popular than aid to Africa. Potential investors from North America, Europe and Asia who have carefully analysed the effects of the removal of preferential trade anticipated for 1992, are now rethinking their investment strategies in the light of the current Eastern European situation.

On the basis of the analysis, it is possible to conclude that the completion of the single European market in 1992 could affect not only aid and investment but also traditional trade relations of African countries with the EU without much opportunity of equal value being offered in return. Although measures to be taken in respect of completing the single market will not be the only influencing factors on African exports to the EU market, it will nonetheless increase competition and intensify the presently manifest trend of Africa's declining share in the EU market. Except for a limited number of cases, African products will have to face a comparatively more hostile environment with the resultant drop in export volumes and values.[11]

On the whole, with the shift in the world trade regime towards global liberalization and away from generalized and selective preferences, there does not appear to be much space afforded, nor any practical instruments available, to support preferences, whether for the African ACP states as the traditional EU-favoured group, or for poor or 'least developed' countries generally. In the bleakest of all possible cases, the African ACP states might be left with highly eroded tariff preferences and strict rules of origin and interpretations of surges which fail to offer any significant stimulus to production and trade for the EU market.

Possible Impact of Other Trading Blocs

While, on the face of it, the movement towards regionalism in other world regions should arouse less concern on the basis of the present structure of African trade, they are no less worrying when Africa's future trade prospects are considered. For example, NAFTA and its possible extension to the rest of Latin America and the Caribbean, and the movement for greater cooperation or integration in East and South Asia and the Pacific Rim of countries, have led to speculations about their possible impact on Africa's future trade with those regions, in particular since they now contain some of the most dynamic economies in the world.

As regards NAFTA, the short-term effects are not likely to be substantial because of the present low level of trade between Africa and NAFTA countries. However, the longer-term effects may be quite significant as transnational corporations (TNCs) take advantage of NAFTA to increase their investment in Latin America, and establish close links between enterprises in North and South America. The progressive extension of NAFTA to other Latin American countries, apart from Mexico, is likely to increase the gains already made in regional integration, while the vision of a free trade area covering the whole of North and South America constitutes a major challenge to Africa that can be met only by a steady and consistent implementation of the Abuja Treaty establishing the African Economic Community. On the other hand, Africa's economic relations with Asian countries will now be greatly influenced by the formation of the Asia-Pacific Economic Cooperation (APEC) which has set itself the objective of achieving free and open trade and investment in the region by 2020.

Briefly stated, the emergence of other regional economic blocs in North America and the Pacific Rim is likely to diminish Africa's access to export commodity markets by raising the average level of protectionism in the advanced countries, stiffen export competitiveness, cause further substitution for Africa's commodity exports and impose losses in terms of trade, higher costs of imports and reduced export earnings from those markets.

As regards the challenge which the growing regionalism poses to Africa, it should be pointed out that the impact will be greatly influenced by current economic developments in Africa and future growth perspectives. Indeed, in the long-term, the impact of regionalism will depend on four interrelated sets of considerations, namely, how quickly African countries can: (i) accelerate the pace of growth and structural change; (ii) raise the general level of productivity; (iii) minimise the losses from the Uruguay Round and take advantage of the opportunities; and (iv) remove the impediments to growth and improve the environment for domestic and foreign investment. Therefore, in the long run, the impact of Europe 1992 and of other possible trading blocs on sub-Saharan African countries depends on their own domestic policies. In this respect, economic integration at the subregional and regional levels may play a great role. Indeed the basic answer to Africa's fears of being left out should be found in practical changes in the direction of Africa's trade away from Europe towards intra-African trade. Such changes would provide the long-term basis for improving Africa's products competitiveness within the continent itself. It is therefore necessary that regional economic integration moves from rhetoric, declarations, resolutions to joint economic programming in production, infrastructure, trade, and so on. A sectoral approach of integration programmes is more important than hoping to continue to hang on to Europe's apron strings, as evidenced within the framework of the European Union–Africa relationship under Lomé.

THE CHALLENGE OF THE LOMÉ CONVENTION

Since the signing in February 1975 of the Lomé I Convention (and the subsequent Lomé II, III and IV) between the ACP countries and the members of the European Union, there has been a continuing debate over whether Euro-African relations are a case of decolonization or dependency, or whether Lomé is an unmixed blessing, establishing a radically new relationship, based on partnership in place of the old, unequal ties, or whether it is a colonial device which perpetuates the client status of Africa.[12] The conclusion of the mid-term review negotiations of the Lomé IV in November 1995 in Mauritius has prompted a more fundamental debate on the future of the EU–African cooperation under Lomé. The debate is focused on two critical issues. First, concern has been expressed about not so much the text of the convention but the practical value of its provisions. Decades of privileged relationships have not brought about development nor solved structural problems. African states remain trapped in processes of economic decline, adjustment, debt and poverty. Second, it has been argued that the problem of economic integration in Africa is compounded by the external orientation of the African states and the tendency towards Euro-Africa integration, rather than pan-African economic integration which has been institutionalized in the Lomé system, particularly in the area of intra-African economic and trade penetration.[13]

Is Lomé an Empty Shell?

Besides the disappointing trade performance between the EU and Africa noted above, in the area of industrial cooperation, the implementation of Lomé provisions has been unsatisfactory. Translating the Lomé arrangements into a coherent set of interventions in support of industrial development and cooperation has not been well accomplished. Often African states are endowed with little more than the rudiments of an industrial sector. On a world scale, African states have a negligible industrial importance (less than 0.5 per cent of global industrial production).[14]

To a great extent, the Lomé Convention would seem to have become an empty shell. In the African countries its impact and image are more problematic: it has tended to generate further inequalities rather than development. Structural problems such as debt and commodity prices are not addressed; trade preferences are eroding; aid budgets are shrinking and subjected to a multitude of conditionalities. At best, 'it has generated into a paternalistic and clientelistic system of rent seeking'. STABEX, the scheme for stabilization of export receipt of the ACP countries is of questionable importance for these countries, considering the sharp contrast between its wide scope and the small amount of money available for it. Not only is it chronically underfunded; it has also had limited if not counter-productive impact on structural transformation (including export diversification). Thus, although the Lomé Convention celebrated its twentieth birthday in February 1995, yet for many African states, the instrument is still 'a mystery', whose potential, both in the realm of aid and trade, remains largely untapped. More serious, however, is the impact of Lomé on the process of African economic cooperation and integration.

Is Lomé a Constraint on Regionalism?

Critically studied, the implementation of the key provisions of the Lomé system would seem to constitute one of the most important constraints, at least in the long run, on the degree of economic cooperation schemes attainable in Africa. This had been seen by some early African leaders, both radical and moderate, long before the emergence of the Lomé regime. President Kwame Nkrumah of Ghana had as early as July 1961 described the Common Market as:

> a European scheme designed to attach African countries to European imperialism, to prevent the African countries from pursuing an independent neutral policy, to prevent the establishment of mutually beneficial economic ties among these countries, and to keep the African countries in a position of suppliers of raw materials for imperialist powers.[15]

This was echoed in 1962 by Prime Minister Sir Abubakar Tafawa Balewa of Nigeria:

> As an African country, we consider that the Common Market is essentially a European affair and has political overtones which cannot appeal to Africans. ... We are distrustful of any institutions which operate in a way to keep Africans perpetually as primary producers ....[16]

On close analysis, these statements are not far off the mark. For the linkages of the Lomé Convention would tend to raise some fundamental questions. For example, to what extent do these relationships facilitate the realization of the objectives of ECOWAS, COMESA or SADC strategy of self-reliance or their goal to function as independent autonomous units? Can it be said that the genuine transformation of African regional schemes would not be constrained in the long run by the logic of their continued dependent relationships with the EU? How do the linkages between the EU and African regional groupings tend to perpetuate (or de-emphasise) the client status of African countries as a consequence of their integration into the international (Western) economic system?

If trade dependence is a characteristic feature of developing countries, such dependence is chronic in the member states of African regional schemes. The overall import and export profiles reveal the heavy dependence of ECOWAS, COMESA, SADC or UDEAC/CEMAC countries on trade with Europe, while intra-regional trade is relatively low. Promotion of intra-regional trade expansion with the consequent reduction of the colonial heritage of dependence on trade with Europe or outside economic blocs has thus become one of the major challenges of the African regional and subregional economic communities. ECOWAS and COMESA have each adopted trade liberalization programmes aimed at promoting intra-regional trade expansion through the elimination of the barriers to trade.

On the other hand, the Lomé arrangement is geared towards intensification or reinforcement of the existing pattern of trade links between Europe and Africa, thereby further discouraging intra-African relationships. Trade with EU is sustained by the measures on the Lomé Convention's special preferences. While these prevail the member states of the African economic communities have been hesitant in the implementation of protocols and programmes on trade liberalization. Hence the difficulty, among other things, in promoting collective self-reliance while the Lomé regime is critically geared towards institutionalization of North-bound vertical orientation of the African economy or Euro-Africanism, symbolizing the continuity of an unequal division of labour between Europe and Africa. It is not surprising, therefore, that Shaw is pessimistic about the future: 'Inter-African trade is unlikely to increase much, other than through smuggling and the black market, until the continent escapes from its colonial heritage of North–South links and produces goods with markets on the continent as well as outside.'[17]

The trend in the pattern of trade relations is reinforced by the impact of the Lomé aid and STABEX provisions. The tying of aid to procurement in the EU countries, and the restriction of payment of STABEX to earnings from exports to EU, encourage increased economic transaction between Europe and Africa, a phenomenon which runs counter to the development of cooperation between the member states of African regional integration schemes.

Besides, although it is generally agreed that regional cooperation and integration is the field *par excellence* in which the EU could play a lead role, as it seems very well placed to perform this role in Africa, member states of the EU – with the exception of France – have not been keen to move into this area. Under Lomé IV, regional integration was seen as a key priority. However, in practice, there has been less enthusiasm. EU support for SADC, for instance, has mainly concentrated on transport and communications. It has been less inclined to move into the more difficult area of regional integration, for instance, by placing a greater emphasis on investment in the productive sectors and trade development.

On the whole, although greater economic self-reliance is a necessity for the regional integration schemes in Africa, since it enables them to escape from the historic dependency on the industrial centres in Europe and facilitates their development, the successful implementation of this strategy within the Lomé framework remains problematical. Lomé, in brief, represents a vertical Euro-African orientation, while ECOWAS, COMESA and ECCAS reflect an interest in horizontal South–South links. Thus, if the main goal of the existing economic integration schemes is greater autonomy and the institutions as catalysts and nuclei for the newly established African Economic Community, then interregional North–South relations, as reflected in Euro-African (ACP) links, are counter-productive. These external challenges to the process of African economic integration discussed so far have been reinforced by a set of internal challenges such as the World Bank/IMF orthodox structural adjustment programmes (SAPs).

THE CHALLENGE OF STRUCTURAL ADJUSTMENT PROGRAMMES: A 'PLUS' OR A 'RISK'?

Promotion of regional economic integration and implementation of the IMF and World Bank-mandated structural adjustment programmes are considered the two key strategies in response to the challenge facing Africa in the last decade of the twentieth century: reversal of the trend in economic decline that has beset the continent since the 1970s. These two elements have become the most salient frameworks for policy analysis and praxis.[18] It is generally acknowledged that if the 1990s are not to become another lost decade for Africa, the continent must make a success of these two policy initiatives.[19] For the most part, understandably, the two strategies have been pursued independently of each other. While SAPs are national responses to national economic crisis and are implemented without regard to their regional consequences, economic integration is a joint effort by groups of contiguous countries to come together with a view to forming large markets. The goals of economic integration have also been pursued with little or no regard for the conduct of national macro-economic policies.

In recent years, questions have been raised as to whether structural adjustment, as Jean Claude Boidin puts it, is 'a plus or risk' for African regionalism.[20] Are SAPs compatible with regional integration or are these two competing preoccupations mutually exclusive? Will SAPs prove to be contributors to integration or will they frustrate efforts to create lasting regional integration? And will the prospects for integration be much improved in the absence of SAPs? This section of the chapter attempts to examine the extent to which the orthodox SAPs constitute a challenge to the determination of African states to work assiduously towards economic integration.

Structural Adjustment: A 'Plus' for Regionalism?

Both the World Bank and the IMF have variously stressed that SAPs are compatible with successful regional integration. Indeed, both SAPs and regional integration are seen as 'imperatives'.[21] Edward Jaycox, the former

Vice-President for the Africa Region of the World Bank, has not hesitated to argue strongly in favour of the positive impact of adjustment on African regionalism.[22] This has been vigorously reinforced by Carol Lancaster in a discussion paper on regional integration in West Africa.[23] The general feeling is that SAPs offer opportunities for progress on regional economic cooperation, which have not been grasped by African states. Policy reforms like trade liberalization, exchange rate rationalization or devaluations, and competitive costs are all measures that will resuscitate national economies and promote economic expansion. Economic recovery and long-term sustainable growth will, in turn, stimulate intra-regional trade and enhance regional integration. The Bank's position is made explicit in its 1989 report:

> A realistic structure of exchange rates is critical to intra-regional trade. Trade among members of the CEAO (whose currency is the convertible CFA franc) currently represents 10 per cent of their total trade. This compares with less than 1 per cent of trade for the other members of ECOWAS, for whom currency convertibility has been suspended because of accumulating debts and delayed settlements.[24]

Evidently, the feeling of the Bank is that the correction of macro-economic imbalances and distortions in the form of overvalued exchange rates, protected and inefficient industries, price controls, and so on, will create an enabling environment for trade, competition and factor mobility, all of which will enhance rather than hinder regional integration.

The official view at the Bank has been echoed quite substantially by Boidin, who notes that the idea of the SAPs is to bring back economic growth by improving the mobility of the factors of production, both of which make regional integration easier. Boidin asserts that:

> This greater mobility will make the national economy more flexible, enabling it to adapt better and faster to the changes that come in the wake of enlargement of the economic area and therefore to benefit from it. Better growth will make the economies less fragile and the operators more dynamic and therefore more willing to face up to competition from the neighbouring countries.[25]

One other area of concern which Boidin highlights is the twin conditionalities of SAPs – trade liberalization and privatization of investment and production – which aim at facilitating imports while expanding exports. Regarding liberalization, Boidin suggests that an across-the-board liberalization will encourage the development of regional trade by reducing the administrative and tariff barriers that are characteristic of Africa.[26] In the case of privatization, Boidin is critical of the central planning of industrial investments by African governments which has led to duplication of industries competing in increasingly restricted regional markets. He argues that this explains the absence of complementarity often observed in neighbouring ACPs.[27] He is in favour of transferring investment decisions to the private sector which will lead to different industrial choices being made in different countries.

Structural Adjustment: A 'Risk' for Regionalism?

To a considerable extent, much of the arguments relating to the positive impact of SAPs on regionalism would appear to be fairly theoretical and based on long-term consideration alone. Regardless of reassuring theoretical arguments, it seems, in practice, that implementation of adjustment policies as designed to date, can lead to a decline in regional cooperation between African countries, as I have sought to show elsewhere.[28]

The experience of recent years shows that the regional element is missing from the adjustment programmes designed for Africa, as it is indeed a national concern with priority put on macro-economic policies. Not only are structural adjustment policies designed and implemented at the national level; the aims of SAPs, which are macro-economic, can only be measured correctly also at national economic level. Besides, both the main instruments of the adjustment policy – monetary and budgetary policies – and implementation of these instruments are essentially matters of national scope affecting all areas of the economy and having their direct impact, in principle, inside the country concerned.

Consequently, not only do the programmes fail to explore collective or regional reform responses, in spite of the general recognition that African countries suffer from broadly similar problems; they also tend to overlook development and transformation objectives such as sustained growth, collective self-reliance or regionalism. The approach of SAPs, therefore, tends to lead African governments and people to overlook the existence of potentially important partners – regional and subregional organizations and local communities. As Da Costa recently put it, 'Every country is thinking as an individual, with all its individual adjustment conditionalities. If integration is to be realized, all countries have to streamline their economies and tackle adjustment as a single unit.'[29]

However, Daddieh rightly remarks that while 'multi-country or regional adjustment is clearly desirable, it is easier said than done'. Regional adjustment raises a fundamental question about how ultimate responsibility for the loans thus disbursed will be assigned, or whose responsibility it is to bring the countries together for the purpose.[30] The effort made by ECOWAS and

COMESA to integrate the two development strategies – economic integration and structural adjustment – fell short of expectations, partly because of underfunding (in the case of the ECOWAS Recovery Programme), and partly because of the continuing dichotomy (and rivalry) between the COMESA and SADC.[31]

One other criticism based on the West African experience suggests that some structural adjustment measures designed solely in the light of their effect on the national economy have had a substantial and sometimes unwelcome effect on the countries next door thus militating against regional integration in the short term. Given the artificial or permeable nature of the borders of sub-Saharan Africa, there is the possibility that trade policy measures implemented in one country can have negative spillover effects on neighbouring countries. Such 'beggar my neighbour' policies are ultimately harmful for the region as a whole. Particularly upsetting for the region are measures involving rapid adjustment of domestic prices and movement of exchange rates. The adverse impact of Gambia's devaluation of Delasi (the national currency) to stimulate its export trade on the country's relations with Senegal, and that of Nigeria's sudden devaluations of 1986–7 of the Naira on neighbouring Benin and Niger are cases in point.[32] Besides, the uncoordinated and at times wide-ranging devaluations of national currencies offset tariff reductions conceded through trade liberalization programmes of regional groupings. Similarly, uncoordinated changes in fiscal policies and structures have disruptive impact on tariff concessions and the arrangements for external common tariffs.

Furthermore, in a period of macro-economic adjustment, the authorities tend to concentrate on short-term objectives and on the instruments of tax policy. This is understandable and probably unavoidable, but it is not really much encouragement to the development of regionalism. Regional integration is an essentially long-term thing and progress towards it primarily depends on the non-budgetary sides of the economic policy – 'trade policy and liberalization of the flow of finance first and the employment policy and administrative reform afterwards', as Boidin has highlighted.[33]

Moreover, macro-economic policy reforms requiring expenditure cutbacks lead to reduced consumer demand, which lowers trade in general. It leads also to reduced public investment, with cuts tending to fall more heavily on such regional projects as exist, because of their usually long-term nature and their lower rate of return. Payments to regional organizations are cut more deeply than ever. In addition, the quest for balance of payments equilibrium will tend to favour hard currency exports and reduce priority for self-sufficiency, both of which will favour exports outside the region. Then, too, as is often argued, since reform programmes are introduced at different times and are implemented at different speeds and intensities, SAPs can increase policy disharmony between neighbours and increase the degree of 'informalization' of trade. Above all, fiscal policies, pressured by needs for new revenue sources, often aim at higher taxes, including taxes on tradable goods, and at better control over the parallel economy. Both can dampen regional trade.

It is worth noting that owing to the reduced emphasis on development planning, the growing privatization of state-owned enterprises and the diminished role of governments in economic activity – another consequence of adjustment policies – some of the basic premises of the accepted model of cooperating among African countries were no longer applicable. Government cooperation in the integration of production and investment activities, uneven as its progress had been, suffered a setback, as national policies curtailed demands, investment and growth.

It has become quite evident that in practice, the structural adjustment policies have not been used to improve intra-African states preferences. More seriously, the liberalization measures they involve reduce the size of the existing preferential margins and thus encourage the development of trade outside the zone more than in it. And since the trade liberalization measures in the orthodox SAPs are decided unilaterally without consultation with neighbouring states or subregional groupings, they tend to increase asymmetry of the access systems operating between neighbouring countries.

Finally, other adjustment measures such as exchange rates, which sometimes become a source of instability for the economic operators, budgetary policies, which are the hard core of the structural adjustment programmes, and the effect of prolonged contraction of public spending on the various budget items – all this has the tendency not only to reduce the contributions to regional and subregional community budgets (which have to be made in foreign exchange), but also to deflect attention away from the process of regional cooperation and integration.

Thus, although structural adjustment policies are designed within a national framework, they are not without their effects on the practical possibilities of regional cooperation or on the prospects of economic integration in the longer term. More immediately, however, the implementation of the first generation of SAPs has created some adverse conditions for regional integration partly because they have not paid sufficient attention to the regional dimension of Africa's economic crisis. What is more, like the Lomé Convention, some parts of the liberalization policies pursued under the SAPs are incompatible with the objective of promoting collective self-reliance through regionalism because they have a tendency to reinforce rather than transcend Africa's historical role in the international division of labour and the extroversion of its political economies. Hence both the SAPs and the Lomé regime present African countries with a central dilemma. The longer the period of the adoption of the World Bank and IMF stabilization and structural adjustment measures, the greater would be the difficulty and the complexity of the efforts by the African states towards the attainment of the goal of developmental regionalism. On the other hand, the challenge posed by the emergence of democratic South Africa is of an entirely different nature, as reviewed below.

THE CHALLENGE OF DEMOCRATIC SOUTH AFRICA

The dramatic changes which have taken place in South Africa since 1990, leading to a radical transformation of the political and social order and the emergence of a democratic regime in May 1994, have presented wide-ranging challenges not only to the country and its citizens, but also the Southern African subregion, the African continent as a whole, and the strategy of regionalism in Africa.[34] The relative size of South Africa's economy compared to the rest of the Southern African subregion and the extensive economic ties it already has with other Southern African countries have led to South African involvement being widely seen as a potential catalytic event which could give new momentum to a programme of subregional and regional economic cooperation and/or integration. The country is in a strong position to act as a broker in achieving a more rational regional framework.

The new government of South Africa has inherited an economy which, compared with most developing countries, is large: only ten such countries have an absolute GDP greater than South Africa. In 1992, Reserve Bank of South Africa data put its GDP at Rand 327.1 billion (US$114.8 billion). The World Bank terms South Africa an 'upper middle income' country with GNP per capita comparable to Venezuela, Argentina, Brazil and Mexico.[35] But it is when compared with the economies of sub-Saharan Africa (SSA) that the size of South Africa's economy becomes quite evident. For within SSA, South Africa's economy is three times larger than the next biggest, Nigeria. Data for 1991 as reflected in a recent *ODI Briefing Paper,*[36] show the following comparisons (in which South Africa is included in data for SSA):

(i)   With just 7% of the total population of SSA and 5% of the total land area of the continent, South Africa accounts for 36% of total SSA GDP;

(ii) South Africa's merchandise exports account for 39% of total SSA exports, its imports for 32% of the total; and

(iii) South Africa produces almost the same value of manufactured goods, and exports twice the value of manufactured goods (if processed minerals are included), as the rest of SSA combined.

According to the Economic Intelligence Unit (EIU), South Africa is one of the world's richest countries in terms of natural resources.[37]

While the new government no doubt has its own internal economic development agenda, if only to satisfy the political imperatives of change, democratic South Africa offers opportunities and challenges for the process of economic integration and development both in Southern Africa and the rest of the continent. For one thing, as President Nelson Mandela has recently stressed, 'South Africa cannot escape its African destiny. If we do not devote our energies to this continent, we too could fall victim to the forces that have brought ruin to its various parts.'[38] In attempting to attract large-scale foreign investment, for instance, which, as recently highlighted by C.L. Stals, Governor of the South African Reserve Bank, is a key to the country's development,[39] South Africa will be forced to take into account its geographical location. As it is part and parcel of Africa, the image of the continent as a whole will inevitably influence the perceptions of foreign investors of the country. South Africa thus has every reason to encourage substantially political stability and especially economic growth elsewhere on the continent.

The period since the 1988 and 1989 negotiations on Angola/Namibia, and more particularly since the unbanning of the organizations of South Africa's liberation movement, has seen a considerable expansion of economic interaction between South Africa and the rest of the continent. The increasing economic relations are reflected not only in trade but also in growing involvement by South Africa in contracts and projects in other African countries and some modest investment. These interactions with virtually all OAU members, plus the prospects which exist for fairly rapid increases in trade, point, first, to the possibility of South Africa establishing (perhaps uniquely) a significant presence as a trading partner across the continent; second, they raise the issue of the potential contribution which closer relations between South Africa and the rest of Africa could make to African development; and third, they provide an opportunity for strengthening the bargaining power of Africa on global economic issues of contemporary significance, such as external debt, commodity prices, environment, and economic integration.

As regards subregional cooperation in infrastructural development, it should be stressed that South Africa needs the subregion in many more ways than is commonly admitted, just as the countries of Southern Africa also need

South Africa. A case in point is South Africa's increasingly desperate need for cheap energy and water to resume growth. Its vast non-renewable energy resources, chiefly coal, may be largely depleted by the year 2000, if rapid industrialization proceeds.[40] It is worth noting that Mozambique has, in recent years, supplied South Africa with as much as 13 per cent of its electricity which is vital to the Transvaal industry. Overall, SADC countries have surpluses of oil, coal and hydro-electricity. Of almost equal importance for South Africa is water. Already, it is in competition for scarce supplies with Botswana and Swaziland, while Mozambique, Namibia and Zimbabwe will need to negotiate with the new South African government over shared rivers and catchment areas.[41]

At the African regional level, there is much that democratic South Africa can offer to influence the shape of continental cooperation and integration in the future. Given its sizeable proportion of the continent's total output, South Africa can play a most important role in forging and accelerating the process of creating those very economic, financial and business links which are the goals of the African Economic Community. Its participation in the Community will not only result in the enlargement of the size of the market, it will also inevitably strengthen it and thereby enhance Africa's bargaining position in the post-Cold War era and in the emerging world of trading blocs, as well as in trade negotiations, especially within the World Trade Organization (WTO) and UNCTAD. Significantly, too, if South Africa's membership and active participation in the Community facilitates the dismantling of trade barriers within Africa, the competitiveness of the African countries with the rest of the world will be improved by increased competition and scale economies.

This chapter has highlighted, albeit briefly, the internal and external challenges to the process of economic cooperation and integration in Africa. It has attempted, among other things, to shed some considerable light on the structural adjustment programmes which, as designed to date, are more of a 'risk' than a 'plus' to regionalism in Africa. As the two are considered key strategies in response to the development challenge facing Africa today, it has become necessary, as will be discussed in the next chapter, to make structural adjustment programmes compatible with regional integration to enable the former to have a positive impact on the promotion of the latter.

As regards Europe 1992, it is quite evident that as more than 50 per cent of the external trade of most African countries is with the EU under preferential arrangement, the trade implications of Europe 1992 for Africa are enormous. And from the trade agreement in the current Lomé IV, it is clear that Africa will sustain net trade losses under the single European market. The Lomé system itself has become increasingly obsolete and irrelevant to Africa of the 1990s and beyond. If anything, it rather reinforces the age-old dependency syndrome of Africa. Like Europe 1992, the emergence of other regional economic blocs in North America and the Pacific Rim is likely to diminish Africa's access to export commodity markets by raising the average level of protectionism in the advanced countries, stiffen export competitiveness, cause further substitution for Africa's commodity exports and impose losses in terms of trade, higher cost of imports and reduced export earnings from those markets. The next chapter focuses special attention on the extent to which Africa can meet the challenges of economic cooperation and integration in the 1990s and beyond. Consequently, it sets out a new direction for Africa.

7 Regionalism in Africa: Towards a New Direction

The new challenges to regionalism, coupled with the obstacles encountered in managing it as a viable development strategy for Africa and lessons derived from past experience, show that existing economic conditions are not particularly favourable to intra-African economic integration. Accordingly, African countries need to emphasize the establishment of an enabling environment for supporting regional and subregional economic cooperation and integration. This requires the removal of internal deficiencies facing groupings in the broad areas of institutional arrangements, and emphasizing objectives, policies and instruments. Thus, if the coming decades are to witness the evolution of a viable dynamic process of intra-African economic cooperation and integration, and if regionalism is to be the basic element of a long-term development strategy for Africa, the revival process needs to be set in the context of a realistic appraisal of past experience and the new regional and global realities.

The purpose of this chapter, therefore, is to identify major issues requiring priority attention for revitalizing as well as adjusting the process of economic cooperation and integration to the new realities of the 1990s and to forge a new direction. The chapter is divided into five closely related sections: (i) towards a new approach; (ii) strengthening national institutional and managerial capacity; (iii) strengthening the institutional capacity of the economic communities; (iv) crucial factors in implementing the treaty of the African Economic Community; and (v) enhancing South–South cooperation. Surely it is time to rethink strategy, review our approach to economic integration, reconsider commitment and management of regionalism in Africa in order to effectively meet the interlocking challenges posed by the global resurgence of interest in regional economic integration in the 1990s and the renewed emphasis being given to it in Africa today.

TOWARDS A NEW APPROACH TO REGIONAL INTEGRATION

It has become quite evident that the traditional or European model of economic integration, recently reinforced by the Cross-Border Initiative, with its emphasis on integration of markets rather than physical infrastructure and production, is inappropriate because of virtually non-existence industrial base in Africa. It is like 'putting the cart before the horse'. The analyses so far point both to the prematureness and inadequacy of the market integration approach in the particular context of underdeveloped Africa, and the dangers that such a strategy has in reinforcing and strengthening the horizontal extensions of some of the existing vertical linkages of the continent with the advanced industrialized countries of the North. Not surprisingly, the success of African economic groupings has so far been rather limited, with little or no impact on the economic growth of the cooperating countries; not even the limited objective of intra-African trade expansion has been achieved in Africa. Therefore, a new approach is required, that is, the integration of the African economies that involves three related dimensions: the integration of physical and institutional structures, of production structures, and of the African markets.

Integration of Physical Structures

There is general consensus on the importance of physical infrastructures which enable and foster efficient operations and sustainable development of national and subregional economies, as well as fair and equitable distribution of products, services and other amenities among various peoples of a country, subregion or region. At the subregional or regional levels, interconnection of infrastructures is a necessary condition for integration of national markets and industries to facilitate increased intra-African trade. Transport and communications development is the key to the integration of physical and institutional structures. To accelerate the goal of integration, efforts should be made to address the problem of disjointed physical space with excessively extroverted transport and communications networks and limited horizontal links between African countries. The opening of lines of communication between the member states of a subregional or regional economic grouping is a prerequisite to the exploitation of the basic strategic materials, especially those located in the hinterland. Rural infrastructure requires particular emphasis as it is vital to the agricultural development of the region. In this regard, stress needs to be placed on development of rural roads, air transportation into centres of importance to agriculture and port handling facilities.

In view of the necessity to develop a heavy transport system for the needs of the industrial base, priority would have to be given to the improvement of navigable waterways (rivers and lakes) and to increasing coastal shipping. Maritime modes of transportation, especially coastal shipping, are important in linking coastal states. Development, in general, is closely linked to international trade, the largest proportion of which is moved by ships. Exports and imports require a sound transportation infrastructure which will ensure an efficient and cost-effective movement of goods. This means that a network of land-based facilities must be available and be linked to properly designed and managed ports so that ships can handle their portion of the system properly. To guarantee that these elements are in place and fit together requires a sound and well-structured maritime administration coupled with well-trained port operators and marine officers. Regional programmes for this transport mode are lacking and efforts to address the deficiency are only now under way. The West and Central African Coastal Shipping Service is a recent development initiative of ECOWAS and UDEAC, together with the Ministerial Conference of West and Central Africa on Maritime Transport (MINCONMAR). The economic communities should investigate the potential for developing regional transportation using inland waterways linking several countries such as the Nile, Zaire and Niger rivers and the lakes Victoria and Tanganyika.

In Africa, where most countries are linked by land, the most important mode of transportation for regional development may be road transport. Hence, the development of inter- and intra-subregional road networks is indispensable. It would involve completing missing segments of subregional and regional road networks, rehabilitating deteriorating infrastructure and placing emphasis on routine maintenance. The development of rail transport calls for similar treatment. Carriage by rail is important for transport of bulk cargoes and heavy low-value primary commodities. Regarding air transport, which is specially important for carrying light-weight manufactured products, and is often the only means of effective movement of persons, goods and services between states, several groupings have proposed establishing joint transport companies to service their regions as well as handle external trade. A case in point was the establishment in May 1989 of a regional airline, Air Mano, by member states of MRU. The launching of Air Mano's operations, originally scheduled for September 1991, had to be postponed owing to political problems in the region.

The development of telecommunications systems is also an essential factor for reinforcing the cohesion of the subregional economic areas. This includes the maintenance of national networks and the interconnection of the earth stations networks of the subregions. Some progress in this direction has been made through the Pan African Telecommunications Network (PANATEL) and the Regional African Satellite Communications System (RASCOM). However, the lack of funds and skilled manpower to maintain the existing facilities has undermined the quality of services.

On the whole, as a priority segment in the process of regional economic integration, cooperation on developing and maintaining efficient, reliable communications linkages, inland (road, rail and air) transport linkages and ocean transport networks regionally should be strengthened because these elements facilitate regional trade as well as minimize the inherent costs. The economic communities could take more initiatives in this direction, while strong commitment and support from member states would be required in tackling the task. The business sector should also be encouraged to participate in the establishment of regional and subregional road, railways, maritime shipping and civil aviation companies. It would help to develop competitive, financially viable and moderately comfortable transportation facilities. If well planned, carefully targeted, efficiently priced and operated, and well maintained, infrastructure systems can play an important role in facilitating subregional and regional economic activities, increasing opportunities for production, increasing equitable distribution of economic opportunities, reducing rural-to-urban migration pressures, as well as minimizing pressures on the environment and reducing poverty.

Closely related to this are energy services which are also essential components in the integration of the subregional economic entities. In this regard, it is necessary to ensure the full exploitation of the hydro-electric energy potential of the subregions and devise a comprehensive programme of inter-connections of power lines within each subregion, in order to meet primarily the needs of the basic and capital foods industries. Sharing energy resources is one particularly suitable area for enhanced regional cooperation. The emerging trend towards intercountry cooperation in various subregions needs to be widened. Governments should put in place regionally oriented policies to accelerate the trend by facilitating private sector initiatives, but also appropriate government interventions in these sectors. A major task will be to identify and promote current best practices within and outside Africa, so that member states will apply them where appropriate. Equally important will be studies that point to opportunities for intercountry cooperation in energy.

Integration of Production Structures

The second high priority is for the economic community schemes to address the weak production structures with virtually no intersectoral links, that is, between the primary and the secondary sectors in general and between agriculture and industry, between mining and manufacturing, in particular. Therefore, the recently revitalized ECOWAS and the newly transformed Eastern and Southern African economic groupings – COMESA and SADC – among others, should now give top priority to production and devote substantial resources to production integration in order to reduce the excessive external dependence, critical lack of productive capacity and internal non-viability of member economies.

It is from the integration of the productive structures that the veritable gains of Africa's self-reliance will be derived. First, it is at this level that the benefits of the economies of scale will be reaped. Second, given the natural complementarities of endowments in Africa, the integration of the productive structures would generate new forward and backward linkages in the process of subregional development. Third, integrating the production structures would alleviate the persistent constraint of financial resources, as it would enable countries to pool resources and establish multicountry programmes in areas like iron and steel and the development of lake and river basins.

To say this is not to ignore or underestimate the importance of market integration in the building up of effective subregional economic schemes. The point at issue is that, on the basis of past experience, attempts to integrate markets through the removal of trade barriers without simultaneous effort to promote a joint approach to the expansion of production capacities, will be largely ineffective. Not only is it important that the two endeavours should proceed simultaneously and be mutually reinforcing, it is also essential that the removal of trade barriers should be pursued in the context of, and as an integral part of agreements and understandings relating to, the planning of production improvements on a subregional basis.

Harmonization of national efforts to improve agricultural productivity, restructure industrial production to rely more on domestic rather than on imported factor inputs, rationalize the production and utilization of energy, and improve facilities for repair and maintenance of plant and machinery, among other things, through subregional efforts to standardize equipment and parts, should be major components of cooperative programmes that ECOWAS, SADC, COMESA and the other economic groupings ought to promote if they are to have any significant impact on the development of member states.

The objective of developing, expanding and diversifying the production capacities of African countries – both for lending support to the process of regional trade liberalization and for promoting overall economic development – cannot be overemphasized. At present, all the developing African countries have mostly commodity-dependent economies. Hence, for some time to come, they will continue to depend on trade in commodities. Joint cooperation in commodity-related development should therefore be an important consideration of such groupings. As emphasized below, cooperation in the production of and trade in food, in particular, deserves special treatment, given the mounting food needs of the African continent as the population expands.

Cooperation programmes and projects of groupings in this area should have strong support from member states. Importantly, too, in the long-term, African countries will have to diversify their production structures into growth sectors of manufactures and services in order to expand the range of consumable and tradable goods. It will no doubt be a slow process, given the present low degree of industrialization in the developing countries of Africa.

Regional industrial development requires, as an immediate priority, the design and implementation of industrial development strategies and policies by groupings. Some of the groupings have begun to formulate plans for industrial development. ECOWAS, for instance, has undertaken inventories of existing industrial activities in the West African subregion as a first step towards a subregional industrial development programme. COMESA has adopted a new regional integration strategy with industrial development as a central goal. Regional industrial development plans need not necessarily focus on establishing comparatively large multinational enterprises, but could help promote specialization between small- and medium-scale enterprises in different member states. The output of these regional industrial enterprises should be geared to serving national, subregional and global markets.

Even within the production integration approach, priorities must be set. Following the objective of establishing a human-centred development, one major priority area of collective self-reliance is that of food self-sufficiency and security. The recurrent food crises in Africa have heightened the need for integration in agriculture designed to provide self-sufficiency in food, the production and distribution of seeds, the local manufacture of agricultural inputs, including animal feed and integrated research and animal health facilities, and food processing and the establishment of food marketing systems on a subregional basis. Indeed, nothing short of a subregional and, subsequently, pan-African common agricultural policy, production and marketing is required.

Production of intermediate and capital goods, especially iron and steel, machine tools, fertilizers, chemicals and pharmaceuticals, building materials, as well as agricultural, transport and construction equipment may constitute another priority. Indeed, the establishment of a solid industrial base with key industries of iron and steel, aluminium, chemical and petrochemical products is necessary for triggering a rapid, self-sustaining process of economic development. This industrialization process is also essential to support energy development (production of cables, manufacture of pylons and transformers), the major infrastructural projects, the construction of transport facilities and basic capital goods.

Finally, integration of production structure is also important in another respect. It constitutes Africa's response to current world trends. In an increasingly competitive world, where it will be ever more difficult to resort to protective measures, a high level of productivity is undoubtedly the key to improved competitiveness of African products in world markets. To this end, integration process in Africa must go beyond the mere integration of markets. It must deal as well, and effectively, with integration of production at the regional and continental levels. This will encourage and facilitate the participation of African countries in the global trend towards the integration of production processes on a worldwide basis, involving the establishment of linkages between production units in different countries. African countries must face the reality that, in a world of free markets and fierce competition, productivity is the king. Therefore, one major task facing African integration groupings in the 1990s and beyond is to improve the productivity of African industries, and to promote regional trade in raw materials and intermediate products.

Integration of Markets

The third priority is to address the cumbersome tariff and non-tariff obstacles to intra-regional trade in order to bring about subregional trade liberalization and market expansion. Trade liberalization is a major building block of economic integration and cooperation. In Africa, its potential remains to be fully realized. This deficiency should be corrected. Coincidentally, the scope for liberalization of trade has widened in the new atmosphere of movement towards general liberalization and opening up of economies in developing countries.

The actual launching and full implementation of trade liberalization programmes deserve high priority in economic groupings. Member states will need to identify and resolve quickly the problems blocking progress. This could be done through measures such as: identification of locally produced products which have major trade potential and concentration of trade liberalization efforts on those products; adoption of less restrictive rules of origin which may enhance the benefits of regional tariff preferences accorded; promotion of a foreign investment policy that is friendly; and adoption of special or differential treatment in favour of the lesser advanced member states – all this should be geared to correcting, rather than compensating for imbalances, particularly through the creation of productive and export capacities.

This should be enhanced by the convergence of economic and monetary policies. In this regard, the multilateral clearing and payments arrangements

– the West African Clearing House (WACH), Central African Clearing House (CACH) and the COMESA Clearing House (CCH) – will have to be revitalized and their operations strengthened. African countries which are not members of the three operational clearing arrangements should be encouraged either to join or to establish their own clearing arrangements, bearing in mind both to avoid proliferation of institutions and the efforts under way to create a single continental economic and monetary arrangement. In this connection, AMU's efforts to create a clearing arrangement deserve the full support of its member states.

Members of clearing arrangements should also be encouraged to allow a large proportion of the goods and services traded among themselves to be cleared by their clearing house. This would help to expand the volume of transactions so channelled. The possibility of establishing limited convertibility schemes among willing member states should be explored with a view to alleviating problems arising from disparities in exchange rate regimes. Although monetary union is a desirable objective, it is likely to evolve only over time, given the complexity of the subject and the current situation in Africa where there are many non-convertible currencies, differing floating exchange rates and with various foreign exchange restrictions. Nonetheless, the economic communities should gradually explore other sectors of financial and monetary cooperation. For example, they could consider establishing, where needed, trade financing institutions to provide short- and medium-term credit for trade in non-traditional products, in particular. Another area for expansion is the mobilization of domestic savings and promotion of subregional or regional capital markets for economic development.

It is reassuring to note that the three related key dimensions involved in the integration of the African economies are now clearly espoused and given the necessary emphasis both in the treaties and priorities of the major post-1990 African economic communities. For example, unlike the 1975 ECOWAS Treaty which put to the forefront a timetabled trade liberalization programme, the revised 1993 ECOWAS Treaty highlights, as a priority concern, production and trade and the building of national development capacities. Similarly, in the 1992 transformed SADC, transport and communications, food, agriculture and industry sectors occupy a central position. In the case of COMESA, the first summit of the Authority of Heads of State and Government held in Malawi, in December 1994, adopted five priorities to be the basis of COMESA's focus for the next five to ten years. Unlike the PTA, which devoted most of its efforts to market integration, the COMESA priorities highlighted physical integration with special attention to development of transport and communications infrastructures and services; significant and sustained increases in productivity in industry; increase of agricultural production; new programmes for trade promotion, trade expansion and trade facilitation; and development of comprehensive, reliable and up-to-date information databases covering all sectors of the economy.[1]

Multispeed Approach

On the whole, in the new phase of adjustment now under way, African countries should advocate an acceleration of the process of economic integration within the subregional and regional groupings. Member states should not be expected or required to participate in economic integration and cooperation activities at the same speed. There should be some flexibility in the sequencing of member states' participation in regional development. Being at different levels of growth and development, member states cannot move at the same speed. Besides, different member states have different interests in relation to the measures envisaged within the context of a regional grouping. It is therefore unrealistic to expect them to move along at the same pace, unless one accepts that one pace will be that of the slowest moving member. The process of arriving at common policies tends to become more complex as the number of participating countries increases. Therefore the process of integration must be based on the concept of multispeed development by which two or more member states can agree to accelerate the implementation of specific treaty provisions or other common agreements, while allowing others to join in later on a reciprocal basis. Future programmes should therefore be pegged on the 'fastest moving member state'. The whole integration process would be tremendously accelerated by encouraging participation of the enterprise sector and a greater role for the service sector.

Greater Role for Service and Enterprise Sectors

Against the background of the current technological revolution, the services sector has emerged as an area of critical importance in the context of structural transformation and industrialization of developing countries. This has been reinforced by the recently concluded Uruguay Round Agreement under which, African countries have to accept an obligation to undertake to liberalize their trade in services, under the General Agreement on Trade in Services (GATS). While services have a great role to play in the promotion of economic cooperation and integration at the regional and subregional levels, as cooperation in services can stimulate and promote regional or subregional trade, especially services directly supportive of trade and goods such as credit and regional payment facilities, clearing houses, information networks, and so on, joint initiatives in the services sector have remained marginal or inoperative in African integration programmes.[2]

Most of the regional and subregional agreements deal with the simple facilitating of services among countries. Cooperation among member states is limited, for the most part to measures aimed at coordinating and harmonizing rules and regulations affecting services activities, the harmonization of institutionalized mechanisms for the exchange of information and experiences, and initiatives promoting joint research and training programmes on services. Thus, for example, there are several regional and bilateral agreements that aim to facilitate services in the various modes of road and rail transport. ECOWAS has adopted a number of decisions with this in mind within the West African subregion. These include the Convention on Interstate Road Transport, the decision on the harmonization of highway legislation, and measures such as the creation of liability insurance for transit and transport operations.

Efforts to promote economic integration in Africa could no doubt be furthered by taking into account the role of services in the integration process. The challenge to develop services at the subregional level stems from the fact that higher growth rates are associated with service sector growth. Therefore, member states of COMESA, ECOWAS and SADC should target key service industries – especially banking, insurance and related services, transport and communications services – for rapid development. Hence, concrete measures are necessary for the development of critical service activities to constitute an important component of integration strategies at the subregional, regional and interregional levels.

To this end, there is a need for: (i) preparation of policy-oriented sectoral studies on different service activities, in close coordination between member countries, which could provide the basis for the development and implementation within integration groupings of appropriate policy measures and mechanisms for joint cooperation in this sector; (ii) development of regional and subregional programmes geared to the improvement of the statistical database on service activities, in particular those related to international exchange; (iii) organization of regional and subregional seminars and workshops on cooperation and integration services; and (iv) continued support for and intensification of concerted effort towards the development of service infrastructure, especially transportation, communications and information services to facilitate such flows.[3] As far as transport is concerned, harmonization and simplification of customs policies and transport documentation, and granting the right of transit to the means of transportation of member countries could constitute good examples of measures to be taken. In the field of tourism, cooperation in promotion and marketing, reduction of travel barriers and promotion of intra-regional flows of tourists could favour cooperation within the subregions.

Of particular significance is the greater role which enterprises or the private sector should play in the integration process in Africa. After all, in countries where production is not predominantly in the hands of government, it is the private sector and the NGOs that must respond to the integration process and implement the changes in production that are the aim. Therefore, with a view to promoting and increasing a more active participation of the business community in the integration process, in particular in trade and industrial cooperation, mechanisms should be established in all the economic communities to encourage the participation of enterprises in the design and implementation of regional trade and production programmes and projects. Enterprises would become aware of, and take advantage of, incentives to produce and create trade within groupings, especially if they were linked into the whole trade liberalization process. The experience of the Latin American Integration Association (ALADI) and the Association of South-East Asian Nations (ASEAN) in involving the regional business community in trade cooperation activities could be of benefit to groupings in Africa. In ALADI, sectoral industrial groups have been organized to review and propose industrial products for preferential treatment. In ASEAN, the business community has been invited to participate in ASEAN's dialogue with its major development cooperation partners on trade and economic cooperation.[4]

In Africa, the promotion and support for the development of effective institutional mechanisms for cooperation among enterprises and their organizations, including business information systems at the subregional, regional and interregional levels, would be required. There would also be the need to develop ways and means to facilitate investment promotion schemes of African countries in the areas of service, industrial and trade-creating joint ventures.

Governments of the member states of the economic groupings need to ensure that an enabling environment exists for the private sector to fulfil its role and potential. Without the appropriate regulatory, legal and legislative framework, the right fiscal and other incentives, the supportive macro-economic climate, it will not be possible to encourage the private sector to become a key stakeholder and an important partner in the integration process of the African economic communities. The security of investment, the predictability of policies, the building of investors' confidence are extremely important. Increasing production and trade in goods and services, as well as diversification should be recognized as the highest priority. The role of the private sector in attaining these objectives will be critical in the future. It is this sector which will invest in productive enterprises, produce the goods and services, and move them across national frontiers. One important way of encouraging the enterprise sector will be to establish closer coordination between regional integration objectives and trade promotion policies. Achieving this effectively will involve a second very important measure, namely ensuring greater participation and deeper involvement of chambers of commerce and industry, as well as other appropriate private sector groups in the policy formulation process.

At the level of the African Economic Community, there is the need to develop a close working relationship that would enable the private sector to contribute to policies on integration, including the preparation of the various protocols and instruments required for the implementation of the AEC Treaty. Article 91(2) of the AEC Treaty which deals with the setting up of a mechanism for consultation with the socio-economic organizations and associations, should be acted upon, as a priority in order to enable the private sector to provide an effective input into the preparation of the various protocols and instruments. This would ensure that policies on integration, as well as the important instruments address the critical concerns of economic operators and thus facilitate continental integration.

It is encouraging to note that the new post-1990 economic communities in Africa which have established mechanisms for this purpose include the COMESA Chambers of Commerce and Industry and the SADC Regional Business Council. Similarly, the revised ECOWAS Treaty has shifted considerably from its exclusive focus on government to government, to involving the private sector. Provisions have thus been made for promotion of active involvement of the private sector and to ensure the harmonization of national investment codes with a view to adopting a single community code. In the case of COMESA, the most important element is that the treaty commits member states to, *inter alia*, (i) promote a continuous dialogue with the private sector at the national and regional levels to help create an improved business environment for the implementation of agreed decisions in all economic sectors; and (ii) provide an opportunity for entrepreneurs to participate actively in improving the policing, regulations and institutions that affect them so as to increase confidence in policy reforms, raise productivity and lower costs at enterprise levels. The new, alternative approach of economic integration in Africa should be enhanced by strengthening and effective management of institutions and structures of economic cooperation and integration.

STRENGTHENING NATIONAL INSTITUTIONAL AND MANAGERIAL CAPACITY

Since integration is multifaceted it needs to be approached from a wide variety of angles. This section and the one that follows attempt to distinguish between different 'actors' on whose action the success of regional initiatives will depend in the coming decades. Regional cooperation and integration must of necessity be the coordinated effort of African governments, African institutions and organizations both national and subregional or regional and the international donor community. Together they must create the enabling environment required for the private sector and the civil society to participate efficiently and effectively.

African Governments and Regionalism

However important the role of the private sector, enterprises or NGOs, the process of integration must begin with and be sustained by governments and politicians. The experience of the last three decades has demonstrated that it is the vision, will, and commitment of those directly involved, and especially of the top political leaders, that have proved to be crucial factors in the success or failures of initiatives in cooperation. Put differently, although the private sector and the regional organizations have a major role to play, it is government action which, through its influence on the other actors, will be the most decisive factor in the present African context.

Many decisions which could have spurred on the cooperation and integration movement have been taken in the past, but have not been implemented. At this point in time, when there is intensified interest in the promotion of regional cooperation and integration, it appears useful to take stock of these decisions and to take measures to implement in order of priority those measures which could advance the integration process. Importantly, too, political commitment to cooperation and integration also means taking the necessary measures to ensure that means to implement regional policies are put into place (for example, expertise to be able to advise on how best to put into practice the commitments of the state in the regional context).

In brief, as one of the important preconditions and features of successful integration and cooperation, strong political commitment is required to advance integration towards common objectives. It is not enough to have a strong motivation in the initial stages. The commitment must be sustained over a long period. In this regard, it is worth noting that the European integration process has been in construction for almost half a century now. The most remarkable feature in this regard was the irreversible nature of progress accomplished. Politicians could not backtrack once the process was engaged.

Strengthening National Integration Structures

For the economic schemes to be effective, regional economic relations must be given a central role in the activities of governments, which must adopt an administrative structure that gives to those responsible for pursuing integration the weight and power they must have if they are to succeed. Thus if regional economic schemes are to yield the expected results, regional cooperation must become an integral part of the national policy making and planning processes. Member countries of regional economic groupings should seek the opportunities offered by regional cooperation to enhance national economic management and performance.

There is the need for synergy to exist between the national and the subregional or regional programmes. However, for this to materialize, member states of the economic community need to develop planning capacity and tools that would enable the national and the regional programmes to complement each other in terms of planning, management and implementation. The national and subregional or regional programmes should complement each other, but remain distinct as there are areas of development that may not lend themselves readily to regional cooperation. Fears of dispersion of effort, duplication, overlap and potential for conflict between what is perceived as national interest and the collective interest at the subregional or regional level could be avoided as long as member states are able to distinguish between their regional obligations and national endeavours.

It is needless to stress that at the national level, member states of groupings should endeavour to give prominence to subregional or regional development in national development plans. This approach would facilitate the adoption of national development policies that make allowance for subregional and regional development objectives. National policies for developing productive capacities, expanding trade and, in general, making structural adjustments should be consistent with subregional and regional integration policies. At the level of groupings, the formulation of development plans and programmes should, as far as possible, ensure a careful reconciliation of the individual interests of member states with those of the group as a whole. Such a linkage could be promoted through the establishment and strengthening of mechanisms for regular dialogue, consultation and exchange of views and experiences on national policies among member states of groupings at the ministerial level as well as at the level of working officials. In the European context, this role is played by Permanent Representatives, who provide feedback to their national administrations and perform a bridge-building function between national policy and union policy.

Undoubtedly, therefore, successful regional integration would depend on the extent to which there exist national and subregional or regional institutions with adequate competence and capacity to stimulate and manage efficiently and effectively the complex process of integration. Weak national institutions may seriously hamper effective cooperation and integration. It is often noted that implementation is lagging behind because of limited administrative and managerial capacity at the national level. In many cases, responsibilities are dispersed over different ministries.[5] A situation may arise where measures agreed in one context are not compatible with measures agreed upon in another.

Therefore, a well-structured national apparatus capable of coordinating involvement of member states in different regional organizations, is vital if they are to exercise a multiplicity of new tasks and roles. Establishing national integration structures in each country will make for better coordination among member states and would facilitate implementation of decisions. It will also make for quicker decisions. Arguably this would lead to easier consultation and harmonization at the subregional or regional level.

As Jeggan Senghor has recently noted, the present common practice of making a unit within the ministry of finance, of planning, of foreign affairs or of trade and industry, responsible for overseeing regional cooperation, 'is no effective alternative to a separate ministry'.[6] It fails to give high-profile recognition to the seriousness of the government's commitment to regional cooperation. At the bureaucratic level, Senghor identifies two shortcomings to this practice. First, the mainstream responsibilities of these ministries understandably tend to dominate their activities and leave regional development issues 'as the residual legatee of their time and effort'. Moreover, the staffing, authority level, backgrounds and qualifications of personnel in these ministerial units 'tend to be far below what is required to make them effective'.[7]

Second, it could be argued that since regional issues frequently cut across the sectoral and functional responsibilities of line ministries, they could be handled through interministerial committees. In practice, however, these committees have proved to be ineffective mainly because first, their composition and powers are limited; and second, their meetings have tended to be significantly irregular. The solution to these problems, therefore, is 'to rise above them' and establish a separate ministry of regional and international economic cooperation answerable directly to the Head of State and headed by a senior minister. It would ensure that regional policies were integrated into all aspects of national policy and that they were implemented according to plan. A separate ministry of economic cooperation and integration might constitute a first step in the direction of better regional cooperation and integration management such as better coordination. Whatever it is called the key issue is that there should be some coordinating machinery in the government responsible for coherence and consistency in regional affairs.

The establishment of national units of the regional economic community schemes in member countries, as evidenced in the ECOWAS subregion, is only a second-best proposition. Not only would this not reflect the need for visible demonstration of national commitment to regional cooperation, it is also hard to believe that it would ever become an accepted part of the national bureaucratic process. Thus, it would be in danger of being even more marginal to the determination of government policies than the units in existing ministries.

The ministry of economic cooperation and integration should have adequate authority to ensure effective implementation of integration measures at the national level as well as implementation of South–South cooperation policies and programmes and to carry out such functions as:

- Coordination of all government relationships with subregional, regional, international economic and development organizations;
- Monitoring and reviewing the member state's involvement and participation in such organizations with a view to making periodic assessments of the costs and benefits from these organizations;
- Coordination of close liaison with relevant ministries, departments, private sector or business community on issues of regional, international and bilateral cooperation;
- Maintenance of close liaison with the top officials of regional and international economic groupings both inside and outside Africa with a view to exchanging information of common concerns and learn from their experience as appropriate;
- Dissemination of regular information on the member state's activities in the area of economic integration and also publicizing through the media various forms of cooperation both inside and outside Africa to the general public.

As regards staffing, it would be necessary to offer career incentives to public servants to attract them to serve in institutions established under cooperation arrangements. The staff would have to be selected with the specific needs of regional integration and international economic cooperation in mind. They must be both narrowly technocratic and at the same time adopt broad perspectives and a multidisciplinary approach to development and its relationship to regional issues. Regionalism, integration and cooperation, whatever it is called, will not succeed if it is seen as a matter of secondary importance; secondary, say, to the important concerns of relationships with the US, with Britain, with France, with the European Union and, particularly in recent years, with the World Bank or the IMF.

Besides the ministry of economic cooperation and integration, there should also be established a consultative body such as a National Commission for Cooperation and Integration (NCCI) for permanent consultation on all issues of subregional, regional and international cooperation under the chairmanship of the Head of State or Government. The NCCI should be composed of government representatives, representatives of socio-economic associations – chambers of commerce and industry, association of manufacturers, employers' unions and all other social and economic operators to provide a democratic framework of regionalism. This institutional machinery would enable the people to find appropriate and adequate channels of participation in the member state's formulation and implementation of cooperation strategies and decisions at the subregional, regional and international levels.

There should be established, also, an Interministerial Coordination Committee (ICC) to formulate national policy and coordinate Government action in the area of subregional, regional and international economic cooperation. It should play a central role in the pursuit of national policies and initiations of economic integration strategies. The membership of the ICC should include ministers of foreign affairs, finance, planning and national development, commerce and industry, agriculture, transport and communications. The point must be stressed that apart from regional institutions, strong institutions at the national level are indispensable for implementing the large and increasingly diverse number of conclusions and recommendations formulated in regional cooperation or integration schemes.

At the risk of repetition, it is worth stressing that national development plans and integration strategies must be formulated in a mutually reinforcing manner, especially with regard to national policies that are linked to the external sector. To promote reflection of subregional programmes in national plans, each country could formally set out, in its statements of national policy or its development plan, explicit objectives relating to subregional or regional cooperation. A country adopting a five-year indicative plan could, for example, outline its strategy for subregional and regional cooperation, laying down specific targets and highlighting the links between such cooperation and national objectives. In addition, there should be regular procedures, including the use of statistical and other indicators, for reviewing performance in meeting goals of cooperation with other countries.

The effectiveness of any subregional or regional initiative depends on how it is perceived, accepted, and implemented at the national level. Member states of the communities should not only incorporate the community decisions into national policies and programmes; they must also collaborate in implementing community infrastructural programmes, such as construction of community roads and railways, telecommunications and other sectors, in their respective areas; strengthening community research centres located in individual countries to meet community needs; constructing segments of community electricity grids within their national boundaries; translating community common policies into national laws and regulations; supporting the community industrial programmes by providing financial support to private entrepreneurs, and mobilizing government institutions, public enterprises, government research centres and universities for the effective implementation of community programmes and projects in their respective areas.

STRENGTHENING THE INSTITUTIONAL CAPACITY OF THE ECONOMIC COMMUNITIES

The institutional deficiencies of the economic communities have already been noted as a critical factor in the management of economic integration in Africa. For there can be no doubt that strong, autonomous institutions play a crucial role in regional cooperation and integration. Strong and independent institutions are required to ensure that the grouping pursues clearly identified regional interests rather than the (sometimes) conflicting interests of different member states. This means that the economic community institutions should be endowed not only with a sufficient amount of automatically available resources and a clear mandate as well as decision making powers; they should also have a well-defined institutional framework and a skilled and competent personnel. This section of the chapter therefore devotes special attention to these critical issues in the integration process. It is aimed at strengthening the institutional and managerial capacity of the economic communities to enable them to respond effectively to the challenges of regionalism in the 1990s.

Rationalization of the Institutional Framework

Groupings are the major instruments for building viable subregional and regional economic cooperation and integration. Enhancing their effectiveness and technical competence is a prerequisite. The first step to strengthening the economic communities appears, therefore, to lie in the genuine rationalization of the present institutional framework with a view to harmonizing the activities of the different subregional groupings. The need to streamline subregional economic schemes was identified in the *Lagos Plan of Action*. It becomes especially relevant in the context of the establishment of a continent-wide economic community.

Given the fragmentation of Africa into small markets, there is no doubt that economic cooperation and integration that would emerge through rationalization and restructuring of the subregional economic institutions would impact positively on the development process of Africa. Hence the urgency for the rationalization of cooperation organizations, not only to prevent costly duplication, but also to establish certainty and a better investment climate, and to meet the challenges posed by the collapse of international commodity prices, declining export earnings for Africa's primary commodities, the slowdown in financial resource inflows, the lack of access to international investments and markets and, above all, the debilitating effect of the debt problem on the economies of the continent and the negative impact on development programmes.

The rationalization and restructuring of Africa's IGOs has become much more compelling and urgent to enable the continent to participate meaningfully and effectively in the emerging world of trading blocs and in the growing global linkages and interdependence. The establishment of a single but effective economic community in each of the subregions that can authoritatively speak for and negotiate on behalf of member states of the subregion on important economic and social issues will better enable African countries to face the difficulties that lie ahead. Since, for example, Africa will be dealing with an increasingly monolithic Europe, it cannot afford to continue to speak with a multiplicity of voices. Rather, the simple logic of economic self-preservation should awaken the countries of the various subregions to the need for greater unity and collective action. The experience under the successive Lomé Conventions is illustrative of the futility of having a multiplicity of customs unions and IGOs struggling to take advantage of the provisions of the Lomé system. The unhealthy rivalry and lack of coordination in the submission of projects for financing by the EU and other donors certainly militates against the effectiveness of the EU's assistance in promoting cooperation and development in the subregions.

Without doubt, rationalization will yield tremendous advantages. First, it will enable the subregional economic communities to contribute more effectively to the economic development of their member states, and reverse the present situation where many of them have little to show to justify their budgets. Second, it will promote the cost-effectiveness of these communities. Besides minimizing the dissipation of scarce resources which member states can ill afford, rationalization will also diminish the scope for persistent conflicts in the objectives and operations of those organizations that have constituted major obstacles to the process of economic integration in Africa.

Above all, rationalization will facilitate the promotion of joint or complementary projects, the exchange of skilled professionals and managerial personnel in the implementation of projects, and more beneficial utilization of educational and technical institutions for the training of high-calibre personnel. Besides, promoting interlinkages among industrial units in the African subregions will accelerate the industrial integration of the economies and contribute to balanced industrial development. And since industrial development holds the key to the economic transformation of the subregions, the need for industrial programming becomes an imperative in an overall economic integration strategy. Given the small size of most African economies, failure to harmonize the industrial programme at the subregional level has obviously retarded structural transformation.

Recognizing the level of sensitivity among the subregional economic communities and other groupings within each subregion, the Economic and Social Commission of the AEC should launch, in each subregion, and with the close involvement of all the economic communities, a programme on long-term coordination and harmonization. To this end, a mechanism, which for want of a better expression might be known as an Integration Committee, should be established in each subregion to be responsible for programme coordination, harmonization and rationalization. The Committee should also be responsible for examining long-term perspective issues on subregional, regional or continental integration. Membership of the Committee should include representatives of the subregional economic communities and other IGOs in the subregion.

The Establishment of Economic and Social Commissions and Community Parliaments

A second crucial step is to strengthen the institutional framework of the subregional and regional communities by establishing economic and social commissions and community parliaments. Functioning as a consultative and advisory body, the economic and social commissions would play an important role in the preparation of programmes, policies and strategies. Composed of active economic agents, the commissions would provide a mechanism for involvement of socio-economic interest groups and organizations in the decision making process at the community level. This would have the potential for inspiring massive support for integration in Africa.

The establishment of community parliaments also gives recognition to the imperative of representation from among the peoples of the member states in deliberations on integration matters. It provides an opportunity for their interests to be brought to bear on the development of the subregional or regional communities. Consequently, the community parliaments would contribute towards democratization by involving representatives of the peoples of the subregions in the integration process. This democratic element is essential for the health and survival of the communities, by preventing them from degenerating into a mere technocratic and almost bureaucratic construction. This is an important step forward since, to date, economic integration issues have been left to governments. These parliaments should represent all the political and social forces, not only political parties but also NGOs such as workers' unions, youth and students' associations, women, professional associations, businessmen, press corps and other identifiable groups. The community parliaments should therefore be endowed with power to decide on the future course of the economic communities.

In sum, the post-1990 economic communities – the revitalized ECOWAS, SADC and COMESA – in particular, are supposed to be designed not only for industrialists, economists and officials but also for the people whose voice would make itself heard through its representatives in parliament, whose job is to understand and to represent the interests of peoples of the subregions grouped together in the communities. Active participation of the peoples, through community parliaments, is a matter of justice. To repeat, the communities should never be the exclusive reserve of specialists and technocrats because their activities embrace the entire economic life of the member states, entail decisions of the most radical nature and have the most varied and widespread repercussions. It is through parliaments that the general public would participate in the work of the economic communities. Through them, the peoples of the subregions would be involved and kept informed of community activities in order to maintain the momentum towards regional integration.

The Importance of Community-owned Resources

A third crucial step towards strengthening of the community institutions is to ensure that the institutions have enough autonomy and own resources to undertake the tasks assigned to them. No serious development endeavours and integration programmes, for that matter, can be exclusively based on foreign assistance. Put differently, an organization to promote integration should have a certain independence from the participating governments so that it can effectively pursue 'community' interest rather than the sum of national interests. This independence requires a claim to own resources to carry out the community tasks. Otherwise the integration organization will constantly have to beg for funding and will not be able to formulate and implement integration policy.

There is a wide range of possibilities as far as the origin of 'own' or autonomous resources is concerned. It may be a percentage of duties levied on goods traded within the subregion, a specific tax for economic integration purposes, a portion of duties levied on goods originating from outside the subregion and other possibilities. The important thing is that such resources should be identified as those of the economic groupings concerned and that member states should have no bearing on them. The European experience shows how important a self-financing mechanism is and no significant progress towards economic integration can be achieved so long as economic groupings in Africa will not have at their disposal a regular and sufficient flow of resources.

Besides 'own' resources, the economic communities would need to initiate a comprehensive strategy for the effective mobilization of extra-budgetary resources, which are vitally important for increasing the scope and impact of their activities.[8] The secretariats have the responsibility to identify and exploit all avenues for obtaining extra-budgetary resources, or search for effective ways and means to bolster their extra-budgetary resources for implementation of community programmes and projects. To this end, the economic communities should not only diversify their sources of extra-budgetary funding but also should: (i) establish effective channels of communication and cooperation relationships with the donor community and development partners to improve relations with them; (ii) strive to report to donors in an effective and timely manner on the implementation of donor-funded projects and programmes; (iii) have profile and project documents prepared in a professional and attractive manner and market these vigorously; and (iv) enter into close dialogue with a diversified number of donors with a view to providing a steady flow of information between the parties and getting the donors interested in the communities' economic integration process.

Training in the Technology of Regional Integration

While financial resources are *sine qua non* for accelerating the process of integration, training or human resources development constitutes the fourth crucial step towards enhancing the capacity of the community institutions. Improving human resource capacity is a key element for the promotion of regional integration and cooperation. Put another way, human resource development and administrative, technical and research capacities are indeed fundamental in any strategy to promote regional cooperation. One aspect is the factual knowledge and skills to effectively set up and run regional integration organizations, as, for example, on monetary matters, customs regulations, quality inspection, standardization and so on. There is thus a need for more training in the technology of regional cooperation and integration.

Training of government officials and technocrats at both the national level and the level of secretariats charged with implementing regional policies as well as finding ways to motivate them, are key factors that may help to achieve the objective of economic cooperation and integration of the 1990s and beyond. A critical mass of dedicated people within the administration at both the national and subregional levels is needed to ensure continuity. Exchange programmes and increased contacts at the personal level also play a major role in building support for subregional cooperation initiatives and in creating a common language between the actors and stakeholders – both public and private – in the countries concerned.

As a priority concern, there is the need for training in the enhancement of the capacity of the communities to strengthen the human resource base and to equip staff members with the skills necessary to enable the secretariats to assume (increasing) responsibility in the identification, design, formulation and implementation of community programmes and projects.[9] Training would also be required in the areas of role and mandate of institutions, budgetary procedures, regional policy analysis and policy formulation, monetary cooperation and competition policy as well as transport policy. In an era when the ability to access and use modern transport and communications technologies is the key to exploiting opportunities in trade and investment, skilled professionals are needed to manage and operate telecommunications infrastructures.

With the objective of bringing about professionally and technically strong community secretariats, a comprehensive training and capacity-building programme targeted to all categories of staff would need to be developed and implemented. Specifically, the following group-training programmes are worth urgent attention: policy management retreat, or seminar on subregional policy analysis and policy development; seminar in general and programme management, on project feasibility studies; computer training and training in the planning, management and evaluation of training programmes; tailor-made training in monetary and financial policy programming techniques; and training in trade promotion, trade facilitation and marketing techniques. Other possibilities may include research on topics related to regional cooperation and integration, establishing special university curricula on economic integration, and founding integration journals. The personnel of the economic communities should be of high professional calibre and commitment, able to produce first-class practical results with solid widespread impact on critical subregional and regional development problems, and thereby establish strong credibility and respected reputation for itself and the institutions it serves.

To ensure that the gains from training programmes are consolidated, steps should be taken to establish a Training and Management Improvement Unit within the secretariats of the communities to plan, conduct, evaluate and generally coordinate regular and specialist training programmes, and undertake management improvement work either on its own, or in collaboration with external institutions or consultants.

Harnessing Information for Regional Integration

The fifth crucial step towards strengthening the institutions of the economic communities is information management. Information, including data, is a tool for development. Timely and reliable information and data are needed for economic policy making in the public sectors, for business decisions by private economic agents and for economic integration policy issues by community top executives. Information technology, driven by the convergence of computers, telecommunications, satellites, and fibre optics, is crucial for the knowledge-based economy of the future.

There is, in the secretariats of a number of communities, an acute lack of awareness of what other African countries can offer to substitute for the products presently being imported from developed countries. Institutionalized access to and quick transmission of information on rules and regulations implemented in partner countries and on bureaucratic procedures, publications and standardized statistical data, for example, are needed to lay the groundwork for effective regional cooperation and integration.

International Community Support

External support to the integration process in Africa constitutes the final crucial step towards strengthening the management of economic cooperation and integration at the subregional and regional levels. Even though the success of regional initiatives ultimately hinges on the will of the sub-Saharan Africa region itself to forge ahead, external support would be required to play an essential role.[10] Consistent with the recognition of the power of regionalism as a tool for Africa's economic development, more and more bilateral and multilateral donors have started to adopt their aid mechanisms to cater for this re-emerging priority. Some are actively exploring new possibilities of intervening in and support of regional activities as, for example, the World Bank and African Development Bank. Others already have firmly established procedures – for example, the UNDP with its multicountry programmes, the EU through the Lomé Conventions, France, Canada, the Scandinavian countries – and the IMF have acknowledged that there may be room for regionalism. But more, much more still needs to be done. Most donors are still far better equipped for cooperation with individual states than with groups of states.

Donors which have not yet established clear-cut procedures should take account of the priority given by Africa itself to regional integration and cooperation in order to ensure effectiveness of resources deployed. Others need to simplify access to regional resources and examine consistency of actions at national and at subregional or regional levels.

Undoubtedly, action by development partners can significantly reduce the constraints caused by policy divergence given their role in determining policy decisions. The interrelationship between regional cooperation and integration and other development policies, especially structural adjustment measures, should be used to ensure that positive measures reinforce, rather than contradict, each other.

It is, however, necessary to stress that donors should, as a matter of principle, avoid supporting projects at national level which hinder the achievement of the objectives of regional projects and programmes. Where efficient procedures exist in the region, donors should promote untied aid (for example, balance of payments support) and thus avoid diverting demand from the region. To make the most effective use of this opportunity, African integration organs should clearly articulate their needs and priorities for the implementation of their objectives.

Considering the major difficulties facing existing integration organs, it could be said that international support for African integration would go a long way if devoted largely to strengthening cooperation and integration in such areas as: (i) rationalization of existing institutions; (ii) the development of multinational projects; (iii) the improvement of regional infrastructure relevant to raising the level of productivity and increasing the competitiveness of African products in world markets; (iv) enhancing manpower resources through the transfer of know-how (exchange programmes between institutions) and research networking; (v) supporting programmes which improve public awareness of regional cooperation and integration as a priority area of African development (publicity campaigns, information on the benefits of regionalism, compensatory policies to be implemented, and so on); (vi) the removal of barriers to trade and factor movements; and (vii) increased cooperation in the area of monetary and financial services.

Of considerable importance, too, is the need for the international community to work towards ensuring that the international trading environment is conducive to the cooperation and integration efforts of the African countries. A key area of action in this regard will be keeping regional cooperation and integration in Africa high on the international agenda.

CRUCIAL FACTORS IN IMPLEMENTING THE AEC TREATY

With the emergence of trade blocs in Europe, America and Asia, it is most likely that future relationships between Africa and these blocs will be guided largely by commercial considerations, with little or no concessionary elements. It is important therefore that Africa should consider that the most important response would be an effective mobilization of Africa's own regional and subregional economic groupings to achieve rapid structural transformation and high levels of productivity and competitiveness. In this regard, acceleration of the implementation process of the AEC Treaty is vital for Africa's survival in a world of trading blocs. Not only does the AEC open a new chapter in Africa's integration; it could also have beneficial effects on the integration process, in particular by 'providing a continental framework for the rationalization of integration organs and institutions'. The successful implementation of the treaty would depend in a large measure on several crucial factors to which member states, who are the signatories of the treaty as well as the target beneficiaries, and who retain the ownership of the AEC, must pay special attention. Among these factors is first, the structure and capability of the single OAU/AEC secretariat to which attention has been drawn in the previous chapter.

Although, as noted above, the Abuja Treaty was ratified in 1994 to pave the way for its implementation, the AEC has still no secretariat of its own to vigorously and effectively pursue the task of implementation. The restructuring of the OAU secretariat to provide for two basic functions – the implementation of the AEC Treaty on the one hand, and performance of political functions on the other – is still under discussion. As indicated earlier in Chapter 5, a single OAU/AEC secretariat with the Secretary-General of the OAU as also the Secretary-General of the AEC, and with the responsibilities for the implementation of the AEC Treaty as well as the pursuit of the expanded political functions of the OAU would not appear to give the all-important AEC the much needed identity, impact and independence of action. The recently assumed new role of the OAU in conflict prevention, management and resolution, on which almost nearly all attention of the organization is being focused, would for a long time continue to dominate the issue of AEC Treaty implementation.

Given the problems and difficulties of a full transformation of the present OAU Secretariat into the secretariat of the AEC, assuming that this is a desirable objective, the continued reliance on the secretariat of a political organization as a secretariat for the AEC will not allow the implementation of the AEC Treaty to have at its disposal, the total services, expertise and commitment available in that secretariat. There are, indeed, serious problems associated with the structure, procedures, and staffing of the secretariat, and with the greater devotion and commitment to political issues almost to the total exclusion of the AEC which up to now has no visibility in the OAU secretariat. Although provision has been made for regular meetings of the chief executives of the OAU, ECA and ADB within the framework of a 'Joint Secretariat' to supplement the capacity of the OAU to cope with the new tasks of implementing the AEC Treaty, it does not appear, on the basis of its present showing, to be an effective mechanism.

What is required is a separate AEC secretariat with its own secretary-general, and a technically equipped and well-trained professional staff, to be responsible for the establishment, servicing and functioning of all other institutions of the community, from the most supreme, the Assembly of Heads of State and Government, to task forces and *ad hoc* bodies set up to deal with specific issues; for taking action on and supervising implementation of the AEC Treaty, protocols, decisions and resolutions of the legislative organs; for initiation of ideas and proposals for action by other institutions, on a vast range of subject areas bearing on the operations of the community and the realization of its aims and objectives; for ensuring that the integration process is on course and that the dynamics of the process are guided and directed towards desirable ends; and in this regard, for formulating policies, plans and programmes and taking charge of their execution.

Indeed, against the background of the major changes evolving on the international political and economic scene which have given new impetus to regionalism, the AEC would require an independent, vibrant secretariat that could provide a new direction to current integration process in Africa, direct the surge of interest on the subject of economic integration into constructive and productive channels and respond to the globalization of the economy and of financial services, as well as the tremendous developments in information technology which threaten to marginalize Africa further. Sharing a secretariat with the OAU, an essentially continental political organ, which operates under severe constraints and suffers from an overwhelming crisis of confidence, credibility and relevance and, above all, has an extremely limited capacity to handle effectively the intricacies and challenges of regionalism of the 1990s and beyond – all this does question our hope for an effective and dynamic single OAU/AEC secretariat and, in fact, the African Economic Community as a whole.

The AEC and the Linking of SAPs with Integration

Besides the factors highlighted above, the AEC should make every effort to improve interactions between structural adjustment and economic integration and that the two must be made to relate to each other positively. In this regard, the AEC will be expected to emphasize those measures which are likely to improve favourable interactions between economic integration and structural adjustment programmes. Improving interactions between the two objectives requires closer economic coordination and harmonization at the regional level, as well as joint action at the regional level to improve the efficiency of the national SAPs.[11]

The AEC action, in this regard, has become necessary, since there has been no serious, systematic attempt by any agency or donor to operationalize effectively ways in which integration and adjustment might be interwoven and made mutually reinforcing. The World Bank's landmark report in 1989, *Sub-Saharan Africa: From Crisis to Sustainable Growth,* places considerable emphasis on regional integration as a means for overcoming the deficiencies of fragmented and small national markets which were economically unviable. Yet IMF/World Bank adjustment programmes in Africa have contained little to translate those worthy thoughts into operational reality. The CBI, sponsored jointly by the World Bank, the EU and the ADB, provides an umbrella under which different experiments are being tried to induce greater regional interaction in trade and investment. But the linkage between the CBI initiatives and adjustment efforts is not particularly clear.[12] Thus throughout Africa SAPs and regional integration have been pursued as two separate initiatives, employing their own distinct modalities, processes and institutional conduits.

However, in view of the links between integration and adjustment, we may ask what is the best way to make sure that these two components of cooperation converge. This quest for convergence raises a number of parallel problems. First, how to ensure that the integration process is sustainable before any significant progress has been made in structural adjustment; and the reverse: how structural adjustment can be facilitated by strengthening regional integration. Second, what forms of integration and economic policy coordination should be given priority. And third, how to ensure that the sequence, the pace and the timetabling of stabilization/adjustment policies (short- to medium-term policies) and integration policies (long-term policies) are compatible and that they converge.

There is no single answer to these three questions. For instance, as regards compatibility and convergence, if a distinction is made between sustainable and unsustainable integration measures, there cannot be a fundamental contradiction between adjustment and integration. However, at least three guidelines may be identified to serve to create the dynamic, mutually enriching relationship between regional integration and structural adjustment. The first involves the coordination of macro-economic and sectoral policies at regional level in order to minimize spillover effects that are damaging to domestic policies (and minimize the transfer of the costs of adjustment to neighbouring countries) and ensure that adjustment and integration policies are mutually reinforcing, though without allowing the pace to be dictated by the lowest reformer. The second involves trade and investment policy harmonization, and the third, attaching regional conditions to structural adjustment programmes (that is, channelling aid for reforms through regional institutions).

The AEC should encourage a thorough review of a regional impact of national macro-economic policies, and also encourage the regional economic communities to play a role in implementing national SAPs, and explore actions that member states can take jointly which would complement or render more efficient their several national SAPs. Although the few attempts made to explore the regional dimensions of SAPs have not been encouraging,[13] the experience still provides a useful starting point for the AEC to examine the question.

ENHANCING SOUTH–SOUTH COOPERATION

Developments on the international scene, characterized, among other things, by the new trading environment ushered in by the Uruguay Round, are creating a radically new world environment which demands not only new initiatives to speed up the process of economic integration in Africa; it also makes it necessary for developing countries to strengthen cooperation among themselves in order to achieve collective self-sufficiency and improve their position in the world economy. Indeed, the changing international relations in the 1990s should make it clear that the era of national, subregional and even regional isolationism is effectively gone.

Interregional cooperation among developing countries can provide additional support to the diversification efforts of African countries. This should involve, for example, (i) promotion of transport and communication networks and facilities, including shipping lines between Africa, Asia and Latin America; (ii) establishment of mechanisms for the financing of South–South trade and investment; (iii) promotion of multinational production and services; (iv) establishment of a network of technical support centres for research, consultancy and training; (v) the design and implementation of programmes of technical cooperation among developing countries (TCDC); and (vi) trade liberalization through the Global System of Trade Preferences (GSTP) and other arrangements.

As articulated in the May 1996 *Strategic Directions for the Economic Commission for Africa* (ECA), 'enhanced South–South cooperation offers many potential gains for Africa's development'.[14] It can hold enormous potential for Africa to capitalize on economic prosperity manifested in other regions of the developing world. South–South cooperation can be successful to the extent that concrete steps are being taken at the country level to forge such collaboration and to the extent that strong public–private linkages take place. While the locus of action in promoting South–South cooperation will mainly be at the national level, with governments and the private sector taking the lead roles, African regional institutions like the ECA can facilitate the process through a mix of measures. As an important aspect of the recent renewal programme to enable the Commission to serve Africa better, ECA can collaborate with the United Nations regional commissions in Asia (ESCAP) and Latin America (ECLAC) in organizing, among other things, investment forums between interested business groups from the three regions. Furthermore, it can collaborate with UNCTAD 'to strengthen the electronic trade network and support and encourage more African countries to link to the network'. And using the resources of its United Nations Trust Fund for African Development (UNTFAD), ECA can facilitate TCDC that enables African countries to learn from the experience of other developing regions about successful innovations in such areas as financial mediation and information technology adaptations.

South–South cooperation also offers unique opportunities for Africa in particular and the South in general to participate and compete in the new global trading system through the building of regional business, production and services ventures. Indeed, as stressed in *The United Nations System-wide Special Initiative on Africa* launched on 15 March 1996, South–South cooperation will also 'strengthen trade and financial links and the exchange of development experiences and scientific and technological innovations between Africa and the other regions of the South'.[15] It is timely therefore to build not only on the United Nations' many years of effort to foster South–South cooperation, stimulating interregional and national actions, but also, notably, the efforts of the South–South Commission, the Bandung Framework for Asia–Africa Cooperation of December 1994, which sprang from the October 1993 Tokyo International Conference on African Development (TICAD), and the recent International Conference on Understanding Contemporary Africa: India and South–South Cooperation held in February 1996 in New Delhi, India.[16]

This chapter has in a nutshell attempted to identify the internal deficiencies and limitations that require priority action to enable the integration process in Africa to respond effectively to the new realities of the 1990s. Past integration efforts hold important lessons for the future. The chapter has therefore stressed the need for an alternative approach to integration that takes into account the realities inherent in the African situation and aims at ensuring adequate and well-maintained economic infrastructure, maintaining sustainable agriculture and food security, and reducing dependence of industrial production on imported materials. More attention has also been focused on strengthening both the national and subregional or regional institutional and managerial capacity which has greatly slowed down the process of integration in Africa.

It should not be thought that the mere signing of an integration treaty will in itself bring development to the signatories. First of all, the integration instruments must be used positively by the member states, collectively and individually. Second, integration provides additional opportunities for national development and can be effective only to the extent that each member state has a set of well-conceived and properly implemented development policies and is capable of effective national economic management. Indeed, if economic integration is to succeed it must function essentially as a mechanism for supporting the national effort at development in each member state. Accordingly, governments must ask themselves how they can use the processes of regional integration and cooperate to underpin and extend the momentum for development which they are trying to generate. Finally, integration benefits member countries only to the extent that the public and private sectors continually undertake jointly and individually certain specific and concrete actions and tasks.

The rationalization and strengthening of the integration organs in the subregions will enhance the capacity of African countries to respond to the global changes and arrest the current trend towards their marginalization in the world economy. The importance of accelerating the process of implementing the African Economic Community Treaty which itself is a new reality, within which the process of intra-African economic cooperation and integration could be structured, has been briefly highlighted. Establishing the AEC will be a formidable task, requiring strong political commitment on the part of member countries along with substantive progress at the subregional levels in the promotion of economic cooperation and integration.

8 Conclusion: Time for Action

The combination of increasing regionalism, globalization of world production, rapid changes in technology and continued liberalization of world trade, has created a situation of great crisis for Africa which demands fundamental changes in policy and perspectives. For in the evolving world trading situation, the real winners will be those countries which are able to keep pace with technological development, creating and maintaining efficient, competitive production structures which would allow them to respond adequately to changing trends in demand in the world markets. The industrialized countries have responded to this challenge well ahead of the developing countries, especially those of Africa, as they have already adopted new policy measures and strategies. In major industrialized countries, a prominent aspect of this response has been a resurgence of interest in consolidation and further enlargement of their economic space so as, first, to stimulate, protect and support the development of the technological capacities; second, to encourage efficient, competitive industries; and third, to engender greater trade expansion. As noted above, this policy thrust has found concrete expression in the emergence and widening of economic arrangements among developed market-economy countries. 'Europe 1992' and NAFTA are two significant examples of such arrangements.

In the case of Africa, the profound changes taking place in the world economy present challenges and opportunities, as well as dangers and possibilities of serious economic, financial and market losses. It could further accentuate the socio-economic crisis of Africa and its increasing marginalization in the international economy, or it could trigger the turn-around process in Africa. To meet the challenge posed by the changing international trading environment of the 1990s and to become an active partner in the world economic system, Africa has to move fast towards pursuit of subregional, regional or continental constituency as the best guarantee of its survival in the increasingly competitive world. To this end, this concluding chapter seeks to do two things: first, to highlight the need for new initiatives to speed up the process of economic integration that would enable Africa to participate in the global trends that are going to shape the future of international economic relations; and second, to stress the imperative need for strengthening

169

the popular base of the process of economic integration as ingredients *par excellence* of sustainable developmental regionalism.

POLICY RESPONSES TO THE EMERGING REGIONAL AGE

As one of the 'best responses' to the growing regionalism in the world, there is great need for Africa to consolidate and strengthen its programmes for regional and subregional cooperation and integration. With a large number of mini-states which collectively account for only a very tiny proportion of world trade, a proportion which has declined even further in the past two decades, there is little doubt that Africa needs regionalism more than other regions. This explains why the strengthening of the integration mechanisms occupies a central position in the 1995 *Cairo Agenda for Action*. The *Agenda* calls on African countries to pool their resources and enhance cooperation, in order to achieve regional economic cooperation and integration so as to be competitive in world trade.[1] It also highlights the need for greater commitment, including more moral, material and financial support, to the various obligations on continental and regional cooperation, in particular on the implementation of the programmes collectively adopted by the member states of the economic groupings. The growth of regionalism has therefore made it more important for African countries to speed up their integration programmes and, in particular, to ensure a steady and consistent implementation of the Abuja Treaty establishing the African Economic Community.

Against the background of the persistence of tariff and non-tariff obstacles, the crucial question that African countries must address is whether they still need to maintain any tariff barriers on their intra-regional trade. Indeed, as Onitiri has recently underscored, now that barriers on extra-regional trade have been substantially reduced in the implementation of SAPs, African countries should aim to 'remove all tariff barriers on goods of regional origin entering intra-regional trade in the shortest time possible'.[2] Although this will still leave a number of non-tariff barriers to tackle, it will no doubt give a major boost to intra-regional trade. This is a measure that African countries should consider most seriously in view of the fact that internal free trade is now a common feature of all major trade blocs in all the continents. It has been achieved in the EU; it will be fully achieved in the Free Trade Area of the Americas (FTAA) by 2005. It will be achieved in ASEAN by 2003, and in APEC by 2010 for developed-country members and by 2020 for developing-country members.[3] Because of the present low level of intra-regional trade among African countries, Africa needs to achieve regional free trade much sooner than the other developing regions.

New initiatives in the process of economic cooperation and integration should also involve, among other things, first, speeding up the liberalization provisions of the subregional economic communities as well as those of the African Economic Community, so that the objectives of complete liberalization of intra-African trade can be achieved much sooner than the year 2000 targeted in the Abuja Treaty; second, encouraging current efforts to rationalize the integration organs at the subregional level; and third, promoting new efforts to achieve the harmonization of macro-economic policies at the subregional level.

In responding to the challenge of Europe 1992 and other emerging changes in the global economy, the African subregional economic communities and African Economic Community should learn from the experience of the European Union itself. The acceleration of the process of European economic integration in recent years stems largely from the growing realization by the European leaders that as the twenty-first century approaches, the nation-state has become increasingly inadequate for creating the right environment for the promotion of welfare and security.[4] The willingness of Europe to put an end to parochial nationalism in the drive for economic integration is paradoxical and instructive for ECOWAS, COMESA, SADC and other subregional economic communities. Given the weakness and smallness of the economies of these groupings, integration and the surrender of sovereignty which it implies are a *sine qua non* for halting the economic decay and ensuring the survival of the member states of these communities in an increasingly competitive international economic system that is divided into blocs. If the marginalization and increasing immiseration of the countries of these economic groupings in the global economy is not to be aggravated, economic integration with an approach appropriate to the African conditions, has to be pursued with greater vigour. In the final analysis, the optimal response of member states of the African subregional and regional economic communities to Europe 1992 and the other trading blocs should be intensification, rationalization and revitalization of their integration process leading to a continental African economic interaction.

Overall, the adverse developments from Europe 1992 and the other regional trading blocs should offer real opportunities to Africa in many areas. They should force African countries to diversify their exports more rapidly; engage in increased export processing; seek alternative export markets; expand intra-African trade; raise the quality of their exports; promote South–South trade and general cooperation; enforce reduction of excessive external dependence through diminished foreign exchange earnings and rising import costs; and increase national and collective self-reliance with growing internationalization of the engine of African development.

Economic integration should no longer be considered as a mere development option in Africa. There is a growing recognition, strengthened by the integration process in Europe, America and South-east Asia, that such integration is a real necessity for the economic survival of the African countries and a key element of successful international competitiveness and trade performance. For these countries, the need for more substantial and sustained collective efforts within integration frameworks cannot be overemphasized; it is essential both for acquiring technical capabilities and for designing competitive, efficient production structures.

Above all, traditional integration strategies, based on the inward-oriented, import substitution, industrial development, will have to be reappraised and reconciled with the new requirements for becoming competitive on an international scale. Regional economic integration should be increasingly seen as an instrument to support medium- to long-term development strategies consistent with increasing the participation of African countries in the world economy. Indeed, the pace of the integration process, in the industrialized countries, should help to instil a sense of urgency regarding revitalization and consolidation of the integration process in Africa. ECOWAS, COMESA, SADC, ECCAS, AMU and especially the AEC would have to rededicate themselves to their integration objectives so as to meet their obligations under integration treaties.

And finally, as regards future Africa–EU relations beyond Lomé IV, it must be stressed that against the background of the major developments that would have taken place in the world economy, in Europe, and in the three regions making up the ACP, by the time the present agreement runs out in the year 2000, to negotiate the old type of Lomé Convention would be like 'putting old wine in a new bottle'. It certainly will not meet the requirement of helping Africa to achieve the structural transformation that will enable the continent to participate more effectively in the global economy. I therefore agree with Onitiri[5] that what will be more in tune with Africa's future needs would be an agreement with Europe that would: (i) contribute substantially to Africa's effort to create a single continental market for goods, services, capital and labour; (ii) provide incentives for small African countries, most of them least-developed, to participate in, and benefit from such a continental market; (iii) support Africa's efforts to create a favourable environment for private foreign investment by expanding infrastructure, particularly transport and communications, promoting cooperation in energy development and utilization and improving the facilities for human resource development; (iv) contribute to ongoing efforts to promote cross-border investment by African and foreign investors; (v) restructure the provisions on industrial cooperation to encourage cross-border agreements between African countries and TNCs to exploit Africa's natural resources for local processing, cross-border trade and exports; and (vi) provide incentives to encourage the growing rank of Africa's private sector to improve and extend their operations, particularly in cross-border activities.

An agreement with such features will be more likely to contribute to improved productivity and increased competitiveness in African countries, promote the inflow of foreign investment, and enable African countries to better face the longer-term challenges of diversification and increased participation in the world market.

TOWARDS SUSTAINABLE DEVELOPMENTAL REGIONALISM

One important lesson to be learnt from the past experience of regional economic cooperation and integration in Africa is the marginalization of the people from the process of regionalism. Hence accelerated recovery with transformation in Africa through subregional and regional cooperation requires a new domestic order with full democratization and popular participation. The pervasive political instability and crisis of legitimacy and civil strife in African countries are incompatible with successful economic cooperation and integration for accelerated recovery and transformation. As one of the common causes of these political problems is often the perceived denial of democratic participation, African countries must open up to ensure the full participation of all sections of their societies in the process of developmental regionalism.[6]

Of special importance is the potential role of the growing NGO sector in changing the structures of Africa's governance in favour of greater democratization and institutional accountability. Alan Fowler has recently examined the extent to which NGOs contribute to the needed democratization of African countries by 'pluralizing and strengthening civil society'.[7] Similarly, observers like Hyden, Frantz and the World Bank have analysed how NGOs help increase diversity of opportunity in society, a prerequisite for the success of market-oriented policies which stress competition and freedom of choice and action.[8] By providing variety and autonomy in associational choice, they promote the formation of interest groups which can challenge monopolistic tendencies and the poor performance of state enterprises and thereby contribute to changing the present situation in favour of more democracy at both the national and economic cooperation and integration levels.

More significant is the need to strengthen the popular base of the process of regionalism in Africa – the need for a group of a popular dynamic in support of regionalism: pressure groups both for participation and mobilization of public opinion in the direction of the economic communities. A group of popular dynamic means a momentum propelling integration forward. It means, as well, an attachment or commitment to integration and action to give effect to the attachment or commitment. Indeed, it is the dynamic that would provide the motivation for actions to promote integration, and support for actions taken. And as long as groups in the African subregions remain more or less on the sidelines or limited participants, there would be little or no dynamic propelling and supporting of the movement towards evolution of subregional economic communities.

To be sure, unless the people of Africa are themselves aware of the process of regionalism and are interested in, and enthusiastic to make an effort, all the extensive and desperate efforts to revitalize or redesign existing arrangements and to create new ones, as evident in recent years, may not improve the current low rate of success.[9] The centrality of the people and their institutions in the process of integration and community building is critical to the process of regionalism. Regional integration in Africa will continue to be a pipe-dream unless the peoples of the subregions determine its content, form and directions; and are themselves its active agent. While the national governments must no doubt be in control of the commanding heights of the economy and must lay down policies and guide the direction of change, ample opportunities should be provided for the active participation of the people in the development process – that is in the conception, planning, programming and implementation. Therefore, the effective mobilization of public support should be regarded as a crucial ingredient in recipes for implementing and maintaining cooperation and integration oriented towards collective self-reliant, indigenous, and self-sustaining development. Hence though ECOWAS, COMESA, SADC and the all-embracing AEC may be powerful means for achieving economic communities and accelerating development in Africa, in the final analysis, man is both the means and the end. The best study of the strategy of economic integration, particularly in the 1990s, a decade of human development strategy, is man.

There should therefore be deliberate efforts on the part of the subregional and regional economic communities in Africa to create active, supporting integration constituencies among, in particular, socio-economic groups in the population: trade unions, professional associations, chambers of commerce, employers' organizations, academical bodies, women's and peasant organizations. These groups must be given the opportunity to mount systematic pressure to generate the necessary political will for sustainable developmental regionalism. In particular, trade unions and employers' associations, which are the fundamental social partners in development and democracy must be given adequate recognition at national, subregional and regional levels. The trade unions may be responsible for broadly based and organized popular opinion favourable to the economic communities. Their support will be dictated by the fact that it is through common economic efforts at the community level that the standards of living may be raised and full employment secured. Apart from articulating popular support, the unions may, when properly organized, be in advance of some of the member governments in giving priority to community over national interests when some elements of choice occur. Indeed, effective and sustainable economic democracy would very much depend on the extent to which these social partners are vigorously empowered and systematically integrated in the development process as articulated in the *African Charter for Popular Participation in Development and Transformation*.[10] The constant pressure of such groups would ensure that the issue of economic integration is kept high on the agenda. The successes of the integration efforts would reinforce the momentum thus built and the integration process could in this way be said to have created its own momentum.

The economic communities in Africa must encourage and devote some of their resources to the foundation of integration journals and promotion of research and seminars in the field of integration. Such an undertaking would in no small measure contribute to the broadening of outlook of socio-economic groups in the subregions as well as the enlargement of their regional understanding, all of which would help to create a favourable nationwide climate for the development of integration movement. As a corollary of this, in order to infuse among the younger generation of Africans a tradition of integrative spirit and thinking, a course on economic integration should be taught as an independent branch of study in all research institutes, schools, colleges, and higher institutions in Africa. And to facilitate communication between the various cultural and linguistic groups, the study of French and English, and possibly Portuguese should be made compulsory in all high schools and colleges. All this would help to create a long-lasting intellectual foundation for the movement towards African economic community.

Closely related to this is the instrumental role which the media and the press should play in the popularization of the economic cooperation and integration schemes to increase the level of awareness of the largest section of the population about the contribution which regionalism can make to African economic and social development. The success of the implementation of the Abuja Treaty establishing the African Economic Community, the new

COMESA and SADC treaties and the revised ECOWAS treaty will depend not only on the actions to be taken by African governments alone, but also on the extent to which the various segments of African society will be sensitized and made aware of the main objectives of these treaties. In this regard, it is the media and the press which, given the requisite enabling environment, should inculcate into all segments of the population what one may term an 'integration ideology' to stimulate responses from the industrial, commercial, agricultural, labour, elite and student leaders.

There is, undoubtedly, the imperative need for a systematic media and press campaign in Africa to highlight: (i) the importance of the AEC, ECOWAS, SADC, COMESA and other subregional communities for Africa's survival in view of the political and economic changes taking place in other parts of the world; (ii) benefits to be derived from communities for African peoples and countries in the short-, medium- and long-term; (iii) the role and contribution of each African in the establishment and success of these communities; (iv) national legal and administrative reforms required for the realization of the objectives of the communities; and (v), the role which the AEC in particular, can play in the global economy. Besides, to stimulate the active participation of the African people in the integration process, the Conference of African Ministers of Information should give top priority to the popularization of the AEC and the subregional economic communities at the national, regional and continental levels. Copies of the AEC Treaty, as well as the ECOWAS, COMESA and SADC treaties should be widely circulated to educational institutions, organs and bodies of the private sector, the military and religious establishments and student organizations. Furthermore, instances of a successful regional economic grouping like the European Union could be pointed out to counter 'fatalistic pessimism', and also show how people in various walks of life can facilitate such cooperation. All this is required not only to dispel apathy arising from insufficient information about the communities, their aims and objectives, but also to limit the intensity of efficacy of the national sovereignty concepts prevalent in Africa and to overcome the lack of political will.

Consequently, one important function that the governments in African countries must perform in order to enhance promotion of the process of economic cooperation and integration is to create the enabling environment for developmental regionalism. Besides creating an environment to facilitate, *inter alia*, the intra-regional movement of goods, services, capital and labour and other customs union or trade matters, there must be an environment for private sector operators with a view to first, involving them more closely in regional initiatives, and second, increasing dialogue between the private sector and government departments and institutions responsible for regional initiatives. Above all, there must be an environment in terms of political freedom and human rights: freedom of speech, or thought, and of association; freedom from economic and personal insecurity; and freedom from arbitrary arrest. Individuals must be able to express new ideas, to articulate thoughts without being molested. It is in such a society that values of self-reliance, dedication and loyalty can be developed. In other words, there must be the democratization of the development process at the national, subregional, and regional levels. What, then, are the indications towards this process in Africa? What are the chances of success of the new regional initiatives? What also are the emerging developments in Africa today? To what extent can they affect the process of regionalism?

THE WAY FORWARD

Once it is admitted that closer regional cooperation and integration is a condition for the development of Africa in the 1990s, the question which arises is why the new regional initiatives should succeed where previous attempts failed. There are indications that the new regionalism has several advantages over the previous one. Indeed, the most obvious advantage is that policy makers today have the benefit of hindsight. Many of the new regional initiatives aim to be more outward-oriented and pragmatic. They also appear to be more sensitive to the context in which implementation must take place. The second most obvious advantage is that both the national and international contents are more conducive to success.

At the national level, the widening influence of democracy has created new possibilities for African populations to take more active part in shaping the economic and the political landscape. This is complemented by economic reforms which favour increased participation of the private sector and productivity gains which should improve the competitiveness of local firms on international markets. The widespread adoption and pursuit of wide-ranging economic reforms by African countries is now a matter of record. These reforms provide an indispensable background for regional cooperation and integration. There is also now developing a gradual progression towards more participatory forms of government. Both these processes need to be encouraged, nurtured and supported by all, including Africa's development partners. The significance of these developments in the present context rests on the fact that they can make an important contribution to the African integration process.

The pursuit of bold structural adjustment and other economic reform policies will remove some of the rigidities in national economic policy, promote flexible responses to the dynamics of internal and international economic relationships and remove distortions which often stand in the way of positive approaches to integration. As noted earlier, inconvertibility of currencies and divergent policy stances have been a major constraint on integration efforts. In the broad trends towards reforms, African countries should now move towards greater harmonization of macro-economic policies and away from the often wrong response of putting restrictions on trade and payments. The requirements of adjustment should not divert attention from long-term developmental and integration objectives. Adjustment programmes should as far as possible take into account their potential impact on regional cooperation and integration.

Although African governments are now moving towards more open participatory forms of governance, there is still a lot of ground to cover qualitatively. There is a need to inculcate a greater appreciation of the fact that it is also possible to make a positive contribution to good government under constitutional rule, even if one is not in the ruling party. These emerging trends can and should be developed and expanded so that participatory government is taken to mean consensus-building and broader consultation of affected sectors in the evolution of policy. Such a development will lay the foundations for subregional and regional contacts at the sectoral levels with the potential to strengthen trade. The major players in the enterprise sector such as the chambers of commerce and industry, the banks, the stock exchanges and others could coordinate their policies much more easily as operational policies and would reflect inputs from the principal participants themselves.

On the international level, there is now a more supportive environment for regional endeavours. The first wave of regionalism basically went against the prevailing mood and was generally considered to be inimical to the GATT philosophy. Today, even traditional sceptics of regionalism are beginning to seriously consider its merits as an instrument for advancing the cause of multilateralism. This more favourable climate comes at a time when the general level of protection in the world economy is, on the whole, lower than it was during the 1960s and 1970s. Consequently, it is now widely accepted that increased regional cohesion through the creation of economically viable areas could reinforce and help sustain the economic and political reforms being undertaken by African countries. Another decisive element stems from the intensification of regional links in other parts of the world, which has reinforced the conviction of African leaders that they must unite in order to enable the continent to participate more fully in the new international relationships.

However, regional efforts alone will not be sufficient to improve the economic prospects of Africa. They can certainly not be considered to be a substitute for national economic adjustment, good governance and the strengthening of the human resources. It is, however, clear from the analysis of experiences in Africa and elsewhere that regional efforts can, under certain conditions, yield significant benefits. It is also clear that many development issues transcend national boundaries and have to be tackled at a regional level. Regional cooperation and integration not only complement national development efforts but also induce positive reactions at national level particularly by creating a more favourable trade and investment climate, and can thus be a part of the solution.

The main theme of this concluding chapter is to stress that if genuine and sustainable economic integration is to be pursued in the 1990s and beyond, the approach to date – the denial of participatory democracy to socio-economic groups in the process of regionalism – should be changed. Not only does the strategy require rethinking, but also the mechanisms need to be reviewed. Regionalism cannot be imposed from above. It has to develop from the grassroots. Hence the importance of encouraging active participation of non-governmental social and economic operators whose relative neglect is undoubtedly one of the major causes of the lack of progress in the process of economic cooperation and integration. Therefore, it is imperative for Africa, in the light of current developments in the rest of the world, to map out a strategy of regionalism which incorporates the human factor and the democratic imperatives in order to face the challenges posed by the emerging regional age and lay the foundation for sustainable development in the twenty-first century. It is time for action.

Notes

CHAPTER 1

1. John Sloan, 'The Strategy of Developmental Regionalism: Benefits, Distribution, Obstacles and Capabilities', *Journal of Common Market Studies*, Vol. 10, No. 2, (December 1971), p. 142.
2. Jaime de Melo and Arvind Panagariya, *The New Regionalism in Trade Policy: An Interpretative Summary of a Conference*, (Washington DC: World Bank and London: Centre for Economic Policy Research, 1992), p. 1.
3. *World Bank Policy Research Bulletin*, Vol. 3, No. 3, (May–July 1992), p. 1.
4. Augusto de la Torre and Margaret R. Kelly, *Regional Trade Arrangements*, (Washington DC: International Monetary Fund, March 1992), p. 41.
5. Paul Krugman, 'Regionalism versus Multilateralism: analytical notes', in Jaime de Melo and Arvind Panagariya (eds), *New Dimensions in Regional Integration*, (Cambridge: Cambridge University Press, 1993), pp. 74–5.
6. Robert C. Hine, 'Regionalism and the Integration of the World Economy', *Journal of Common Market Studies*, Vol. xxx, No. 2, (June 1992), p. 120.
7. *Ibid.*
8. Allan Bollard and David Mayes, 'Regionalism and the Pacific Rim' *Journal of Common Market Studies*, Vol. xxx, No. 2, (June 1992), pp. 196-7.
9. Jaime de Melo and Arvind Panagariya and Dani Rodrik, 'The New Regionalism', *Finance and Development*, Vol. 29, No. 4, (December 1992), p. 37.
10. *Ibid.*
11. B. Hettne and A. Inota, 'The New Regionalism: Implications for Global Development and International Security', UNU/WIDER, Helsinki, 1994. Cited in Percy S. Mistry, 'Open Regionalism: Stepping Stone or Millstone toward an Improved Multilateral System?', in Jan Joost Teunissen (ed.), *Regionalism and the Global Economy: The Case of Latin America and the Caribbean*, (The Hague: FONDAD, 1995), p. 13.
12. C. Braga, 'The New Regionalism and its Consequences', (Washington DC: World Bank, August 1994). Cited in Mistry 'Open Regionalism'.
13. This section of the discussion benefited greatly from Mistry, 'Open Regionalism'.
14. Jaime de Melo, Arvind Panagariya and Dani Rodrik, 'The New Regionalism: a Country Perspective', in de Melo and Panagariya (eds), *New Dimensions*, p. 159.
15. De Melo and Panagariya, *The New Regionalism*, p. 12.
16. For details see John Whalley, 'Regional Trade Arrangements in North America: CUSTA and NAFTA', in de Melo and Panagariya (eds), *New Dimensions*, pp. 352–87. Also John Whalley, 'CUSTA and NAFTA: Can WHFTA BE FAR BEHIND?', *Journal of Common Market Studies*, Vol. xxx, No. 2, (June 1992), pp. 125–41.
17. For details see S.K.B. Asante, 'Africa and the Brave New World of Regionalism', *West Africa*, (10–16 September 1990).
18. H.M.A. Onitiri, *Regionalism and Africa's Development*, UNCTAD Study, (November 1995).

19. See 'The America drift towards free trade', *The Economist*, (8 July 1995).
20. ECA, *African Charter for Popular Participation in Development and Transformation*, (Arusha, 1990).
21. UNDP, *Human Development Report* series, (New York and Oxford: Oxford University Press, 1990, and so on).
22. Jean-Claude Boidin, 'Regional Cooperation in the face of Structural Adjustment', *Courier*, No. 112, (November–December 1988), p. 67.
23. S.K.B. Asante, 'New Hope for Africa: Pan-African Economic Community', *Development and Cooperation*, No. 4, (December 1992), pp. 21–2.

CHAPTER 2

1. A. Antonio Dadome and Luis E. di Marco, 'The Impact of Prebisch's Ideas on Modern Economic Analysis', in Luis E. di Marco (ed.), *International Economic and Development: Essays in Honour of Raul Prebisch*, (New York: 1972), p. 27.
2. See, for example, Bela Balassa, *The Theory of Economic Integration*, (Homewood, III: Richard D. Irwin, 1961); John Pinder, 'Positive and Negative Integration: Some Problems of Economic Union in the EEC', *World Today*, (24 March 1968); and George C. Abangwu, 'Systems Approach to Regional Integration in West Africa', *Journal of Common Market Studies*, Vol. 13, Nos 1, 2 (1975), pp. 117–25.
3. Fritz Machlup, 'A History of Thought on Economic Integration', in Fritz Machlup (ed.), *Economic Integration: Worldwide, Regional, Sectoral*, (London: Macmillan, 1978), p. 62
4. *Ibid.*, p. 63.
5. Pinder, 'Positive and Negative Integration', p. 90.
6. See J. Tinbergen, *International Economic Integration*, (Elsevier, Amsterdam, 1954).
7. Willem Molle, *The Economics of European Integration: Theory, Practice, Policy*, (Aldershot, Hants: Dartmont Publishing Co. Ltd, 1994), p. 8.
8. Bingu W.T. Mutharika, *Toward Multinational Economic Cooperation in Africa*, (New York: Praeger, 1972), p. 15.
9. *Ibid.*, See also B.T.G. Chidzero, 'The Meaning of Economic Integration in Africa' *East Africa Journal*, (December 1965), p. 23.
10. E.B. Haas, 'The Study of Regional Integration: Reflections on the Joy and Anguish of Pretheorizing', *International Organization*, Vol. 24, No. 4, (Autumn 1970), p. 610.
11. Isebill V. Gruhn, *Regionalism Reconsidered: The Economic Commission for Africa*, (Boulder: Westview Press, 1979), p. 15.
12. Molle, *The Economics of European Integration*, p. 10.
13. Ali M. El-Agraa, *The Theory and Measurement of International Economic Integration*,(New York: St. Martin's Press, 1989), p. 2.
14. Joseph Frankel, *Contemporary International Relations Theory and the Behaviour of States*, (London: Oxford University Press, 1973), p. 48.

15. Jacob Viner, *The Customs Union Issue*, (New York: Carnegie Endowment for International Peace, 1950); and R. Lipsey, 'The Theory of Customs Union: A General Survey', *Economic Journal*, Vol. 70, (September 1960), pp. 496–513.
16. See, for example, Dudley Seers, 'The Limitations of the Special Case', *Bulletin of the Oxford Institute of Economics and Statistics*, (May 1963), p. 83.
17. H.M.A. Onitiri, 'Towards a West African Economic Community', *Nigerian Journal of Economic and Social Studies*, Vol. 5, (1963), p. 33.
18. Amitai Etzioni, *Political Unification: A Comparative Study of Leaders and Forces*, (New York: 1964), pp. 318–21.
19. Roger D. Hansen, 'Regional Integration: Reflections on a Decade of Theoretical Efforts', *World Politics*, Vol. 21, No. 2, (January 1969), p. 261.
20. Joseph S. Nye, Jr. 'Comparing Common Markets: A Revised New-Functionalist Model', *International Organizatgion*, Vol. 24, No. 4, (Autumn 1970), pp. 831–2.
21. E.B. Haas, *The Uniting of Europe: Political, Social and Economic Forces 1950–57*, (Stanford: Stanford University Press, 1958), p. 13.
22. Felippe Herrera, 'Economic Integration and Political Reintegration', in Mildred Adams, (ed.), *Latin America: Evolution or Explosion?*, (New York: Dodd, Mead, 1963), p. 99.
23. James D. Cochrane, *The Politics of Regional Integration: The Central American Case*, (New Orleans: Tulane University Press, 1969), Preface.
24. Donald Rothchild, 'The Political Implications of the Treaty' *East African Economic Review*, Vol. 3, No. 2, New Series, (December 1967), p. 14.
25. Mutharika, *Toward Multinational Economic Cooperation*, p. 15.
26. James Nti, 'ECOWAS: An Approach to Regional Economic Cooperation'. A Talk at the 18th Induction Course for newly recruited Foreign Service Officers, Lagos, Nigeria: July 1980.
27. See for example, Ahmed, A.H.M. Aly, *Economic Cooperation in Africa: In Search of Direction*, (Boulder/London: Lynne Rienner Publishers, 1994); S.K.B. Asante, *The Political Economy of Regionalism in Africa: A Decade of the Economic Community of West African States [ECOWAS]*, (New York: Praeger, 1986); R.I. Onwuka and A. Sesay (eds), *the Future of Regionalism in Africa*, (London: Allen and Unwin, 1986).
28. For example, World Bank, *Accelerated Development in Sub-Saharan Africa: An Agenda for Action*, (Washington DC: The World Bank, 1981); and especially, *Sub-Saharan Africa: from Crisis to Sustainable Growth*, (Washington DC: The World Bank, 1989), pp. 148–62. Also, the European Community, *The European Community and Africa*, (Brussels: 1984).
29. Organization of African Unity (OAU), *Lagos Plan of Action for the Economic Development of Africa, 1980–2000*, (Geneva: Institute of Labour Studies, 1981).
30. Robert S. Browne and Robert J. Cummings, *The Lagos Plan of Action vs The Berg Report: Contemporary Issues in African Development*, (Washington DC: Howard University African Studies Program, 1984), p. 37.
31. E. Oteiza and F. Sercovich, 'Collective Self-reliance: selected Issues', *International Social Science Journal*, Vol. 28, No. 4, (1976), p. 666.
32. Ruth Schachter Morgenthau, 'The Developing Status of Africa', *Annals of the American Academy of Political and Social Science*, Vol. 432, (July 1977), p. 87.
33. See United Nations, 'Developing Countries and Levels of Development', E/AC.54/L.81, 1975.

34. Ann Seidman, 'Africa and the World Economy: Prospects for Real Economic Growth', *Issue*, Vol. 8, No. 4, (Winter 1978), p. 46.
35. Faezeh Foroutan, 'Regional Integration in Sub-Saharan Africa: past experience and future prospects', in Jaime de Melo and Arvind Panagariya (eds), *New Dimensions in Regional Integration*, (Cambridge: Cambridge University Press, 1993), p. 234.
36. World Bank, *World Development Report 1994*, (New York: Oxford University Press, 1994), p. 188.
37. Colin McCarthy, 'Regional Integration: Part of the Solution or Part of the Problem?' in Stephen Ellis (ed.), *Africa Now: People, Policies, Institutions*, (London: James Curry Ltd, 1996), p. 215.
38. Adebayo Adedeji, *Africa, The Third World and the Search for a New Economic Order*, Turkeyen Third World Lectures, (Georgetown, Guyana, November 1976).
39. ECA, *African Alternative Framework to Structural Adjustment Programmes for Socio-economic Recovery and Transformation*, E/ECA/CM.15/6 Ref.3, Addis Ababa, July 1989.
40. Adebayo Adedeji, 'Comparative Strategies of Economic Decolonization in Africa', in Ali A. Mazrui (ed.), *General History of Africa, VIII: Africa Since 1935*, (London: Heinemann, 1993), p. 408.
41. For details see George Padmore (ed.), *History of the Pan-African Congress*, (London: 1963).
42. Adedeji, 'Comparative strategies', p. 408.
43. S.K.B. Asante, 'Pan-Africanism and Regional Integration', in Ali A. Mazrui (ed.), *General History of Africa, VIII: Africa Since 1935*, p. 724.
44. Kwame Nkrumah, *Towards Colonial Freedom*, (London: Heinemann, 1962), p. 33; see also S.K.B. Asante, 'Kwame Nkrumah and Pan-Africanism: The Early Phase, 1945–1961', *Universitas*, Vol. III, No. 1, (October 1973).
45. For details, see Asante, 'Pan-Africanism and Regional Integration', p. 724.
46. Kwame Nkrumah, *Africa Must Unite*, (New York: Praeger; London: Heinemann, 1963), p. 163.
47. See S.K.B. Asante, 'Towards A Continental African Economic Community by the Year 2000?', in Christopher Fyfe (ed.), *African Futures*, (Edinburgh: University of Edinburgh), 1987, p. 78.
48. Adedeji, 'Comparative strategies', p. 408.
49. *Ibid.*
50. *West Africa*, London, (30 June 1980), p. 1174.
51. Timothy M. Shaw and Paul Goulding, 'Alternative Scenarios for Africa', in T.M. Shaw (ed.), *Alternative Futures for Africa*, (Boulder, Colo.: Westview Press, 1982), p. 97.
52. Association for Public Administration and Management (ed.), *Regional Cooperation in Africa: Problems and Prospects*, (Addis Ababa: 1977), p. 10.
53. T.M. Shaw, 'The Political Economy of African International Relations', *Issue*, Vol. 5, (Winter 1975), pp. 29–38.
54. T.M. Shaw, 'Regional Cooperation and Conflict in Africa', *International Journal*, Vol. 30, No. 4, (Autumn 1975), pp. 667–8.
55. Organization of African Unity, *LPA*, para. 10.
56. J.B. Zulu and S.M. Nsouli, 'Adjustment Programmes in Africa', *Finance and Development*, Vol. 21, No. 1, (March 1984), p. 5.

57. World Bank, *Accelerated development*, p. 3; and UN Committee for Programme and Coordination, *Proposed Revisions to the System-wide Plan of Action for African Economic Recovery and Development*, Thirty-fourth Session, E/AC.51/1994/7, 9 August 1994.

58. J.K. Nyerere, *Non-alignment in the 1970s*, (Dar-es-Salaam: Government Printer, 1970), p. 12.

59. UN Doc. A/Res/320/(S–vi), 9 May 1974.

60. For a full-scale study of ECOWAS, see Asante, *The Political Economy of Regionalism in Africa*.

CHAPTER 3

1. For details see S.K.B. Asante, *The Political Economy of Regionalism in Africa: A Decade of the Economic Community of West African States (ECOWAS)*, (New York: Praeger, 1986), pp. 94–7.

2. See PTA/COMESA, *PTA/COMESA Welcome South Africa*, undated, pp. 3–4.

3. PTA/COMESA, *Final Communique of the Eleventh Meeting of the Authority of the Preferential Trade Area for Eastern and Southern African States*, Lusaka, Zambia, January 1993.

4. PTA/COMESA, *Eighteenth Meeting of the PTA Council of Ministers*, Lusaka, Zambia, January 1993.

5. PTA/COMESA, *Final Communique on the Twelfth Meeting of the Authority of the Preferential Trade Area for Eastern and Southern African States*, Kampala, Uganda, 6 November 1993.

6. COMESA, *Review Study of the Implementation of the Common Market for Eastern and Southern Africa (COMESA) Monetary Harmonization Programme*, COMESA/ECA/95/1, 30 October 1995.

7. COMESA, *Report of the Second Meeting of the COMESA Council of Ministers*, COMESA/CM/II/3, Lusaka, Zambia, April 1996.

8. Augusto de la Torre and Margaret R. Kelly, *Regional Trade Arrangements*, (Washington DC: IMF Occasional paper 93, March 1992), p. 16.

9. *Ibid.*, p. 17.

10. Andras Inotai, *Regional Integration among Developing Countries Revisited*, (Washington DC: The World Bank, Country Economics Department, April 1991), p. 9.

11. *Ibid.*

12. Faezah Foroutan, ' Regional integration in Sub-Saharan Africa: Past experience and future prospects' in J. de Melo and A. Panagariya (eds), *New Dimensions in Regional Integration*, (Cambridge: Cambridge University Press, 1993), pp. 264–5.

CHAPTER 4

1. Ahmed A.H.M. Aly, *Economic Cooperation in Africa: In Search of Direction*, (Boulder/London: Lynne Rienner Publishers, 1994), p. 35.

2. Jacques Pelkmans and Marc Vanheukelen (eds), *Coming to Grips with the Internal Market*, (Maastricht: European Institute of Public Administration, 1986).

3. Augusto Lopez-Claros, 'The European Community: On the Road to Integration', *Finance and Development*, Vol. 24, No. 3, (September 1987), p. 36.

4. S.K.B. Asante, 'Regional Economic Cooperation and Integration: The Experience of ECOWAS', in Peter Anyang' Nyong'O (ed.), *Regional Integration in Africa: Unfinished Agenda*, (Nairobi: Academy of Science Publishers, 1990), p. 127.

5. Cited in Arthur D. Hazlewood, 'Economic Integration: Lessons for Afrifan Recovery and Development', in O. Teriba and P. Bugembe (eds), *The Challenge of African Recovery and Development*, (London: Frank Cass, 1990), p. 592.

6. See S.K.B. Asante, *African Development: Adebayo Adededji's Alternative Strategies*, (London: Hans Zell Publishers, 1991), pp. 100–1.

7. Ademola Ariyo, 'Tariff Harmonization, Government Revenue and Economic Integration within ECOWAS: Some Reflections', *Development Policy Review*, Vol. 10, (1992), p. 171.

8. United Nations, *Statistical and Economic Information Bulletin for Africa*, No. 9, UN E/CM.14/SE 1B9; International Financial Statistics, IMF, January 1978. Details in Table 1, UNCTAD preliminary report on *Trade Liberalization Options and Issues for the ECOWAS*, p. 39.

9. Aly, *Economic Cooperation in Africa*, p. 46.

10. *Ibid.*, p. 48.

11. UNDP project document on *Project of the Preferential Trade Area for Eastern and Southern Africa*, July 1987.

12. Hazlewood, 'Economic integration: lessons for African recovery and development', p. 601.

13. Steven Langdon and Lynn K. Mytelka, 'Africa in the Changing World Economy', in Colin Legum *et al.* (eds), *Africa in the 1980s: A Continent in Crisis*, (New York: McGraw-Hill for Council on Foreign Relations 1980s Project, 1979), p. 179.

14. ECA, *Report of the ECA Mission on the Evaluation of UDEAC*, Libreville, Gabon, 1981.

15. OAU, *Lagos Plan*, p. 128.

16. Edward G. Stockwell and K.A. Laidlaw, *Third World Development: Problems and Prospects*, (Chicago: Nelson-Hall, 1981), pp. 251–96.

17. John P. Lewis, 'Overview: Development Promotion: A time for regrouping', in John P. Lewis and V. Kallab (eds), *Development Strategies Reconsidered*, (New Brunswick and Oxford: Transaction Books, 1986), p. 29.

18. Asante, 'Regional Economic Cooperation and Integration'.

19. ECOWAS, *Final Report of the Committee of Eminent Persons for the Review of the ECOWAS Treaty*, ECW/CEP/TREV/VI/2. Lagos, June 1992.

20. Aly, *Economic Cooperation in Africa*, p. 69.

21. *Ibid.*, p. 70.

22. Jeggan Senghor, 'Cooperation in Africa: Generating Action at the Unit-Level', *DPMN Bulletin*, Vol. II, No. 1, (April 1994), p. 3.

23. Adebayo Adedeji, 'Economic Integration in Africa: Expectations, Results, Problems and Perspectives'. Address to ADB Symposium on African Economic Integration, Abuja, Nigeria, May 1989.

24. See UNCTAD/ECDC/228, *Regional and Subregional Economic Integration and Cooperation Among Developing Countries: Adjusting to Changing Realities*, 6 August 1992.
25. See Asante, *African Development*, pp. 204–5; Asante, 'Popular Participation and Regionalism', London-based *West Africa*, (19–25 November 1990).
26. E.B. Haas, *The Uniting of Europe: Political, Social and Economic Forces, 1950–57*, (Stanford: Stanford University Press, 1958); L.N. Lindberg, *The Political Dynamics of European Economic Integration*, (Stanford: Stanford University Press, 1963).
27. J. Lodge and V. Herman, 'The Economic and Social Committee in EEC Decision-making', *International Organization*, Vol. 34, No. 2, (Spring 1980), pp. 266–84.
28. Stephen Holt, *The Common Market*, (London: Hamish Hamilton, 1967), p. 66.
29. Abdul A. Jalloh, 'Regional Integration in Africa: Lessons from the Past and Prospects for the Future'. *Africa Development*, Vol. 1, No. 2, (1976), pp. 48–53.
30. Abdul A. Jalloh, 'The Politics and Economics of Regional Political Integration of Equatorial Africa', (Berkeley: PhD diss., University of California, 1969), p. 300.
31 W.P. Avery and J.D. Cochrane, 'Innovation in Latin American Regionalism: The Andean Common Market', *International Organization*, Vol. 27, No. 2, (Spring 1973), p. 205.
32. Werner Feld, 'National Interest Groups and Policy Formation in the EEC', *Political Science Quarterly*, Vol. 81, No. 3, (September 1966), pp. 392–411.
33. Joseph S. Nye, Jr., 'Comparing Common Markets: A Revised Neo-Functionalist Model', *International Organization*, Vol. 24, No. 4, (Autumn 1970), p. 809.
34. For details, see Roger W. Fontaine, *The Andean Pact: A Political Analysis*, Vol. 5, *The Washington Papers*, (Beverley Hills/London: 1977), pp. 33–4. See also W.P. Avery, 'Oil, Politics, and Economic Decision-making: Venezuela and the Andean Common Market', *International Organization*, Vol. 30, No. 4, (Autumn 1976), pp. 541–71.
35. R. Colin Beever, *Trade Unions and Free Labour Movement in the EEC*, (London: Chatham House; PEP, 1969), pp. 18–19.
36. Nye, 'Comparing common markets', p. 809.
37. Adebayo Adedeji, 'Collective Self-reliance in Developing Africa: Scope, Prospects and Problems'. Paper presented at the Conference on ECOWAS, Lagos, Nigeria, 23–27 August 1976.

CHAPTER 5

1. For an earlier analysis of the future of the African Economic Community see S.K.B. Asante, 'Towards a Continental African Economic Community by the Year 2000?', in Christopher Fyfe (ed.), *African Futures*, (Edinburgh: Edinburgh University, 1988), pp. 71–106. See also Asante, 'New Hope for Africa: Pan-African Economic Community', *Development and Cooperation*, (4/1992), pp. 21–2.
2. S.K.B. Asante, 'Kwame Nkrumah and Pan-Africanism: The Early Years', *Universitas*, Vol. 3, No. 1, (October 1973); see also Asante, 'Pan-Africanism

and Regional Integration', in Ali Mazrui (ed.), *UNESCO General History of Africa: VIII: Africa since 1935*, (California: Heinemann, 1993), pp. 724–43.

3. S.K.B. Asante, 'Africa and the Brave New World of Regionalism', *Development and Cooperation*, (February 1991).

4. ECA, *Policy Convergence for Regional Economic Cooperation and Integration: Implementation of the Treaty Establishing the African Economic Community*, E/ECA/CM.20/15, 21 April 1994.

5. S.K.B. Asante, 'Comparative Analysis of the Treaties of the African Economic Community and the Economic Community of West African States', in Jeggan C. Senghor (ed.), *ECOWAS: Perspectives on Treaty Revision and Reform*, (Dakar: IDEP Working Papers No. 3, November 1993), pp. 15–22.

6. Article 3 of the *Treaty Establishing the African Economic Community*.

7. UNDP, *Human Development Report* series, (New York and Oxford: Oxford University Press, 1990 *et al.*); ECA, *African Charter for Popular Participation in Development and Transformation*, (Arusha, Tanzania: 1990).

8. Article 5 of the *Treaty*.

9. Article 4(1).

10. R.H. Green and G.K. Krishna, *Economic Cooperation in Africa: Retrospect and Prospect*, (Nairobi: Oxford University Press, 1967), p. 44.

11. Article 14.

12. UNCTAD, *Economic Integration among Developing Countries, Trade Cooperation, Monetary and Financial Cooperation and Review of Recent Developments in Major Economic Cooperation and Integration Groupings of Developing Countries*, TD/BC.7/AC.3/10, 12 December 1990.

13. Article 16.

14. J.B. Wilmot, 'Supranationality and the Decision-making Process in ECOWAS', in Jeggan Senghor (ed.), *ECOWAS: Perspectives on Treaty Revision*, p. 25.

15. *Ibid.*, p. 26.

16. *Ibid.*

17. *Ibid.*, p. 33.

18. Asante, 'New Hope for Africa: Pan-African Economic Community', p. 21.

19. Cited in Pierre-Claver Damiba, 'Africa: The Challenges Ahead'. Paper presented at the UNDP Cluster Meeting of African Ministers of Planning, Lusaka, Zambia, 4–6 July 1991.

20. Organization of African Unity, Report of the Seventeenth Extraordinary Session of the Council of Ministers, *Relaunching Africa's Economic and Social Development: The Cairo Agenda for Action*, Doc. CM/1892, presented to the Council of Ministers, Sixty-second Ordinary Session, Addis Ababa, Ethiopia, 21–23 June 1995.

21. S.C. Dube, *Modernization and Development: The Search for Alternative Paradigms*, (London and New Jersey: Zed Books, 1988), p. 6.

22. Thierry G. Verhelst, *No Life Without Roots: Culture and Development*, (London and New Jersey: Zed Books, 1990).

23. IDEP, *Rationalization of West African Intergovernmental Organizations*, (Dakar: IDEP, May 1994).

24. C. Fred Bergsten, Robert O. Keohane and Joseph S. Nye Jr, 'International Economics and International Politics: A Framework for Analysis' *International Organization*, Vol. 29, No. 1, (Winter 1975), p. 3.

25. See *Africa South of the Sahara, 1995*, (London: Europa Publications Ltd, 1994), p. 113.
26. H.M.A. Onitiri, 'The African Economic Community: Implementation of the Treaty: Priorities, Strategies, Programmes and Policies', undated.
27. ECA, *Proposals for the Implementation of the Abuja Treaty Establishing the African Economic Community*, E/ECA/CM/19/7, 18 February 1993.
28. *Ibid.*
29. Onitiri, 'The African Economic Community'.
30. *Ibid.*
31. World Bank, *Initiating Memorandum for a Proposed Framework for Bank Assistance in Support of Cross-Border Initiatives to Promote Private Investment, Trade and Payments in Eastern and Southern Africa and the Indian Ocean*, (Washington DC: The World Bank, April 1994).
32. Robert Davies, 'Approaches to Regional Integration in the Southern African Context', *Africa Insight*, Vol. 24, No. 1, (1994), p. 13.
33. World Bank, *Intra-regional Trade in Sub-Saharan Africa*, (Washington DC: World Bank Economic and Finance Division, Technical Department, Africa Region, 1991).
34. O. Saasa, 'Economic Cooperation and Integration Among Developing Countries: An Overview', in O. Saasa (ed.), *Joining the Future: Economic Integration and Cooperation in Africa*, (Nairobi: ACTS Books, 1991), pp. 7–26.
35. F. Cheru, *The Not So Brave New World: Problems and Prospects of Regional Integration in Post-Apartheid Southern Africa*, (Johannesburg: SAIIA, 1992), p. 31.
36. D. Keet, 'International Players and Programmes for - and against - Economic Integration in Southern Africa', *Southern African Perspectives*, South Africa, Cape Town: Centre for Southern African Studies, No. 36, (June 1994), p. 16.
37. Anthoni van Nieuwkerk, 'Big or Small, Open or Closed? A Survey of Views on Regional Integration', in Gregg Mills, Alan Begg and A. van Nieuwkerk (eds), *South Africa in the Global Economy*, (Johannesburg: SAIIA, 1995), pp. 250–1.
38. Robert Davies, 'The Significance of Theoretical Debates on Regional Cooperation and Integration in the Transformation of Southern Africa'. Paper presented at Ruth First Memorial Symposium, University of Western Cape, 17–18 August 1992.

CHAPTER 6

1. Jaime de Mello and Arvind Panagariya, 'The New Regionalism', *Finance and Development*, Vol. 29, No. 4, (December 1992), pp. 37–40.
2. See Unilag Consultant, *The Potential Effects of the 1992 Single European Market on Members of ECOWAS*, (Lagos: University of Lagos Press, 1990).
3. Salim Ahmed Salim, 'Africa: The Challenges of European Economic Integration', *The 1990 Guardian Lecture*, (Lagos, Nigeria: June 1990).
4. John Ravenhill, 'When Weakness Is Strength: The Lomé IV Negotiations', in I. William Zartman (ed.), *Europe and Africa: The New Phase*, (Boulder and London: Lynne Rienner Publishers, 1993), p. 59.

5. Carol Cosgrove, 'Has the Lomé Convention Failed ACP Trade?', *Journal of International Affairs*, Vol. 48, No. 1, (1994), p. 227.
6. Cited in Shada Islam, 'Inside the Magic Circle', *South*, No. 111, (January 1990), p. 17.
7. Cited in *ibid.*
8. Allechi M'Bet, 'The CFA Franc Zone in the Context of Europe After 1992'. Paper presented at the fifth symposium of the special commission on Africa organized by the African Academy of Sciences, in collaboration with the African Development Bank, Abidjan, Côte d'Ivoire, September 1989.
9. For details see P. Economou *et al.*, 'Europe 1992 and Foreign Direct Investment in Africa', in William Zartman (ed.), *Europe and Africa*, pp. 95–119.
10. For details see S.K.B. Asante, *African Development: Adebayo Adedeji's Alternative Strategies*, (London: Hans Zell Publishers, 1991), pp. 198–200.
11. ECA, *The Completion of the European Internal Market by 1992: Possible Consequences for Africa*, ECA/ECO/EUR/90 Rev. 1, 1990.
12. For details see S.K.B. Asante, 'Africa and Europe: Collective Dependence or Interdependence?', in A. Sesay (ed.), *Africa and Europe: From Partition to Interdependence or Dependence?*, (London *et al.*: Croom Helm, 1986), pp. 183–221; S.K.B. Asante, 'The Lomé Convention: Towards Perpetuation of Dependency or Promotion of Inter-dependence?', *Third World Quarterly*, Vol. 3, (October 1981).
13. S.K.B. Asante, 'Whither Africa? Euro-African Integration or African Regional Cooperation?', *Development and Cooperation* (5/1986), pp. 9–11.
14. J. Bossuyt, G. Laporte and G. Brigaldino, *European Development Policy After the Treaty of Maastricht: The Mid-term Review of Lomé IV and the Complementarity Debate*, ECDPM occasional paper, 1993, p. 40.
15. Cited in Asante; 'Whither Africa', p. 10.
16. *Ibid.*
17. Timothy M. Shaw, 'The Revival of Regionalism in Africa: Cure for Crisis or Prescription for Conflict', *Jerusalem Journal of International Affairs*, Vol. 11, No. 4, (1989), p. 86.
18. Cyril Daddieh, 'Structural Adjustment Programmes and Regional Integration: Compatible or Mutually Exclusive?', in K. Mengisteab and B.I. Logan, (eds), *Beyond Economic Liberalization in Africa: Structural Adjustment and the Alternatives*, (London *et al.*: Zed Books Ltd 1995), p. 248.
19. African Development Bank, *African Development Report 1993*, (Abidjan: African Development Bank, 1993), p. 144.
20. Jean-Claude Boidin, 'Regional Cooperation in the Face of Structural Adjustment', *The Courier*, No. 112, (November–December 1988), p. 67.
21. Edward V.K. Jaycox, *The Challenges of African Development*, (Washington DC: World Bank, 1992), pp. 65–7.
22. Edward V.K. Jaycox, 'Economic Recovery in Sub-Saharan Africa: Assessing the Joint Effort'. Keynote address to the Inter-Agency Task Force on the United Nations Programme of Action for African Economic Recovery and Development [UN-PAAERD], Washington DC, February 1988.
23. Carol Lancaster, 'Fostering Regional Integration in West Africa: The Economic Community of West African States'. A Discussion Paper, October 1989.
24. World Bank, *Sub-Saharan Africa: From Crisis to Sustainable Growth*, (Washington DC: World Bank, 1989), pp. 159–60.

25. Boidin, 'Regional cooperation', p. 67.
26. *Ibid*, pp. 67–8.
27. *Ibid*.
28. See S.K.B. Asante, 'Structural Adjustment Programmes and Regionalism in Africa', *Development and Cooperation*, (6/1991), pp. 13–14. See also Asante, *African development*, pp. 173–4.
29. Peter Da Costa, 'A New Role for ECOWAS', *Africa Report* 36, No. 5, (September–October 1991), pp. 38–9.
30. Daddieh, 'Structural Adjustment Programmes', p. 262.
31. African Development Bank, *African development report*, p. ii.
32. Boidin, 'Regional Cooperation', p. 68.
33. *Ibid*, p. 69.
34. For details see S.K.B. Asante, 'The United Nations Economic Commission for Africa, South Africa and Africa: A New Era for Cooperation and Development'. Text of an address delivered at the University of Pretoria, South Africa, October 1994.
35. Cited in *ODI Briefing Paper*, 'Economic Policies in the New South Africa', (April 1994).
36. *Ibid*.
37. The Economic Intelligence Unit, *The New South Africa: Business Prospects and Corporate Strategies*, (June 1994).
38. Nelson Mandela, 'South Africa's Future Foreign Policy', *Foreign Affairs*, Vol. 72, No. 5, (November/December 1993), p. 89.
39. See *The Economist*, (2 September 1995). Extracts from Address by Dr C.L. Stals, Governor of the South African Reserve Bank, at the Seventy-fifth Ordinary General Meeting of Shareholders of the Bank on 22 August, 1995.
40. African Development Bank, *African development report*, p. 141.
41. *Ibid*.

CHAPTER 7

1. ECA, *Progress Report by the Regional Economic Communities: COMESA: A Successful Venture in Regional Integration*. First Session of the Conference of African Ministers Responsible for Trade, Regional Cooperation, Integration and Tourism, Addis Ababa, 14–16 February, 1996.
2. UNDP/UNCTAD African MTN Project: RAF/87/157, *Services in Africa: Prospects for Trade, Regional Cooperation and Technical Assistance in the Post-Uruguay Round*, International Conference on the Uruguay Round of Multilateral Trade Negotiations, Tunis, Tunisia, October, 1994. See also *The Courier*, No. 156, (March–April 1996), pp. 36–40.
3. UNCTAD TD/B/C.7/94; TD/B/C.7/AC.3/7, *Report of the First Session of the Meeting of the Heads of Secretariat of Economic Cooperation and Integration Groupings of Developing Countries*, Geneva, April, 1989.
4. *Ibid*.
5. See for example, S.K.B. Asante and W.A. Ndongko, *Report of UNECA-MRAG Mission to Kenya on Rationalization of Institutional Mechanisms for Regional*

and International Economic Cooperation, ECA/MRAG/94/54/Mr, Addis Ababa, August 1994.

6. Jeggan C. Senghor, 'Cooperation in Africa: Generating Action at the Unit-Level', *Bulletin of the Development Policy Management Network* (DPMN), Vol. II, No. 1, (April 1994), p. 3.

7. *Ibid.*

8. For details see S.K.B. Asante, *UNECA-MRAG Preliminary Mission Report on Current ECOWAS Cooperation Programmes: A Framework for Action*, ECA/MRAG/94/36/MR, Addis Ababa, June, 1994.

9. See S.K.B. Asante and M.J. Balogun, *Report of Mission on ECOWAS Management Training Needs and Training Programmes*, Addis Ababa, October, 1991; also Asante and Balogun, *Report of Mission on PTA Treaty Review and Enhancement of Capacity of PTA Secretariat*, ECA/MRAG/92/6, Addis Ababa, May 1992.

10. Global Coalition for Africa, *Outline of a Programme of Action to Promote Regional Cooperation and Integration in Sub-Saharan Africa*, Doc. GCA/AC.3/No.9/06/1993, GCA Meetings, Cotonou, Benin, June 1993.

11. H.M.A. Onitiri; 'Changing Political and Economic Conditions for Regional Integration in Sub-Saharan Africa', Paper presented at AERC Workshop on Trade, Policy and Regional Integration, Nairobi, December 1993.

12. For an illuminating study on linking SAPs with regional integration, see Percy S. Mistry, 'Regional Dimensions of Structural Adjustment in Southern Africa', Paper prepared for a Fondad Conference on Regional Integration in Africa, Johannesburg, South Africa, February 1996.

13. Onitiri, 'Changing Political and Economic Conditions'.

14. ECA, *Serving Africa Better: Strategic Directions for the Economic Commission for Africa*, E/ECA/CH.22/2, Addis Ababa, May 1996.

15. United Nations, *United Nations System-wide Special Initiative on Africa*, E/ECA/CM.22/5, Addis Ababa, March 1996.

16. See S.K.B. Asante, *Mission Report on Conference on Understanding Contemporary Africa: India and South-South Cooperation*, ECA/MRAG/96, Addis Ababa, March 1996.

CHAPTER 8

1. Organization of African Unity, Relaunching Africa's Economic and Social Development: The Cairo Agenda for Action, ECM/2 (xvii) Rev. 4, Cairo, Egypt, March 1995.

2. H.M.A. Onitiri, 'Regionalism and Africa's Development', study prepared for UNCTAD, November 1995.

3. *Ibid.*

4. Unilag Consultant, *The Potential Effects of the 1992 Single European Market on Members of ECOWAS*, (Lagos: University of Lagos Press, 1990), p. 46.

5. Onitiri, 'Regionalism and Africa's Development'.

6. For details see S.K.B. Asante, 'Democracy, Development and Regionalism in Africa', in S.F. Coetzee, B. Turok, E.P. Beukes (eds), *Transition to Democracy:*

Breaking Out of Apartheid, (Johannesburg: Institute for African Alternatives and Africa Institute of South Africa, 1994), pp. 183–207.

7. Alan Fowler, 'The Role of NGOs in Changing State-society relations: Perspectives from Eastern and Southern Africa', *Development Policy Review*, Vol. 9, No. 1, (March 1991), p. 53.

8. G. Hyden, *No Shortcuts to Progress: African Development Management in Perspective*, (Berkeley, CA.: University of California Press, 1983), p. 119; R. Frantz, 'The role of NGOs in Strengthening Civil Society' in A. Drabek (ed.), 'Development Alternatives: The Challenge of NGOs', *World Development*, suppl. 15, (Autumn 1987), p. 121; World Bank, *Sub-Saharan Africa: From crisis to sustainable growth*, (Washington DC: The World Bank, 1989), p. 61.

9. S.K.B. Asante, *The Political Economy of Regionalism in Africa: A Decade of the Economic Community of West African States* (ECOWAS), (New York: Praeger, 1986), pp. 200–5.

10. ECA, *African Charter for Popular Participation in Development and Transformation*, E/ECA/CM.14/11, Arusha, Tanzania, February 1990.

Select Bibliography

PRINTED PRIMARY SOURCES

Adedeji, Adebayo, *Africa, The Third World and the Search for a New Economic Order,* Turkeyen Third World Lectures, Georgetown, Guyana, November 1976.

African Development Bank, *African Development Report, 1993,* Abidjan, Côte d'Ivoire: African Development Bank, 1993.

——, *Economic Integration in Southern Africa,* Oxford: 1993.

Asante, S.K.B., *Report on a Study and Appraisal of the Impact of the UN Economic Commission for Africa on African Development: Policy-making, Programming and the Execution of Projects, 1958–1985,* Addis Ababa: ECA, December 1987.

——, *Mission Report on International Conference on Understanding Contemporary Africa: India and South-South Cooperation,* New Delhi, ECA/MRAG/96, Addis Ababa, March 1996.

——, *UNECA-MRAG Preliminary Mission Report on Current ECOWAS Cooperation Programmes: A Framework for Action,* ECA/MRAG/94/36/MR, Addis Ababa, June 1994.

——, *Regionalism in West Africa: A Case for Rationalization and Restructuring,* ECA/MRAG/TP/92/ 25, Addis Ababa, April 1993.

Asante, S.K.B. and Balogun, M.J., *Report of Mission on ECOWAS Management Training Needs and Training Programmes,* Addis Ababa, October 1991.

——, *Report of Mission on PTA Treaty Review and Enhancement of Capacity of PTA Secretariat,* ECA/MRAG/92/6, Addis Ababa, May 1992.

Asante, S.K.B. and Ndongko, W.A., *Report of UNECA-MRAG Mission to Kenya on Rationalization of Institutional Mechanisms for Regional and International Economic Cooperation,* ECA/MRAG/94/54/MR, Addis Ababa, August 1994.

——, *UNECA-MRAG Mission Report on the Initiatives of the Republic of Seychelles on Economic Integration: Determining Factors and the Way Forward,* ECA/MRAG/95/107/MR, Addis Ababa, November 1995.

Asante, S.K.B., Balogun, M.J. and Ndongko, W.A., *Draft Proposal for the Establishment of African Centre for Regional Economic Integration at the University of Ghana,* ECA/MRAG/95/MR, Addis Ababa, February 1995.

COMESA, *Review Study of the Implementation of the Common Market for Eastern and Southern Africa (COMESA) Monetary Harmonization Programme,* COMESA/ECA/95/1, 30 October 1995.

——, *Report of the Second Meeting of the COMESA Council of Ministers,* COMESA/CM/11/3, April 1996.

ECA, *Progress Report by the Regional Economic Communities: COMESA - A Successful Venture in Regional Integration.* First Session of the Conference of African Ministers Responsible for Trade, Regional Cooperation, Integration and Tourism, Addis Ababa, 14–16 February 1996.

——, *Serving Africa Better: Strategic Directions for the Economic Commission for Africa,* E/ECA/CM.22/2, Addis Ababa, May 1996.

——, *Policy Convergence for Regional Economic Cooperation and Integration: Implementation of the Treaty Establishing the African Economic Community*, E/ECA/CM.20/15, Addis Ababa, 21 April 1994.

——, *Proposals for the Implementation of the Abuja Treaty Establishing the African Economic Community*, E/ECA/CM.17/7, Addis Ababa, February 1993.

——, *Report of the ECA Mission on the Evaluation of UDEAC*, Libreville, Gabon, 1981.

——, *African Charter for Popular Participation in Development and Transformation*, E/ECA/CM.14/11, Arusha, Tanzania, February 1990.

——, *The Completion of the European Internal Market by 1992: Possible Consequences for Africa*, ECA/ECO/EUR /90/Rev.1, 1990.

——, *Rationalization of the Operations of PTA, SADCC and the Lusaka-based MULPOC: A Proposal*, ECA/MULPOC. Lusaka, VII/7, 22 April 1984.

——, *African Alternative Framework to Structural Adjustment Programmes for Socio-economic Recovery and Transformation*, E/ECA/CM.15/6, Rev.3, Addis Ababa, July 1989.

Economic Intelligence Unit, *The New South Africa: Business Prospects and Corporate Strategies*, June 1994.

ECOWAS, *Final Report of the Committee of Eminent Persons for the Review of the ECOWAS Treaty*, ECW/CEP/TREV/ vi/2. Lagos, Nigeria, June 1992.

Global Coalition for Africa, *Outline of a Programme of Action to Promote Regional Cooperation and Integration in Sub-Saharan Africa*, Doc.GCA AC.3/No.9/06/1993, GCA Meetings, Cotonou, Benin, June 1993.

IDEP, *Rationalization of West African Intergovernmental Organizations*, Dakar: IDEP, May 1994.

Mandaza, Ibbo *et al.*, *The Joint PTA/SADC Study on Harmonization, Rationalization and Coordination of the Activities of the Preferential Trade Area for Eastern and Southern African States (PTA) and the Southern African Development Community (SADC)*, Harare, July 1994.

Organization of African Unity, *Relaunching Africa's Economic and Social Development: The Cairo Agenda for Action*, ECM/2 (xvii) Rev.4, Cairo, Egypt, March 1995.

——, *Lagos Plan of Action for the Economic Development of Africa, 1980–2000*, Geneva: Institute of Labour Studies, 1981.

PTA/COMESA, *PTA/COMESA Welcome South Africa*, Lusaka, Zambia: PTA/COMESA, undated.

——, *Final Communique of the Eleventh Meeting of the Authority of the Preferential Trade Area for Eastern and Southern African States*, Kampala, Uganda, 6 November 1993.

UNCTAD, *Report of the First Session of the Meeting of the Heads of Secretariat of Economic Cooperation and Integration Groupings of Developing Countries*, TD/B/C.7/AC.3/7, Geneva, April 1989.

——, *Regional and Subregional Economic Integration and Cooperation Among Developing Countries: Adjusting to Changing Realities*, UNCTAD/ECDC/220, 6 August 1992.

——, *Economic Integration Among Developing Countries, Trade Cooperation, Monetary and Financing Cooperation and Review of Recent Developments in Major Economic Cooperation and Integration Groupings of Developing Countries*, TD/B/C.7/AC.3/10, 12 December 1990.

UNDP, *Human Development Report* series, 1990–1995, New York and Oxford University Press, 1990 *et al.*

UNDP/UNCTAD, *Africa MTN Project Services in Africa: Prospects for Trade, Regional Cooperation and Technical Assistance in the Post-Uruguay Round,* International Conference on the Uruguay Round of Multilateral Trade Negotiations, RAF/87/157, Tunis, Tunisia, October 1994.

Unilag Consultant, *The Potential Effects of the 1992 Single European Market on Members of ECOWAS,* Lagos: University of Lagos Press, 1990.

United Nations Committee for Programme and Coordination, *Proposed Revisions to the System-wide Plan of Action for African Economic Recovery and Development,* Thirty-fourth Session, E/AC.51/1994/7, 9 August 1994.

United Nations, *United Nations System-wide Special Initiative on Africa,* E/ECA/CM.22/5, Addis Ababa, March 1996.

——, *Developing Countries and Levels of Development,* E/AC.54/L.81 1975.

World Bank, *Initiating Memorandum for a Proposed Framework for Bank Assistance in Support of Cross-Border Initiative to Promote Private Investment, Trade and Payments in Eastern and Southern Africa and the Indian Ocean,* Washington D.C., World Bank, April 1994.

——, *Accelerated Development in Sub-Saharan Africa: an Agenda for Action,* Washington D.C.: World Bank, 1981.

——, *Sub-Saharan Africa: From Crisis to Sustainable Growth,* Washington D.C.: World Bank, 1989.

——, *World Development Report 1994,* New York: Oxford University Press, 1994.

——, *Intra-regional Trade in Sub-Saharan Africa,* Washington D.C.: World Bank Economic and Finance Division, Technical Department, Africa Region, 1991.

UNPUBLISHED PAPERS

Adedeji, Adebayo, 'Economic Integration in Africa: Expectations, Results, Problems and Perspectives'. Address to African Development Bank Symposium in African Economic Integration, Abuja, Nigeria, May 1989.

——, 'Collective Self-reliance in developing Africa: Scope, Prospects and Problems'. Paper presented at the Conference on ECOWAS, Lagos, Nigeria, 23–27 August 1976.

Asante, S.K.B., 'The United Nations Economic Commission for Africa, South Africa and Africa: A New Era for Cooperation and Development'. Text of an address delivered at the University of Pretoria, October 1994.

——, 'European Union–Africa ACP Lomé Convention: Expectations, Reality and Challenges of the Twenty-first Century'. Paper prepared for European Centre for Development Policy Management (ECDPM) international conference on the Future EU–ACP relations Beyond Lomé IV, Maastricht, June 1996.

Damiba, Pierre-Claver, 'Africa: The Challenges Ahead'. Paper presented at the UNDP Cluster Meeting of African Ministers of Planning, Lusaka, Zambia, 4–6 July 1991.

Davies, Robert, 'The Significance of Theoretical Debates on Regional Cooperation and Integration in the Transformation of Southern Africa'. Paper presented at Ruth First Memorial Symposium, University of Western Cape, 17–18 August 1992.

Jalloh, Abdul A. 'The Politics and Economics of Regional Political Integration of Equatorial Africa', PhD dissertation, University of California: Berkeley, 1970.

Jaycox, Edward V.K., 'Economic Recovery in Sub-Saharan Africa: Assessing the Joint Effort'. Keynote address to the Inter-Agency Task Force on the UN Programme of Action for African Economic Recovery and Development (UN-PAAERD), Washington D.C., February 1988.

Lancaster, Carol, 'Fostering Regional Integration in West Africa: The Economic Community of West African States'. A discussion paper, 6 October 1989.

M'Bet, Allechi, 'The CFA Franc Zone in the Context of Europe After 1992'. Paper presented at the fifth symposium of the special commission on Africa organized by the African Academy of Sciences, in collaboration with the African Development Bank, Abidjan, Côte d'Ivoire, September 1989.

Mistry, P.S., 'Regional Dimensions of Structural Adjustment in Southern Africa'. Paper presented for a FONDAD Conference on Regional Integration in Africa, Midrand, South Africa, February 1996.

Nti, James, 'ECOWAS: An Approach to Regional Economic Cooperation'. A talk at the 18th Induction Course for newly recruited Foreign Officers, Lagos, Nigeria, July 1980.

Onitiri, H.M.A., 'The African Economic Community: Implementation of the Treaty: Priorities, Strategies, Programmes and Policies', undated.

——, 'Regionalism and Africa's Development', UNCTAD study, November 1995.

——, 'Changing Political and Economic Conditions for Regional Integration in Sub-Saharan Africa'. Paper presented at AERC Workshop on Trade, Policy and Regional Integration, Nairobi, December 1993.

SECONDARY SOURCES: BOOKS

Adedeji, Adebayo, 'Comparative Strategies of Economic Decolonization in Africa', in Ali Mazrui (ed.), *UNESCO General History of Africa, VIII: Africa Since 1935*, California: Heinemann, 1993.

Aly, Ahmad, A.H.M., *Economic Cooperation in Africa: In Search of Direction*, Boulder/London: Lynne Rienner Publishers, 1993.

Asante, S.K.B. *The Political Economy of Regionalism in Africa: a Decade of the Economic Community of West African States (ECOWAS)*, New York: Praeger, 1986.

——, *African Development: Adebayo Adedeji's Alternative Strategies*, London, *et al*: Hans Zell Publishers, 1991.

——, 'Democracy, Development and Regionalism in Africa', in S.F. Coetzee, B. Turok, E.P. Beukes (eds), *Transition to Democracy: Breaking Out of Apartheid*, Johannesburg: Institute for African Alternative and Africa Institute of South Africa, 1994.

——, 'Adebayo Adedeji's Ideas and Approaches to African Development', in Bade Onimode and Richard Synge (eds), *Issues in African Development: Essays in honour of Adebayo Adedeji at 65*, Ibadan, Nigeria: Heinemann Educational Books (Nigeria), Plc., 1995.

——, 'Regional Economic Cooperation and Integration: The Experience of ECOWAS', in Peter Anyang' Nyong'o (ed.), *Regional Integration in Africa: Unfinished Agenda*, Nairobi: Academy of Science Publishers, 1990.

——, 'Africa and Europe: Collective Dependence or Inter-dependence?', in A. Sesay (ed.), *Africa and Europe: From Partition to Interdependence or Dependence?*, London: Croom Helm, 1986.

——, 'CEAO-ECOWAS: Conflict and Cooperation in West Africa', in R.I. Onwuka and A. Sesay (eds), *The Future of Regionalism in Africa*, New York: St. Martin's Press, 1985.

——, 'Towards a Continental African Economic Community by the Year 2000?' in Christopher Fyfe (ed.), *African Futures*, Edinburgh: Edinburgh University Press, 1988.

——, 'Pan-Africanism and Regional Integration', in Ali Mazrui (ed.), *UNESCO General History of Africa: VIII: Africa Since 1935*, California, Heinemann, 1993.

——, 'Comparative Analysis of the Treaties of the African Economic Community and the Economic Community of West African States (ECOWAS)', in J.C. Senghor (ed.), *Perspectives on Treaty Revision and Reform*, Dakar: IDEP Working Papers No. 3, November 1993.

——, 'The SADC Parliamentary Forum and the Process of Economic Cooperation and Integration in Southern Africa', in AWEPA, (ed.), *SADC Parliamentary Forum*. AWEPA: African-European Institute, 1994.

Balassa, Bela, *The Theory of Economic Integration*, Homewood III: Richard D. Irwin, 1961.

Beever, Colin R., *Trade Unions and Free Labour Movement in the EEC*, London: Chatham House, PEP, 1964.

Bossuyt J., Laporte, G. and Brigaldino, G., *European Development Policy After the Treaty of Maastricht: The Mid-term Review of Lomé IV and the Complementarity Debate*, ECDPM occasional paper, 1993.

Braga, C., *The New Regionalism and its Consequences*, Washington D.C.: World Bank, August 1994.

Browne, Robert, S. and Cummings, Robert J., *The Lagos Plan of Action Vs The Berg Report: Contemporary Issues in African Development*, Washington D.C.: Howard University African Studies Programme, 1984.

Cheru, F., *The Not So Brave New World: Problems and Prospects of Regional Integration in Post-Apartheid Southern Africa*, Bradlow Series 6. Johannesburg SIIA, 1992.

Cochrane, James D., *The Politics of Regional Integration: The Central American Case*. New Orleans: Tulane University Press, 1969.

Daddieh, Cyril, 'Structural Adjustment Programmes and Regional Integration: Compatible or Mutually Exclusive?', in K, Mengisteab and B.I. Logan (eds), *Beyond Economic Liberalization in Africa: Structural Adjustment and the Alternatives*, London *et al.*: Zed Books Ltd, 1995.

Dadome, A. Antonio and di Marco, Luis E. 'The Impact of Prebisch's Ideas on Modern Economic Analysis', in Luis E. di Marco (ed.), *International Economic and Development: Essays in Honour of Raul Prebisch*, New York, 1972.

De la Torre, Augusto and Kelly, Margaret R., *Regional Trade Arrangements*, Washington D.C., IMF Occasional paper 93, March 1992.

De Melo, J. and Paragariya, A., *The New Regionalism in Trade Policy: An Interpretative Summary of a Conference*, Washington D.C.: World Bank and London: Centre for Economic Policy Research, 1992.

——, (eds) *New Dimensions in Regional Integration*, Cambridge: Cambridge University Press, 1993.

Dube, S.C., *Modernization and Development – The Search for Alternative Paradigms*, London and New Jersey: Zed Books Ltd 1988.

El-Agraa, Ali M., *The Theory and Measurement of International Economic Integration*, New York: St. Martin's Press, 1989.

Economou, P. *et al.*, 'Europe 1992 and Foreign Direct Investment in Africa', in William Zartman (ed.), *Europe and Africa: The New Phase*, Boulder and London: Lynne Rienner Publishers, 1993.

Etzioni, Amitai, *Political Unification : A Comparative Study of Leaders and Forces*, New York: 1964.

Fontaine, Roger W., *The Andean Pact: A Political Analysis*, Vol.5, *The Washington Papers*, Beverly Hills/London: 1977.

Foroutan, Faezeh, 'Regional Integration in Sub-Saharan Africa: past experience and future prospects', in Jaime de Melo and Arvind Panagariya (eds), *New Dimensions in Regional Integration*, Cambridge: Cambridge University Press, 1993.

Frankel, J., *Contemporary International Relations Theory and the Behaviour of States*, London: Oxford University Press, 1973.

Green, R.H. and Krishna, G.K., *Economic Cooperation in Africa: Retrospect and Prospect*, Nairobi: Oxford University Press, 1967.

Gruhn, Isebill V., *Regionalism Reconsidered: The Economic Commission for Africa*, Boulder: Westview Press, 1979.

Haas, E.B., *The Uniting of Europe: Political, Social and Economic Forces, 1950–57*, Stanford: Stanford University Press, 1958.

Hazelwood, Arthur D., 'Economic Integration: Lessons for African Recovery and Development', in O. Teriba and P. Bugembe, (eds), *The Challenge of African Recovery and Development*, London: Frank Cass, 1990.

Herrera, Felippe, 'Economic Integration and Political Reintegration', in Mildred Adams (ed.), *Latin America: Evolution or Explosion?*, New York: Dodd, Mead, 1963.

Holt, Stephen, *The Common Market*, London: Hamish Hamilton, 1967.

Hyden, G., *No Shortcuts to Progress: African Development Management in Perspective*, Berkeley, California: University of California Press, 1983.

Inotai, Andras, *Regional Integration Among Developing Countries Revisited*, Washington D.C.: World Bank, Country Economics Department, April 1991.

Jaycox, Edward, *The Challenges of African Development*, Washington D.C.: World Bank, 1992.

Kahnert F., *et al.*, *Economic Integration among Development Countries*, Paris: OECD Centre, 1969.

Krugman, Paul, 'Regionalism versus Multilateralism: Analytical Notes', in Jaime de Melo and Arvind Panagariya, (eds), *New Dimensions in Regional Integration*, Cambridge: Cambridge University Press, 1993.

Langdon, Steve and Mytelka, Lynn K., 'Africa in the Changing World Economy', in Colin Legum, *et al.*, (eds), *Africa in the 1980s: A Continent in Crisis*, New York: McGraw-Hill for Council on Foreign Relations 1980s Project, 1979.

Lewis, John P., 'Overview: Development Promotion: A time for regrouping', in John P. Lewis and V. Kallab, (eds) *Development Strategies Reconsidered*, New Brunswick and Oxford: Transaction Books, 1986.

Machlup, Fritz, 'A History of Thought on Economic Integration', in Fritz Machlup, (ed.), *Economic Integration: Worldwide, Regional, Sectoral*, London: Macmillan, 1978.

McCarthy, Colin, 'Regional Integration: Part of the Solution or Part of the Problem', in Stephen Ellis, (ed.), *Africa Now: People, Policies, Institutions*, London: James Curry Ltd, 1996.

Mistry, Percy S., *Regional Integration Arrangements in Economic Development: Panacea or Pitfall?* The Hague: FONDAD, 1996.

Molle, Willen, *The Economics of European Integration: Theory, Practice, Policy*, Aldershot, Hants: Dartmont Publishing Co. Ltd, 1994.

Mutharika, Bingu W.T., *Toward Multinational Economic Cooperation in Africa*, New York: Praeger, 1972.

Nkrumah, Kwame, *Towards Colonial Freedom*, London: Heinemann, 1962.

——, *Africa Must Unite*, New York: Praeger; London: Heinemann, 1963.

Nyerere, J.K., *Non-alignment in the 1970s*, Dar-es-Salaam: Government Printer, 1970.

Padmore, George, (ed.), *History of the Pan-African Congress*, London: 1963.

Pelkmans, Jacques and Vanheukelen, Marc (eds), *Coming to Grips with the Internal Market*, Maastricht: European Institute of Public Administration, 1986.

Ravenhill, John, 'When Weakness is Strength: The Lomé IV Negotiations', in I. William Zartman, (ed.), *Europe and Africa: The New Phase*, Boulder and London: Lynne Rienner Publishers, 1993.

Saasa, O., 'Economic Cooperation and Integration Among Developing Countries: An Overview', in O. Saasa, (ed.), *Joining the Future: Economic Integration and Cooperation in Africa*, Nairobi: ACTS Books, 1991.

Shaw, T.M. and Goulding, Paul, 'Alternative Scenarios for Africa', in T.M. Shaw, (ed.), *Alternative Futures for Africa*, Boulder, Colo: Westview Press, 1982.

Stockwell, E.G. and Laidlaw, K.A., *Third World Development: Problems and Prospects*, Chicago: Nelson-Hall, 1981.

Teunissen, Jan Joost, (ed.), *Regionalism and the Global Economy: The Case of Latin America and the Caribbean*, The Hague: FONDAD, 1995.

Tinbergen, J., *International Economic Integration*, Elsevier, Amsterdam: 1954.

van Nieuwkerk, Anthoni, 'Big or Small, Open or Closed? A Survey of Views on Regional Integration', in Gregg Mills, Alan Begg and A. van Nieuwkerk, (eds), *South Africa in the Global Economy*, Johannesburg: SAIIA, 1995.

Verhelst, Thierry G., *No Life Without Roots: Culture and Development*, London and New Jersey: Zed books Ltd, 1990.

Viner, Jacob, *The Customs Union Issue*, (New York: Carnegie Endowment for International Peace, 1950.

Whalley, John, 'Regional Trade Arrangements in North America: CUSTA and NAFTA', in J. de Melo and A. Panagariya, (eds), *New Dimensions in Regional Integration*, Cambridge: Cambridge University Press, 1993.

Wilmot, J.B., 'Supranationality and the Decision-making Process in ECOWAS', in J.C. Senghor (ed.), *ECOWAS: Perspectives on Treaty Revision*, Dakar, IDEP Working Papers No. 3, November 1993.

SECONDARY SOURCES: ARTICLES

Abangwu, George C., 'Systems Approach to Regional Integration in West Africa', *Journal of Common Market Studies*, Vol. 13. Nos 1 and 2 (1975).

Ariyo, Ademola, 'Tariff Harmonization, Government Revenue and Economic Integration within ECOWAS: Some Reflections', *Development Policy Review*, Vol. 10, 1992.

Asante, S.K.B., 'The Lomé Convention: Towards Perpetuation of Dependency or Promotion of Inter-dependence?', *Third World Quarterly*, Vol. 3, October 1981.

——, 'Whither Africa? Euro-African Integration or African Regional Cooperation' *Development and Cooperation*, 5/1986.

——, 'Kwame Nkrumah and Pan-Africanism: The Early Years', *Universitas*, Vol. 3, No. 1, October 1973.

——, 'Africa and the Brave New World of Regionalism', *West Africa,* London 10–16 September 1990.

——, 'New Hope for Africa: Pan-African Economic Community', *Development and Cooperation*, No. 4, December 1992.

——, 'How Relevant is Lomé After the Year 2000?', *West Africa*, London, December 18–25 December 1995.

——, 'Structural Adjustment Programmes and Regionalism in Africa', *Development and Cooperation*, No. 6, 1991.

Avery, W.P. and Cochrane, J.D., 'Innovation in Latin American Regionalism: The Andean Common Market', *International Organization*, Vol. 27, No. 2, Spring 1973.

——, 'Oil, Politics, and Economic Decision-making: Venezuela and the Andean Common Market', *International Organization*, Vol. 30, No.4 Autumn 1976.

Bergsten, C. Fred, Keohane, R.O. and Nye Jr J.S., 'International Economics and International Politics: A Framework for Analysis', *International Organization*, Vol. 29, No. 1, Winter 1975.

Boidin, Jean-Claude, 'Regional Cooperation in the face of Structural Adjustment', *The Courier*, No. 12, November–December 1988.

Bollard, A. and Mayes, D., 'Regionalism and the Pacific Rim', *Journal of Common Market Studies*, Vol. xxx, No. 2, June 1992.

Chidzero, B.T.G., 'The Meaning of Economic Integration in Africa', *East African Journal* December 1965.

Da Costa, Peter, 'A New Role for ECOWAS', *Africa Report*, Vol. 36, No. 5, September–October 1991.

Davis, R., 'Approaches to Regional Integration in the Southern African Context', *Africa Insight*, Vol. 24, No. 1, 1994.

De Melo, J. Panagariya, A., and Rodrick, Dani, 'The New Regionalism', *Finance and Development*, Vol. 29, No. 4, December 1992.

Dudley Seers, 'The Limitation of the Special Case', *Bulletin of the Oxford Institute of Economics and Statistics*, May 1963.

Feld, Werner, 'National Interest Groups and Policy Formation in the EEC', *Political Science Quarterly*, Vol. 81, No. 3, September 1966.

Fowler, A., 'The Role of NGOs in Changing State-society Relations: Perspectives from Eastern and Southern Africa', *Development Policy Review*, Vol. 9, No. 1, March 1991.

Haas, E.B., 'The Study of Regional Integration: Reflections on the Joy and Anguish of Pre-theorizing', *International Organization*, Vol. 24, No. 4, Autumn 1970.

Hansen, Roger D., 'Regional Integration: Reflections on a Decade of Theoretical Efforts', *World Politics*, Vol. 21, No. 2, January 1969.

Hine, Robert C., 'Regionalism and the Integration of the World Economy', *Journal of Common Market Studies*, Vol. xxi, No. 2, June 1992.

Islam, Shala, 'Inside the Magic Circle', *South*, No. 111, January 1990.

Jalloh, Abdul A., 'Regional Integration in Africa: Lessons from the Past and Prospects for the Future', *Africa Development*, Vol. 1, No. 2, 1976.

Keet, D., 'International Players and Programmes for – and against – Economic Integration in Southern Africa', *Southern African Perspectives*, 36, Cape Town: Centre for Southern African Studies, June 1994.

Lipsey, R. 'The Theory of Customs Union: A General Survey', *Economic Journal*, Vol. 70, September 1960.

Lodge, J. and Herman, V., 'The Economic and Social Committee in EEC Decision-making', *International Organization*, Vol. 34, No. 2, Spring 1980.

Lopez-Claros, A., 'The European Community: On the Road to Integration', *Finance and Development*, Vol. 24, No. 3, September 1987.

Morgenthau, Ruth Schachter, 'The Developing Status of Africa', *Annals of the American Academy of Political and Social Science*, Vol. 432, July 1977.

Nye Jr, J.S., 'Comparing Common Markets: A Revised Neo-Functionalist Model', *International Organization*, Vol. 24, No. 4, Autumn 1970.

Onitiri, H.M.A., 'Towards a West-African Economic Community' *Nigerian Journal of Economic and Social Studies*, Vol. 5, 1963.

Oteiza E. and Sercovich, F., 'Collective Self-reliance: selected issues', *International Social Science Journal*, Vol. 28, No. 4, 1976.

Pinder, John, 'Positive an Negative Integration: Some Problems of Economic Union in the EEC', *World Today*, 24 March 1968.

Rothchild, Donald, 'The Political Implications of the Treaty', *East African Economic Review*, Vol. 3, No. 2, New Series, December 1967.

Salim, Ahmed Salim, 'Africa: The Challenges of European Integration', *The 1990 Guardian Lecture*, Lagos, Nigeria, June 1990.

Seidman, Ann, 'Africa and the World Economy: Prospects for Real Economic Growth', *Issue*, Vol. 8, No. 4, Winter 1978.

Shaw, T.M., 'The Political Economy of African International Relations', *Issue*, Vol. 5, Winter 1975.

——, 'Regional Cooperation and Conflict in Africa', *International Journal*, Vol. 30, No. 4, Autumn 1975.

——, 'The Revival of Regionalism in Africa: Cure for Crisis or Prescription for Conflict', *Jerusalem Journal of International Affairs*, Vol. 11, No. 4, 1989.

Sloan, John, 'The Strategy of Developmental Regionalism: Benefits, Distribution, Obstacles and Capacities', *Journal of Common Market Studies*, Vol. 10, No. 2, December 1971.

Zulu, J.B. and Nsouli, S.M., 'Adjustment Programmes in Africa', *Finance and Development*, Vol. 21, No. 1, March 1984.

Index